CONFEDERATE PHOENIX

Confederate Phoenix

*Rebel Children and Their
Families in South Carolina*

Edmund L. Drago

FORDHAM UNIVERSITY PRESS
NEW YORK   2008

Library of Congress Cataloging-in-Publication Data

Drago, Edmund L.
   Confederate phoenix : rebel children and their families in South Carolina / Edmund L. Drago.
     p. cm.—(Reconstructing America series ; no. 13)
   Includes bibliographical references and index.
   ISBN 978–0-8232–2937–6 (cloth : alk. paper)
   1. United States—History—Civil War, 1861–1865—Participation, Juvenile.
2. South Carolina—History—Civil War, 1861–1865—Participation, Juvenile.
3. United States—History—Civil War, 1861–1865—Children. 4. South Carolina—History—Civil War, 1861–1865—Children. 5. Child soldiers—South Carolina—History—19th century. 6. Children—South Carolina—History—19th century. 7. Teenagers—South Carolina—History—19th century. I. Title.
   E585.C54D73 2008
   973.7083—dc22

2008023277

Printed in the United States of America
10 09 08   5 4 3 2 1
First edition

Contents

Acknowledgments

A variety of people have made this book possible, beginning with my wife, Cheryle Drago. Jason Anderson's expertise as a computer consultant was invaluable. Paul Cimbala suggested I send the manuscript to Fordham University Press. Director Robert Oppedisano was very supportive. Joan Cashin's review of the manuscript was crucial. The College of Charleston Foundation provided me a semester to work on the research. Likewise, I received a summer grant from the Institute for Southern Studies at the University of South Carolina. Some very fine archivists and librarians opened important doors for me: Jane Aldrich (South Carolina Historical Society); Michael Elder and William R. Erwin (Duke University, Special Collections Library); Henry G. Fulmer (South Caroliniana Library, University of South Carolina); Harlan Greene (Avery Research Center); Susan King (City Archives, Charleston); Michael Kohl (Strom Thurmond Institute, Clemson University); David-Moltke Hansen and Tim Williams (University of North Carolina, Chapel Hill); Michael Phillips (College of Charleston); and Gina White (Winthrop University). Ethel Trenholm Seabrook Nepveux graciously shared her knowledge of the Trenholm genealogy with me.

My colleagues at the College of Charleston took valuable time out of their busy teaching schedules to read various chapters of the manuscript. None was more giving of his time and expertise than Stuart Knee. I thank Christophe Boucher, Jason Coy, Robert Crout, Marvin Dulaney, John Fortune Dunn, Marie Fitzwilliam, Caroline Hunt, L. Wayne Jordan, Chris Lamb, Bernard Powers, and Anne C. Rose. Finally, I want to thank my friends Clarence Walker and James Michael Russell for their support.

I am fortunate that Fordham University Press under Robert Oppedisano chose to publish my book. I enjoyed working with his supportive staff, including Eric Newman, Mary-Lou Elias Peña, Loomis Mayer, and Katie Sweeney, along with freelance editor Gregory McNamee.

Abbreviations

CCA	Charleston City Archives, Charleston, South Carolina
CCL	Charleston County Library, Main Branch, Charleston, South Carolina
CLS	Charleston Library Society, Charleston, South Carolina
CSA	Confederate States of America
CSC	Special Collections, Clemson University Libraries, Clemson, South Carolina
CSR	Compiled Service Records of Confederate Soldiers Who Served in Organizations from the State of South Carolina, Microcopy No. 267, National Archives, Washington, D.C.
CSW	Letters Received by the Confederate Secretary of War, 1861–1865, Record Group 109, Microcopy No. 437, 151 reels, National Archives, Washington, D.C.
KKK Reports	U.S. Congress, *Testimony Taken by the Joint Select Committee to Inquire into the Condition of Affairs in the Late Insurrectionary States*, vols. 3–5 (Washington, D.C.: Government Printing Office, 1872)
LC	Library of Congress, Washington, D.C.
NA	National Archives, Washington, D.C.
NAACP	National Association for the Advancement of Colored People
OR	*The War of the Rebellion: A Compilation of the Official Records of the Union and Confederate Armies*, 128 vols. (Washington, D.C.: Government Printing Office, 1880–1901; additions and corrections inserted in each volume, 1902)
SCDAH	South Carolina Department of Archives and History, Columbia
SCDMH	South Carolina Department of Mental Health, South Carolina Lunatic Asylum, Admissions, 1828–1876, Physician's Records, 1860–1874, SCDAH
SCHS	South Carolina Historical Society, Charleston
SCL	South Caroliniana Library, University of South Carolina, Columbia

SCAL   Special Collections, Marlene and Nathan Addleston Library,
                College of Charleston, Charleston, South Carolina
SCV   South Carolina Volunteers
SCWRPL   Special Collections, William R. Perkins Library, Duke Uni-
                versity, Durham, North Carolina
SHS   Southern Historical Collection, University of North Caro-
                lina, Chapel Hill
UDC   United Daughters of the Confederacy
UDC *Recollections* United Daughters of the Confederacy, South Carolina Divi-
                sion, *Recollections and Reminiscences, 1861–1865 Through
                World War I*, 12 vols. (n.p., 1990–2002)
UNC   University of North Carolina, Chapel Hill
USC   University of South Carolina, Columbia

Introduction:
Les Enfants de la Guerre

"Like previously unseen ghosts," James Marten saw, "children peer out from Civil War photographs."[1] His pathbreaking book brought them back from the unseen world by showing how the war reverberated through all aspects of their lives.

What happened to children on the state and local level, however, remains relatively elusive. I have chosen to examine Rebel children and their families in South Carolina, where the war erupted. Composed of a black majority, South Carolina earned the reputation as the most militant Confederate state. Seceding first, it was home to some of the region's most influential politicians. Charleston, its chief port and most populous city, spent much of the war under siege. It became the symbol of Southern resistance. Fierce fighting took place along the coast. During Sherman's march, the state capitol in Columbia went up in flames. White South Carolinians did more than their share of fighting and dying.[2]

When South Carolina leaders urged their people to war in 1860, they encouraged a commitment with consequences unimaginable at the time. They gambled with the future of the children of their state and lost. In January 1864, a woman from Cottage Home captured the people's angst with the lament: Had they foreseen the present "list of the precious youths that have fallen, it would have chill[ed] our hearts. Thousands have passed away—many more are passing. The wail of orphan and widow reach our ears from all parts of the Confederacy. Sisters mourning the loss of precious brothers—while parents, are weeping for their children." In a state that prided itself on a military ethos that had God's blessing, such sacrifices could not have been in vain.[3]

The late dean of South Carolina history, George Rogers, captured and reflected why Carolinians felt compelled to honor the sacrifices of their ancestors in the Lost Cause. In the 1990s, he explains, "Families were shattered. Mothers lost one, two, even three sons in a single battle. A grandfather, a father, a brother disappeared at a crucial moment in life. All were models of virtue and honor to those left behind to mourn their passing. They were worthy of remembrance. Their motives came from within, from what they had been. They had believed that life was God's will. They could not shirk their duties. There were no excuses. They admired their leaders. They were part of a world that is no more."[4] Thus, some white South Carolinians are offended by those who brand their ancestors' efforts as immoral.

South Carolina Rebel children played a critical role in the Civil War drama. Children under the age of fifteen composed more than 40 percent of the state's white population. Boys and girls engaged in activities once reserved for adults only. They made their patriotic presence felt. They relished their contributions. Lee Cohn Harby, born in 1849, told a Sumter gathering of the Daughters of the Confederacy in 1901 that scenes from her childhood were burned into her mind. Her playmates passed quickly from play to war. Each week was full of emotions and stirring events. It seemed the children were aging a year each month. Fourteen-year-old boys took up arms; little girls assumed the responsibilities and tasks normally assigned to grown women. Perhaps like children in other wars, Harby and her friends integrated war into their make-believe world of play. Scholars would call Harby's mindset "a children's world." At times their activities were destructive. In their play, boys at the Charleston Depot killed more civilians in South Carolina than Sherman's troops. Children were also victimized. Their households were wracked, if not shattered, by disease, death, and deprivation. Thousands of fathers and brothers died in the conflict or returned home maimed.[5]

"Phoenix" is a fitting metaphor to describe how white South Carolinians viewed their efforts to preserve their ideal of the good society. The vision entailed states' rights, low taxes, and a subordinate role for blacks. A pristine republic, born in 1860, would rise out of the fire and ashes of the war and Reconstruction. Fire was seared in the collective memory of white South Carolinians: the Charleston fire of 1861, the hurling of Greek fire on Charleston, the burning of Columbia in February 1865, and the mammoth explosion of the Northeastern Railroad Depot in Charleston that very month. "Phoenix," implying resurrection and immortality, has remained ubiquitous in the rhetoric of white South Carolinians as they faced such threats to their core values as the Emancipation Proclamation, federal intervention, the depression of the 1890s, the civil rights movement, and the Cold War. The Conservative Revival (1980–2000) is a testimony to the strength of their vision.

Scholars have thoroughly documented the role black Carolinians played in the Civil War saga. Black children also suffered hardships, deprivation, and dislocation. Many of their fathers and brothers were forced to work on fortifications; others went off to war as body servants. Children and women replaced them in the fields. Carolina slaves contributed to the demise of slavery and hastened their liberation; they ran away singly and in groups. Some youngsters donned blue uniforms and returned to fight for their freedom. In freedom, South Carolina blacks sought a better life for themselves and their children.

They reunited with long-lost relatives and formalized their marriages. They established their own churches and schools. From the collective memory of black South Carolinians came a liberationist legacy.[6]

Emancipation affected the entire society across race and class lines. Slavery tied white and black Carolinians at the hip, with whites maintaining the upper hand. It would take emancipation to alter the relationship. The life of Robert Smalls illustrates this point. A favored slave, born in Beaufort, Smalls was allowed to hire himself out as a stevedore in Charleston. His work ethic impressed his owner and other influential whites in the city, so much so that they allowed him to purchase his wife and set up a residence in the city. He eventually became a skilled pilot, navigating ships through Charleston Harbor. Such largess did not end glaring injustices. Smalls was not allowed to learn to read or write, his marriage was not legally recognized, and most of his pay went to his owner. Chafing under these and other restrictions, Smalls with a group of like-minded friends and relatives seized a Confederate ship, *The Planter*. They constituted a "family of liberation." The North was electrified; the South was stunned. The enterprising pilot was made an officer in the Union army, further enraging Southerners.[7]

Smalls helped the Northerners probe for weaknesses in Charleston Harbor's defenses. Likewise, he piloted the black Fifty-fourth Massachusetts Regiment to Morris Island, where they demonstrated their fighting tenacity at Fort (Battery) Wagner on July 18, 1863. When the war ended, Smalls allowed the wife of his former master to remain in her former home at Beaufort, which he had purchased. The freedman thrived in the milieu that emancipation and Reconstruction provided. He learned to read and write. He became one of the state's premier politicians. In Congress he called for federal intervention to stop Ku Klux Klan violence in the state. He remained in the U.S. House of Representatives for decades. For blacks, Smalls represented the potential of emancipation. For many white South Carolinians, he symbolized their fears of black Republican rule.[8]

Black Republicanism, imminent with the presidential election of Abraham Lincoln, aroused the farmers of the Upcountry and the rest of the Upstate to close ranks and to shelve temporarily their common dislike of the planter aristocrats of the Lowcountry coastal districts. Stirred up by their evangelical preachers, these yeomen went to war to defend their families and communities. Upcountry households bore the brunt of the casualties. Many of their men died outside of the state.[9]

South Carolina white women instinctively realized the revolutionary potential of emancipation on their households and status. For decades proslavery propaganda proselytized that mayhem would be the logical outcome of abolitionism. During the war, white women saw the society gradually coming apart; their personal security seemed threatened by runaway slaves and invading Yankees. With slavery abolished, women and children in farming households worked harder, while their men found themselves competing with black laborers, sharecroppers, and landowners.[10]

The war and Reconstruction encouraged parents to cooperate in the raising of their children. The society was not immune to modernization. The patriarchy had already been undergoing changes in the decades before the war. Younger planters were more inclined to accept a kinder, gentler patriarchy. They as well as their wives were more open to progressive ideas about childrearing, which were emanating from the North and Europe. Evangelical seminaries for females encouraged elite women to become agents of change. Likewise, consumerism subtly undermined traditional childrearing; children wanted the newest fashions, toys, and gadgets, and their parents tended to indulge them. Yeoman families were probably less inclined toward progressive childrearing than their more affluent urban neighbors. Despite serious challenges to patriarchal authority posed by these outside influences and the war, the patriarchal ideal prevailed. A crushing and humiliating defeat thwarted the modernization process. Elite women placed the prewar patriarchy on a pedestal in their "Lost Cause" rhetoric. In the process they enlarged their own spheres of influence.

Conflicting legacies as symbolized by the Confederate flag and the Emancipation Proclamation bedevil the state still. Carolinians are not of one mind when it comes to the issue of legacy and what they should tell their children about the war and its aftermath. Collective memory is never static but constantly changing as groups reevaluate their past to explain the present and shape the future. On one hand, most white South Carolinians perceived in 1865 that their state was conquered and occupied by Northerners, who proselytized Black Republicanism. On the other hand, most black Carolinians saw the war and Reconstruction as liberating. Memories of the past still follow these fault lines as the state debates symbols of the war, particularly, at this time, the Confederate flag and its place in the public sphere. In 2007, when a black minister was confronted with evidence of black Confederates and slaveowners, he noted, "It doesn't change the fact you did wrong." *Confederate Phoenix* unfolds the struggle of South Carolinians coming to grips with the legacy of a destructive war.[11]

1

Children as a Factor in War Strategy

Confederate leaders made children central to why they seceded and went to war. Jefferson Davis, in his farewell speech to the U.S. Senate on January 21, 1861, defended Southern secession as a necessary action to protect their inherited rights and their "sacred duty to transmit [this legacy] unshorn to [their] children." Contemporaries used the words "fever" and "whirlwind" to describe the phenomenon, which reached its peak in April 1861 with the firing on Fort Sumter. There was no turning back, no resource rejected. Both warring factions played the children's card throughout the conflict.[1]

From the outset, Northerners and Southerners saw themselves as fighting a righteous and godly war. They branded each other as slayers of women and children. Perceptions, distorted by hatred, ruled the day. South Carolinians took every opportunity to highlight real or imagined Yankee atrocities against women and children. While Carolinians extolled the heroics of their young as patriotic, Yankees perceived this encouragement as a perverse manipulation of youth. For Confederate Carolinians, the war entailed the participation of future generations of children in the building of a new nation. As casualty figures mounted and the chances of success dwindled, a legacy of hate was nurtured and passed on.

Propaganda fed on itself. Southern newspapers catalogued Federal atrocities, which were reprinted throughout the Confederacy. Editorials inevitably appeared alongside these items. Elite women recorded and embellished such atrocity stories in their diaries. Boys and girls politicized by the war sought ways to participate in the movement. Children were active in the public sphere in large numbers, some less than seven years old. They helped in Soldiers' Relief and a campaign led by South Carolina women to finance the building of the Ironclad *Palmetto State*.[2]

The secessionist fever, which gripped the state especially in the months leading up to the firing on Fort Sumter, produced a kind of giddiness associated with childhood. Grace Elmore, returning from a trip to New York, indignantly recalled how the Yankees described South Carolina as a spoiled child, an analogy widespread in the North. Children readily succumbed to this fever even before the firing on Fort Sumter. Milledge L. Bonham, son of the future Confederate governor, was five or six when the secession ordinances were passed. For the lad, secession and possible war were play on a grand scale. Boys were rabid secessionists. They organized military units, marched, and crafted toy guns and swords. Although they were politically naive and did not know what Black Republicanism meant, secession unleashed their wild side. Milledge and his young friends modified a cannon barrel into a play weapon. He fired it at an Edgefield celebration of secession, causing the gun carriage and barrel to break. These youngsters reiterated the rhetoric of the adults to justify their action. In February 1861 a Yorkville newspaper reported a boy ending his composition with "give me liberty, or give me death." The war whirlwind even swept up the slaves. Some, in a "perfect fever of excitement," sought "permission to accompany the volunteers."[3]

Youngsters joined vigilance associations and drilled in units. Their female counterparts lionized these "Juvenile Soldiers." Imbued with Byronic romanticism, the "little misses" presented flags to the "boy troopers." Girls of Columbia, under the age of sixteen, gave a concert at Methodist Hall, honoring Hampton's Legion as it left for Charleston. Something grand and historic was sweeping through their communities, promising to bring independence and prosperity in its wake. Desiring to participate, they envied those young men, lucky enough to be part of the Fort Sumter drama.[4]

On November 15, 1860, Union Major Robert H. Anderson was ordered to Fort Sumter. Given Anderson's background as a Kentuckian, his superiors felt his appointment would soothe the fears of South Carolinians. Anderson understood that Fort Moultrie on Sullivan's Island would most certainly be attacked; he prepared a contingency plan. On December 18, 1860, Governor Francis W. Pickens began preparations to counter a possible removal of the garrison to Fort Sumter. Two days later South Carolina seceded from the Union. Federal troops manning the two garrisons were branded as a threat from a foreign nation.[5]

Finding himself in an untenable position, Anderson decided to move his garrison from Fort Moultrie to Fort Sumter, a securer place to defend. His subsequent action might best be called misdirection. First, he convinced those outside of the fort and his own troops that Fort Moultrie would be defended. His order to evacuate women and children from Fort Moultrie to Fort Johnson appeared chivalrous, an effort to move the weak out of harm's way. On December 26 the women and children left for their destination. But Anderson had ordered the officer in charge to delay their disembarkation, ostensibly until suitable accommodations were found for them. With all eyes on Fort Johnson, Anderson began covertly moving the Moultrie garrison to Sumter during the twilight hours. Once the last soldier reached Sumter, guns were fired as a signal to recall the schooners back. Much to their chagrin, some of the schooner captains, Southerners, detected the ruse, but they were caught by surprise.[6]

Thanks to the chivalry of Governor Pickens, the remaining women and children on Fort Sumter were allowed to leave. Anderson requested that a New York steamer be allowed to remove them to Charleston. The major said he would not have enough food to feed them and that they might get sick. Meanwhile, he hoped the secretary of war would agree to bring the women and children to New York. He said they would "embarrass me should I deem it proper to make any sudden move." On February 3, 1861, twenty women and children boarded the *Marion* for Hamilton, New York. Their departure enabled the garrison to have "an ample supply of pork and bread." The success of Anderson's stratagem raised the cry for action to a crescendo in the city. Individual Charlestonians, including youngsters, began to take matters into their own hands. Consequently, some children narrowly escaped being killed by random shootings.[7]

Patriotic youth were moved by the fervor of eighteen-year-old Thaddeus S. Stawinski. Just a week after entering the freshman class at South Carolina College, the boy and his father joined the army. Young Stawinski was part of the Columbia Artillery stationed at Fort Moultrie. He was killed by an accidental gunshot wound. His obituary offered up to young men a role model by memorializing his last words of mourning as he was carried to the hospital: "Friend, O, how sorry I am you are to attack Fort Sumter without me!" The obituary noted: "The sympathy of the whole community is with [the family] in their bereavement."[8]

On April 11, 1861, the Charleston battery was "thronged with spectators of every age and sex." Nothing comparable had occurred on American soil since the War of 1812. It resembled a set from a Verdi opera. Some mothers, wives, and their children waited nervously inside their homes. The bombardment increased their apprehensions. Cannons boomed all the time. One child, too young to talk, mimicked the sounds of the guns. Youngsters, such as twelve- or thirteen-year-old Peter Lelain, were drawn to the spectacle. The Upcountry youth had joined his brother, a member of the Palmetto Guards. The boy himself fired seventeen times.[9]

The firing on Fort Sumter signaled the birth of a Confederate nation, purified of Northern imperfections. Long before the war prominent Southern preachers were preparing the way for secession. They were instrumental in the regional division of the evangelical churches in the 1840s. The South's premier theologians, such as Basil Manly and James H. Thornwell, became wedded to a defense of slavery and endorsed secession. Baptist Basil Manly (1798–1868) began his career preaching in Edgefield District in the Upcountry. As early as

1861 the Provisional Congress of the Confederacy named him chaplain; he presided over the ceremony that made Jefferson Davis the president of the Confederacy. His biographer hailed him "Chaplain to the Confederacy." He passed on his legacy to his scion, Basil Manly Jr., who willingly followed in his footsteps. With the father's help, Manly Jr. and another fervent disciple, J. P. Boyce, established the Southern Baptist Theological Seminary at Greenville, South Carolina; it was a dream fulfilled for the senior theologian, who taught biblical studies there during the war.[10]

The decision to exempt more than three hundred South Carolina preachers before the end of the war was a shrewd move. White Carolinians were ripe for a theological interpretation of the war. Adults bought books with titles like *Armageddon; or, the United States in Prophecy.* Some looked to the prophecies of Nostradamus to describe the crisis of 1861. As God's spokesmen, preachers provided Confederates the prism to equate patriotism with religion and righteousness. Through their preaching, religion became the underpinning for both propaganda and patriotism. Thus they were able to mobilize support and sustain the ongoing commitment to the cause.[11]

Thomas Smyth, a Presbyterian minister-theologian from Charleston, confirmed what nearly all Confederates thought about the fall of Fort Sumter. In his treatise "The Battle of Fort Sumter: Its Mystery and Miracle—God's Master and Mercy," he summarized their beliefs. God's Providence protected them from harm. The battle served "as a single proof of the powerful providence of God; and, secondly, as a pledge and promise of God's continued providence and protection over us." Smyth graphically expressed their pent-up hatreds and fears. He condemned "the fanatical, unholy, and atheistic crusade against God's Word and providence and the vital institution of the South." He loathed a Northern patriotism that threatened "to pour twenty millions of Goths and Vandals, and mercenary hirelings, and with an ocean's mighty sweep before its irresistible deluge every living inhabitant of the South."[12]

Journalists as well as preachers played a significant role in fueling the war fever. The press on both sides showed no shame in using children as war propaganda. From the beginning, writers and newspapers in the North and South invoked children in their jeremiads. Major Anderson, once viewed as an officer and gentleman by the people of Charleston, became a villain. However, in the North, he was an "Idol. Little children [were] brought to look at him, and any one that [could] only touch him [were] made happy." Southern-born Yankee generals were special targets of Confederate wrath. Emma Holmes of Charleston praised the resolution of the Virginia legislature to buy up the land where General Winfield Scott was born, so that no other children would ever be born there. The schoolteacher went farther, declaiming that the spot should be plowed and sowed with salt, so that not even a blade of grass could grow. In turn, Northerners described Charleston as a nursery for the rebellion. General Henry W. Halleck urged General William T. Sherman to burn the Lowcountry port city, sow the soil with salt, so that it could never again be the cradle of secession. This exhortation became indelibly marked in Confederate memory.[13]

Carolinians were deluged with newspaper accounts of the heroics of Southern boys and girls. Honor and courage was a theme often repeated. In May 1861 "a Brave Virginia Boy" kept "vandal Black Republicans" from destroying the dry-dock gates in Portsmouth by cutting "the connection between the lighted fuse and the powder." That same month the Charleston *Daily Courier* reported that a boy, around eleven years old, who was born in the Palmetto State but now lived in Tennessee, proudly wore the Confederate cockade. He wanted a Charleston pistol; Governor Francis Pickens obliged him. About three weeks later the paper informed its readers that as soon as the lad returned home from school and opened his gift, he "shot the pistol, first in honor of the donor and then in honor of South Carolina." Optimistically he declared, "The South has the right and God on her side, and will come out victorious." In May 1862 a newspaper reported that a fourteen-year-old member of the Home Guards was shot while defending his mother's grave. In October of that year another fourteen-year-old lad, dressed as a farmer and armed with a double-barreled shotgun, captured a Union officer in New Orleans. During the same month the Memphis *Appeal* reported that a ten-year-old boy in Jackson, Tennessee, struck a Yankee on the head for insulting his mother. Young girls were applauded for their compassion. In March 1863 the *Confederate Baptist* told the story of a little girl, "an angel," who helped a wounded soldier in central Georgia. The man had lost a leg at Sharpsburg (Antietam) and was famished. She asked him if he had children. He said yes, three, with tears in his eyes. Confederate newspapers further aroused readers with descriptions of the perfidy of Northern troops on these heroic young people. "The hireling hordes of Lincolnites" were blamed for firing on Baltimore women and children. In July 1861, teacher Emma Holmes claimed that little schoolchildren were being beaten for hurrahing Jefferson Davis. A Charleston newspaper affirmed her accusation by reporting that a fourteen-year-old youth was shot at Frankfort, Kentucky, for the same offense.[14]

Victories became an occasion to proclaim the war a crusade for children. After the First Bull Run (First Manassas), a Charleston divine paid tribute to the dead and those fighting for "the happiness of little children and the security of women." In March 1862 an editorial in a Charleston newspaper damned "Our Enemies," the Yankees for committing "one of the blackest pages in the book of crime" by imprisoning women . . . treat[ing] them with brutal rudeness, [furthermore] rough hands have smitten little children in the face for wearing certain colors." Holmes hailed the governor of Missouri for raising 50,000 state militiamen to repel invaders who killed women and children. On the firing in St. Louis, an editorial took the Yankees to task for plundering Southern homes of food, teaching children "to believe that there is no harm in robbing Southerners."[15]

The Vicksburg campaign and the fall of New Orleans brought an escalation in anti-Yankee vituperation. In June 1862 the *Courier* reported the charge of a Mississippi paper that a commander in the U.S. Navy had demolished "a little village." The indictment concluded: "The practice of slaying women and children as an act of retaliation, has, happily, fallen into disuse with the disappearance of three Indian tribes." General Benjamin F. Butler was roundly condemned when he ordered women who cursed his soldiers to be treated as women of the street. His demeaning order made it "very difficult to make a Southern boy believe that he [was] too young to kill a Yankee." Aroused, little children in New Orleans taunted the general by singing the "Bonnie Blue Flag." Children delighted adults by parodying the general. Mary Chesnut wrote that one young lad, imitating Butler, crossed his eyes, making himself repulsive. Although his antics successfully drew laughter from the adults, the boy was no doubt expressing his gut feelings. His father was a prisoner of war. Emma Holmes compared the occupation of New Orleans with France's "Reign of Terror." Female schools were entered and searched. At the Battle of Secessionville near Charleston (June 16, 1862), Louisianans shouted, "Remember Butler," as the Twenty-fourth Regiment, South Carolina Volunteers, Infantry routed the Yankees.[16]

The Confederate press scavenged Northern propaganda mills for grist. One tasty tidbit savored by the *Courier* came from the *New York Times*, which chastised a Minnesota man for baptizing his child Stonewall Jackson. "Cannot the Copperhead be content with their own infamy," the *Times* asked, "without entailing its scrofulous mementoes upon posterity?" In turn, the *Courier*, reacting to the Emancipation Proclamation, reprinted from a Pennsylvania paper the editorial "The Slave Market Outdone," which claimed that a white man tried to sell his two sons as substitutes, "one almost a mere child."[17]

Such rhetoric, based on real or hyped incidents, served several purposes. First, it dehumanized the enemy. Second, it bolstered the belief of the Confederate citizenry in the righteousness of their resistance. Third, such stories were designed to make the North think twice before trying to subdue such a heroic and united people. Finally, by invoking children, it encouraged readers to support the cause to the bitter end. After the Battle of First Bull Run, the *Courier* ran an item from a Virginia correspondent stating that the Confederates found

30,000 pairs of handcuffs. Surmising that they would be needed to subdue the South and its children, the writer threatened: "There is scarcely a two year's old boy among us who does not know how to fire a gun, and would be found willing to do it in [defense] of our right." How could the South come to terms with such a barbaric opponent? Stories of heroic youth were written to stiffen soldier's backbones. During the siege of Charleston, a local newspaper observed that a sick young child put an ax to her "baby home" rather than let the "vandal" foe get it. The paper reasoned, "If such is the spirit of a half dead child of South Carolina, *the men of the Palmetto State cannot be conquered.*"[18]

The formula was simple. Build a Children's Crusade as a bulwark against the Yankees. In 1863 the *Courier* believed "The Hope of the Country" required children to "acquire a holy hatred of the Yankees and it will grow up with and into every fibre of the heart." After hearing a child sing anti-Yankee lyrics set to the tune of "Yankee Doodle," a Northern officer wondered, "How can we expect to restore the Union when even the children hate us so?" In reply, the Charleston organ concluded, "God bless and spare the children, and keep them in the same mind as long as the Yankees continue as they are or grass grows or water runs."[19]

Children became an underpinning for a sustained war effort. In February 1862 a writer proposed: If you love your freedom, home, wife, children, and God, you must "strike, strike, quick and hard." Take to the swamps to make an "altar to God" never to give up. Never make "terms with the vile wretches who invade and destroy our homes." He promised, "We will make our children and our children's children, swear undying hatred and never ending hostility to the whole accursed Yankee nation." In March 1864 the Yorkville *Enquirer* reprinted how the Yankees, hailing the death of General P. G. T. Beauregard's wife, exclaimed, "There is one less left to spawn forth a brood of traitors."[20]

Lincoln's decision to emancipate the slaves convinced Confederates that such fanaticism was not only godless but also a threat to generations to come. In 1862, the flippant remarks of Union General David Hunter provided more grist for Southern propaganda mills. Planters would rather "lose one of their children than a good negro," the general told his superior. A year later Hunter contested the notion that Southerners were fighting for freedom; he charged slaveowners with seducing slaves and then selling or killing their offspring. He challenged Jefferson Davis: "Is this the kind of liberty" you are fighting for, he asked, "the liberty to kill these children with impunity, when the murder cannot be proven by one of pure white blood"? By 1863 Southerners were committed to raising Yankee-hating children from birth. That year a Presbyterian minister, a South Carolinian, issued a clarion call: "Let the spirit of resistance be infused, with its mother's milk into the baby in its cradle. Let it mingle with the plays of childhood."[21]

In such a milieu and with severe reservations, Charlestonians reevaluated their public-school system. The future Confederate secretary of war, C. G. Memminger, who had helped establish the system, had staffed the schools with Northern-born trained teachers. But in July 1863 an article in a Charleston newspaper, spread in the Upcountry by the Yorkville *Enquirer*, charged that such teachers had hurt the cause and should have been sent home earlier. Yankee school "marms" and tutors who dealt with taboo subjects were anathema. In 1863 a Yankee teacher, formerly employed by one of the distinguished families, said that incest was common among planters. In 1864 the Yorkville newspaper, raising the fears of miscegenation, hoped that the Yankee schoolmistresses would never be allowed to teach in the South again. The obsession with racial intermarriage continued after the war. In June 1866 a Charleston newspaper reported, "An ex-slave of Beauregard's is said to have married a New England school marm." It quipped: "She must have chosen her Beau-regardless of color."[22]

Such hatred inspired the women and children in the state to undertake a fundraising effort to build a Confederate ironclad—actually, a sloop. The fall of Port Royal and the siege of Charleston made South Carolina women fear for their families, so they took on the defense of their hearth themselves. In March, a Columbia contributor to the gunboat cause warned that women must give their all or submit to subjugation. She asked: "Must Southern Women have children to leave them only to the heritage of slaves? Submit! No, never! Sooner let the blood of men, women and children seal the covenant of our liberties." In 1862 women and children engaged in a remarkable effort to raise funds for a South Carolina ironclad. Charleston and Columbia women led the effort. The women staged Gunboat Fairs; silver, jewelry, and other valuable items were donated.[23]

Elite children raised and donated money. But according to the Charleston *Courier*, children throughout the state participated in the Ladies Gunboat Campaign. The newspaper listed the names of donors. Three little girls gave five dollars for a Bible to be used on the gunboat. Twelve-year-old Willie P. from Edgefield donated one dollar. He hoped he would be old enough to be aboard the ironclad when the first guns were fired. Another child offered a ring to the raffle. Three "little girls" went to bed "supper less" to be able to give two dollars. The "Young Ladies" of Belle Haven Institute in Columbia donated twenty-two dollars to build and equip the ironclad.[24]

Most children vied for the approval of adults, but their fear and hatred of Northerners were real enough, even palpable. Three-year-old Minnie Bryce, giving a dollar, wished that "every Yankee will be shot that comes to burn the houses." Ten-year-old M. M. Kemme offered five dollars with the hope that all the other boys would donate as well "to free our coast of the Yankee invaders." A boy, "ambitious of driving a nail in the contemplated turtle or ram," gave a dollar. The Carolina Zouaves, "youthful corps of Charlestonians," presented eleven dollars. They were disappointed that they were "too young to be her crew." The Second Class of the Male Department at the Friend Street School in Charleston donated twelve pounds of lead with the wish that "each bullet may find its mark in the persons of the vile invaders of South Carolina." By early October the ladies had raised $30,268.93. On October 11, 1862, they christened the ironclad *The Palmetto State*.[25]

Children were also active in Solders' Relief and the Free Market. Mrs. Sallie (Sarah Flournoy Moore) Chapin, who wrote a fictional account of a Confederate boy based on her own experiences, headed the Solders' Relief Society in Charleston. She took pride in the juvenile group who called themselves "The Hive of Busy Bees." No person over sixteen could join. Gender conventions prevailed. The "little patriots" paid their dues in Confederate money. Five-year-old "Little Lillie" was the youngest member. Generously the children also supported the Free Market system, an attempt to aid poor families. In April 1863 Charleston's market was spending ten thousand dollars to assist eight hundred poor families, with soldiers at the front. The children of refugee families were most inclined to help. In May 1863 a ten-year-old girl refugee in Sumter raised twenty-five dollars by raffling off her baby house on behalf of the Free Market and Soldiers' Relief. The most striking manifestation of youthful patriotism, though, came in the form of sacrifices made by the "Boy Soldiers."[26]

2 Boy Soldiers and Their Families

B oy" was a nebulous term in Southern society in the 1860s. All black males were "boys." On the other hand, the "boys of '64" became a nostalgic term to describe Confederate veterans. "Mere boy" meant males under twenty. "Boyish" was used to describe women soldiers. "Boys" also appealed to the maternal instincts of Southern women, who saw them as the nation's sons. The age of sixteen had been the enlistment standard during the American Revolution, but nearly a century later this statute did not fit the changing attitudes about childhood and their impact on demographics. In 1861 the Confederacy formally defined boys by forbidding enlistment to males under seventeen without the consent of their parents. In joining the army, South Carolina boys embarked on an early entrance into manhood by demonstrating self-sufficiency. In this chapter, "boy soldier" is a generic term specifically applying to youth who entered the army under age seventeen. Their total number is almost impossible to determine, but it did not exceed five thousand.[1]

In 1905, embarking on a history of the "Boy Soldiers of the Confederacy," Susan Hall had planned to focus on all boys under twenty, but to her dismay she found so many under sixteen that she revised the cutoff age to eighteen. As she discovered, the vicissitudes of civil war profoundly effected the transition from boyhood to manhood and the stability of the patriarchal family. The Conscription Act of April 1862 challenged the common law's definition of a minor. Fathers demanded the right to have the service of their minors until they became twenty-one. In October 1862 the South Carolina Supreme Court ruled against this common law of parental rights. The judges, acknowledging that underage children were serving in the army, cited "public necessity" as the basis for the ruling. Under the Conscription Act of April 1862 male residents of the state between the ages of eighteen and thirty-five were subject to the draft. Those under eighteen or over thirty-five and already serving had to remain an additional ninety days. In July 1862 persons under eighteen and over thirty-five who reenlisted either for three years or the duration of the war could not be discharged. Those who enlisted for twelve months or shorter terms would be discharged only after the original commitment was met. In September 1862, shortly after the Battle of Antietam, the Confederacy extended the upper enlisted age to forty-five. In the middle of February 1864, persons ages seventeen to fifty were required to serve.[2]

In the first year of the war, Confederate leaders, including Jefferson Davis, did not want to sacrifice the "Corn Seed" of the new Confederate Republic. Davis preferred that boys under eighteen be kept home as a reserve for home defense. After Second Bull Run (Second Manassas), General Wade Hampton encouraged students in his Legion to return to college. Union General George B. McClellan shared Hampton's sensibilities. As late as June 1862, when the Yankees threatened South Carolina, people in Virginia and the eastern part of South Carolina were livid when their reserve corps of old men and boys were offered into action.[3]

When the draft age was adjusted downward to seventeen in February 1864, some people charged that the authorities purposely allowed one-third to one-half of the men on their muster rolls to be away from their commands, so that boys of fifteen and old men of sixty would have to take their places. Instead of seeking peace negotiations, the public reluctantly bowed to the necessity of recruiting boys and old men as soldiers. In May 1864, Mary Chesnut noted that only a raw militia of boys and old men confronted the Yankees as they landed at Coosawatchie. In December 1864, a Spartanburg women reported that the fourteen-year-old boys had marched off to stop the enemy. Haunted by the specter of defeat, some elite women were only too eager to send boys into the fray. In March 1865, Emma Holmes demanded that every able boy should take up arms and fight the Yankees to the death rather than be subjected to their domination. With the support of friends, some parents resisted the pressure. In 1864 a dear friend counseled Mary Harth to keep her eager son Willie out of the army until he had to go. Mrs. A Howell warned her that the boy might end up being shot down on the battlefield and buried in a shallow hole.[4]

Some parents gave their consent but regretted it. B. W. Warren of Charleston noted that a general was organizing four companies of youths to defend the city and the coast. The father sent his sixteen-year-old son to what he thought was a kind of training school. He never imagined that his boy would be marching off to war. In 1862, when the concerned father learned that these companies were to become part of a regular regiment advancing to Virginia, he requested his son's release. Poorer parents allowed their sixteen-year-old boys to enter the war as substitutes. In the case of G. W. Bussey, he took his father's place in the army so that the elder Bussey could care for his mother.[5]

Despite warnings from older brothers to stay in school, male siblings, brimming with martial spirit, badgered their parents for their consent or just ran off to enlist. In April 1862, sixteen-year-old Jefferson Strait of Chester District, South Carolina, persuaded his parents to let him join his older brother George

Lafayette Strait of the Catawba Guard, Company A, Sixth Regiment. The boy's mother had real misgivings; she asked George to watch over him. She also told Jefferson he must no longer act like a child; he was filling a man's position. Other patriotic parents became disillusioned. Mrs. William P. Goodman lamented not keeping in school her sixteen-year-old Willie: "I let him go because I saw the necessity of raising an army and very many were holding their sons back, [but I] now feel as if I had almost a right to my child . . . to send him to school."[6]

Like many conflicts, the Civil War offered boys in the North and South a ticket to manhood and adventure. But in the South underage boys, living in a slave society circumscribed by a code of chivalry and honor, knew instinctively that military service in this war was an opportunity to manhood, freedom, and glory they could not reject. Going to war to protect their mothers and sisters freed them from imposing constraints. For Frank Mixson, running away became an obsession. Mixson and youths like him joined a company of Minute Men in Barnwell District. He was not yet fourteen; his father had died when he was six. Thinking the Rebels would lose without him, Frank ran away to join the unit. He walked some twenty-seven miles in his quest for glory, but his guardian retrieved him. In April 1861 he tried to join Colonel Johnson Hagood's First South Carolina Volunteers. The colonel told him to go home but eventually let him become part of the unit. He probably admired the small boy's spunk. Others like Mixson ingratiated their way into the army. Their youthful enthusiasm was appealing to some veteran soldiers. Lawrence Guffin of Abbeville was a scout for the Confederates at age thirteen. Nicknamed "Babe," he claimed he was "one of [General] Hampton's special scouts."[7]

Parents chiefly attributed their sons running away to join the army to enticement and peer pressure. In September 1861, on behalf of his "heart-broken" wife, John Stackley begged for the return of their fifteen-year-old son Jacob. The mother claimed that the youth had been enticed to enlist. A month later a Mr. Moore asked Jefferson Davis for the return of his sixteen-year-old Elijah, who had joined Company F, Third Regiment, South Carolina Volunteers (SCV). The same month Abner Porter claimed his sixteen-year-old son James was induced to enlist by members of Captain Miller's Company. So it went on until the end of the war. In 1864 John W. Rose, only fifteen years old, just left home and joined the Twelfth Regiment, SCV, without parental consent. The family obtained a lawyer to try to get the runaway back. In 1865 Nancy Owens of Pickens District wanted her son exempt, but her husband could not assist because he was in the service. William, not yet sixteen, had run off with a group of sixteen-year-old boys to join the army.[8]

Some parents managed to get their underage children returned, but the process took time. First, they had to go through the chain of command with an affidavit establishing the soldier's age. Some reached the Secretary of War through individual Congressmen; others sent petitions, usually signed by neighbors, requesting a discharge. Several parents wrote directly to Secretary of War George Randolph and President Davis. Randolph had a reputation as a hard-liner. He was determined to keep as many boots in the field as he could. He demanded that the mother of a ten-year-old boy prove that she had not given her consent. Some youngsters were equally determined to stay in service. John Scroggins, only fourteen years old, ran away from his home in York District to join the Fifth South Carolina Regiment at Cold Harbor in April 1864. His mother got him discharged, but the boy had a mind of his own. In August he was accepted by Company D, Third Battalion, South Carolina Reserves, and was assigned to guard duty at Florence prison.[9]

Boy soldiers were compelled to serve several months, sometimes twelve, before they were returned to their parents who had successfully petitioned for their release.

Benjamin S. Nesmith of Williamsburg entered the army at age fifteen or sixteen. He was not discharged at Knoxville, Tennessee, until he had finished his full term of twelve months. Others were more fortunate. Newton F. Walker of Spartanburg District entered the service in August 1861 but was discharged February 12, 1862. A Lancaster youth, David Kennerly, was fifteen years old when he enlisted in July 1862 but was discharged in September. That year Roland R. Wilson of Kershaw District enlisted in Camden. His size (he was six-foot-two) concealed his age. But the young farmer was later discharged as underage. In January 1863, Sophia Divver, a widow, wanted her sixteen-year-old son Young H. returned home. He was a private in the Sixteenth Regiment, General Nathan Evan's Brigade. He received his discharge on April 2, 1863. William C. Hill was fifteen when he enlisted. On January 1, 1863, he was finally discharged for "being a non-Conscript," but only after being taken prisoner and paroled in 1862.[10]

For boy soldiers, militias, local and state, became an important conduit into the army. As early as 1841, white males between sixteen and sixty could be called into the militia. Youths of sixteen also served on slave patrols. The militia eventually absorbed the slave patrols. In the 1850s the South Carolina militia was required to meet annually. The exercise became a spectacle in which white males, planters and yeomen alike, showed their prowess. Thus, sixteen was a marker for young males to begin their quest for manhood even before the war. Although youth under the age of seventeen were ineligible for conscription in February 1864, they were required to serve militia duty. Martial law also brought numbers of boys and old men into the army during the war. In May

1862 martial law was proclaimed in Charleston. City authorities went from door to door registering males between sixteen and eighteen. The militia became a ready reserve. In 1863 the Charleston *Mercury* advocated letting men of eighteen go into the army while allowing youths of sixteen to enter the militia. The manpower squeeze mounted during October 1863. Governor M. L. Bonham, faced with raising an additional five thousand troops, called up the state militia. Boys under eighteen in the militia would be required to fight, or at least stay an additional ninety days in service. In February 1864 the enrolling officer of York required all males between sixteen and sixty to report. That month the Confederate Congress required men between the ages of seventeen or eighteen and forty-five through fifty to enroll themselves in "a reserve for the State Defense and detail duty." They were not required to serve outside their states.[11]

Another venue for youngsters to serve in the war was the Marine School, established in 1859 to train homeless vagrants to become sailors. The school ship was the *Lodebar*, designed to become a seagoing equivalent of the state military academy. It was this vessel that carried Confederate officials to the surrender at Fort Sumter. Some eager students, seven in all, infused with war fever, ran away to enlist in the army; their average age was fifteen. Those that graduated served on blockade runners, including the *Chicora*, as well as on various privateers, such as the Charleston-based *Nashville*. Other youngsters, though neither students nor graduates of the school, also served on the high seas. They were able to sign up as captain's boys on blockade runners. In March 1864 Eugene DeBerry, a sixteen-year-old from Sumter, wanted permission from the secretary of war to serve as a fireman on a vessel bound from Wilmington to Nassau or Bermuda.[12]

Authorities were sometimes circumspect about using youngsters in certain situations. Most boys served in noncombat roles. In March 1862 Lawrence Hill, thirteen, enlisted as a drummer boy in Columbia. One year later the Twenty-fourth Regiment advertised for five good fifers, lads between the ages of fourteen and eighteen; they needed parental consent. A drum corps consisted of a fife, bass drum, and a snare drum. Perky drummer boys appealed to parents and children alike. J. C. Dowling told his sister Rebecca that her son should grow up fast to become a drummer boy for their regiment. In 1863, "The Story of a Drummer Boy" appeared in Charleston newspapers. Jimmy was present at the aftermath of the Battle of Fort Wagner in July. The slight lad joined his comrades in looking for plunder. Tired from a long day's work, he fell asleep, only to be captured by a black man three times his size. He met Yankee General Quincy Gillmore and was then transferred to Hilton Head, where the Northerners sent him home. Asked how he was treated, he replied: "Oh, Bully, pickled beef, and pickled pork, sometimes fresh beef, coffee and a gill of whiskey four times a day." Another lad, John Quinn, was born in Ireland, fifteen years old; he served in Company E, First Butler's South Carolina Infantry as a musician. When he had enlisted at Fort Moultrie in September 1862, he was two inches short of five feet tall. Discharged in July 1864, he appeared again on a report of Rebel deserters and refugees in March 1865.[13]

According to A. S. Salley's compilation, drummer boys were an exception. His three volumes on South Carolina troops included 121 musicians. Ages were available for forty-five of them. Only four were under eighteen; none under fifteen. Seventeen, or 14 percent, were black. They served in a number of South Carolina regiments. Some performed in the regimental bands of Johnson Hagood's and Maxcy Gregg's SCV regiments. The paucity of white youngsters is understandable. The role of Civil War musicians was multipurpose and dangerous. The bandsmen played reveille, breakfast call, assembly, and taps. Some held jobs as barbers, waterboys, and carriers. They also attended the wounded. Life as member of the band was sometimes dangerous. Eighteen-year-old musician Alex Whisnant enlisted in Greenville in April 1861. He was a private in Company B, Second South Carolina Infantry. He was wounded at Gettysburg, where he was taken prisoner on July 3, 1863. He was paroled at the end of the war at Greensboro, North Carolina, on May 2, 1865.[14]

Youngsters served as orderlies and mail carriers. In August 1863, Joseph Darlington of Due West, Abbeville District, age fourteen, wrote to Jefferson Davis, asking to be an orderly to some colonel, "or any place where I can be of service to the Confederate States." He told Davis he was tired of staying home when he could be useful in the army since he was educated enough to "understand Latin." The youth added that one of his brothers had died, while another had not been heard from since Gettysburg. This just made the waiting unbearable. Frederick Gates was a student at Newberry College when the call for volunteers came for the sixteen-year-old boys. He served as an orderly to General M. C. Butler. Robert M. Bullock was a mail carrier in Company F, Seventh South Carolina Regiment. Sixteen-year-old J. W. Pratt of Due West acted as a courier between Castle Pinckney and old St. Michael's Church. He carried messages from the sentinels stationed to watch Charleston Harbor.[15]

Boy soldiers also guarded forts, railroads, and Union prisoners. J. A. M. Gardener belonged to a company of 120 youths, mostly sixteen-year-olds, who guarded railroads. Two other sixteen-year-olds, Duncan McLaurin and Adolphus Miles Copeland, found themselves stationed at Florence Prison. N. S. Courtney from Chesterfield was only sixteen when he guarded Yankee prisoners at the same facility, a hardening tour of duty. He returned home on detail picking up deserters.[16]

The youths were prone to disease. In July 1864 a company of about a hundred boys left Newberry to join Confederate service. During the fall, seven died from yellow fever. Charles W. Williamson of Spartanburg District entered the army before he was sixteen. He was a member of Company C, Edwards' Regiment, SCV. On August 24, 1862, suffering from chronic diarrhea, he entered the CSA general hospital. He returned to duty about a week later. On June 21, 1863, he was admitted to a hospital in Richmond for "exhaustion." He remained there for several weeks. Typhoid was another serious problem. On August 20, 1862, John Wakefield's father wanted the boy released for medical reasons. Earlier that month he had been admitted to Chimborazo Hospital No. 5 in Richmond for typhoid fever. He was granted a thirty-day furlough. Measles struck some underage soldiers with a vengeance. Fourteen-year-old Vinton Carter was a farm laborer from Cokesbury, Abbeville District. He enlisted as a private in Greenville on April 7, 1861. Just three months after arriving at Manassas Junction, he contracted measles.[17]

A profile of fifty-six youths under age seventeen who died paralleled the mortality patterns of soldiers of all ages (see Table 2.1). The Upcountry was hardest hit because it furnished so many soldiers. Thirty-four boy soldiers, or nearly two-thirds, came from the Upstate. More died of disease than were killed in action.

Some boy soldiers were simply too young and physically immature to shoulder adult responsibilities. Private George Mercer of Company E, Fifth Regiment, SCV, was found sleeping at his post. He was part of the Charleston troops under General P. G. T. Beauregard. Private Mercer had the misfortune of walk-

Table 2.1
Confederate Mortality Rate

	Soldiers of All Ages	Under Seventeen Years of Age
Killed in Action	5,226 (28.04 percent)	19 (33.93 percent)
Died of wounds	2,647 (14.2 percent)	3 (5.36 percent)
Died of disease	6,755 (36.24 percent)	29 (51.79 percent)
Died in prison	1,408 (7.55 percent)	2 (3.57 percent)
Accidental	155 (0.83 percent)	1 (1.78 percent)
Murdered	28 (0.15 percent)	0
Executed	9 (0.05 percent)	0
Suicides	3 (0.02 percent)	0
Killed in duels	2 (0.01 percent)	0
Died of exposure	2 (0.01 percent)	0
Unrecorded	2,404 (12.9 percent)	2 (3.57 percent)
Total[18]	18,639	56

ing guard duty at Charleston Harbor after the slave Robert Smalls had absconded with the Confederate *Planter.* Under article 46, the soldier could have been put to death. A military tribunal described him as "a youth scarcely able to bear arms, and not of sufficient intelligence to understand the duties of a sentinel." His age was thought to be sixteen or seventeen, but witnesses described him as younger. He claimed he was fourteen. "A mere youth," he had walked his post without shoes over an oyster bed for five successive days and nights. He was spared.[19]

"Boy" connotes innocence, but boys on both sides made particularly malleable soldiers. Some were quick studies. General William T. Sherman referred to youngsters who fought in his armies as his devils. Among themselves, they referred to him as "Uncle." Underage soldiers in Hampton's Legion proudly identified themselves as "Hampton's scouts." Youngsters in the Georgia state militia were called "Joe Brown's Pets," after the governor. Some officers balked at losing a good boy soldier. In 1862 Captain Andrew Butler rebuffed a mother's contention that her boy entered without her consent. Butler responded, "The sympathy & patriotism in times like these would seem to direct that the Petitioners ought to furnish from their own abundant sources to the Widows whose sons are in service."[20]

Boy soldiers were present at most major battles after Fort Sumter, beginning with Fort Walker and Port Royal (1861) and ending with Sherman's March through the Carolinas. Colonel John A. Wagener's fifteen-year-old son Julius, a private, was active during the Union naval attack on Fort Walker. When the Palmetto banner on Ft. Walker was shot down, Julius replanted it. Thirteen men were killed and about the same number wounded. The state legislature awarded the youngster with a cadetship. Boy soldiers were at the critical Battle of Secessionville (June 16, 1862), which halted the Yankee advance on Charleston. Rebel soldiers were outnumbered thirteen to one. Hiram L. Baggott was "severely" wounded; his older brother J. M. was killed there. Eventually Hiram retuned to his company. James Hunt served as a standard bearer in Maxcy Gregg's Regiment, First SCV. During the Battle of Chickahominy, Virginia (June 27, 1862), the sixteen-year-old was mortally wounded. As the war continued, most of the boy soldiers who had enlisted as underage youth grew up fighting, many dying as young men over the age of seventeen and others returning home with their wounds.[21]

Antietam maimed and killed its share of boy soldiers. Richland's Joseph G. McKee enlisted as a private in April 1861. He was wounded in action both in the Seven Days Campaign and Antietam. On October 1, 1862, he was captured and paroled at Fort McHenry Prison, Maryland. After being in and out of hospitals, including Chimborazo, he returned to active duty on July 30, 1863.

Wounded again in 1864, he was sent to Richmond, this time Jackson Hospital. He was killed in action at Petersburg. His brother served in the Second South Carolina Infantry.[22]

Gettysburg took its toll, too. James B. Pitts of Newberry, Company D, Thirteenth Regiment, was wounded there on July 1, 1863. Captured and paroled, he returned to Newberry as an enrolling officer, but only temporarily. On September 23, 1864, he was admitted to the Episcopal Church Hospital at Williamsburg, Virginia. Robert Pearson, Second Regiment, Kershaw's Brigade, was also wounded and captured at Gettysburg. His arm was amputated. John Wakefield, sixteen when he enlisted in September 1861 in Company I, Fourteenth Regiment, South Carolina Rifles, died on July 5, 1863, of wounds.[23]

Willie P. Goodman of Edgefield, South Carolina ended up at Gettysburg by a circuitous path. His family was originally from Connecticut. In March 1863 Mrs. Goodman requested the release of her son from Company D, Fourteenth Regiment, SCV, McGowan's Brigade. These exemption requests were a constant source of contention between the state and the Confederate government. The concerned mother wanted her son to attend the South Carolina Military Academy. He had applied for the academy when he was fourteen. She had allowed the sixteen-year-old boy to enter the army because the country was in peril. He followed his father into the service. Willie spent twenty consecutive months in the Confederate army. He never came home on a furlough. He was slightly wounded at Shepardstown, Maryland, but refused to report himself hurt. The boy was captured after the Battle of Gettysburg on July 14, 1863, at Falling Waters, Maryland. A month later he was sent to the Old Capitol Prison, Washington, D.C., where he remained for a year. He was transferred to Fort McHenry and then moved to Point Lookout, both in Maryland. At last, he was exchanged at City Point, Virginia, in early March 1865. Like so many other parents who had caved in to the demands of their young sons, Mrs. Goodman must have rued her decision long after the war ended.[24]

Boy soldiers serving in the local and state militia were not free from danger; some did not escape capture and imprisonment. Thomas B. Chaplin, a cotton planter from the Port Royal region, and his three sons joined the local militia to stop the Yankee invasion. Private Eugene Chaplin, age sixteen, was captured and imprisoned in February 1865. Although he was paroled in March, he later died from the ill treatment he received in prison. Willie and other young POWs were lucky to survive, but their ingenuity sometimes made a difference. Lewis J. Langford was sixteen when he enlisted in the army. Sherman's troops captured him. He was in prison for five months, where he contracted the measles. Subsisting on hardback, he took meat and biscuits from the bowl of the cook's dog. Unlucky youngsters ended up at hellholes such as Fort Delaware Prison, where inmates used the camp's privy to fish for survival. Despite such ingenuity, the terrible conditions took their toll, with individuals dying of congestion of the lungs and other illnesses.[25]

By late 1864 conditions were becoming critical in South Carolina. Governor A. G. Magrath issued a proclamation allowing sixteen-year-olds to fight. The Battle of Honey Hill (late November and early December 1864) and the ensuing campaign to stop advances of the Union army into Georgia and South Carolina necessitated the use of boys. Some five thousand Union soldiers were sent from Hilton Head to facilitate Sherman's march toward Savannah by cutting off reinforcements from the city. The specific objective was to sever the Charleston and Savannah Railroad at Honey Hill, near Grahamville Station, South Carolina. On November 30, 1864, the Confederates, some 1,400 strong, threw back a much larger Union army that numbered 5,500 men. The assault continued the next day. The Yankees retreated, but skirmishes continued into December. Another decisive engagement came on December 6 and 7 at a trestle where the railroad crossed over Tulifinny Creek. Cadets from the Citadel manned the right of the line where the two-hour contest was fiercest. Heavy casualties were inflicted on the Yankees. The cadets remained active, participating in the final campaigns of the war.[26]

The boys of Company C, State Militia, Second South Carolina, learned their lessons from military manuals; they received no uniforms or tents. Their mission was to counter Yankee troops landing along the coast from Savannah to Charleston. They were tested at Honey Hill. W. A. Wall, who had enlisted in 1864, remembered digging foxholes large enough to hold four men. The youths felt exhausted as they drove the enemy back. Next they marched to Coosawatchie to guard the Charleston and Savannah Railroad. With no freshwater supply available, they got rainwater from the same ditches used by the horses. Here the boys bathed, washed their clothes, and obtained both their drinking and cooking water. Wall's shoes and clothes were worn out. He went three days without food but was proud to claim that his unit was the youngest and the last to muster out in March 1865. He was not yet sixteen.[27]

The First, Second, and Third Regiments of South Carolina Troops were organized at Camden in August 1864. Lawrence W. Taylor was assigned to Captain A. C. Goodwyn, Company K, Bonham Guards, Third Regiment. Taylor rose from private to captain, one of the youngest in the state. Most of his regiment's service was at Charleston, Green Pond, Adams Run, Salkechatchie, Pocotaligo, and Grahamville. The Battle of Honey Hill remained vivid for him decades later. In telling his story, he wanted to shed light on the heroism of boy soldiers. His big moment came the night after the battle ended. He was ordered to lead a group of one hundred men, in truth, mostly boys, in an advance picket to see if the Yankees were going to renew the attack. His commander told him that it was a chance for the boys to be part of history. The unit was camped near a swamp. The night was cold. The Yankees advanced, terrifying Taylor, but they halted. They were securing the retreat of the Federals to their gunboats. With the threat subsiding, Taylor and his soldiers relaxed. They were exhausted from the marching and fighting. Taylor tried to nap between the rains. When he woke up the next morning, he found himself between two dead black Federal soldiers.[28]

Governor Magrath realized the futility of properly organizing and training young men in regiments to fight in so short a time. On February 7, 1865, Magrath pronounced some regiments "the tombs of these children." Irate parents threatened to take their boys home. The governor concluded, "My plain and obvious duty would be to disband them by my proclamation." After four years of war, observers conceded that the boy soldiers had acquitted themselves well, many heroically, and needed respite. "A Plea for Young Soldiers" was issued by a Spartanburg newspaper in April 1865. Several hundred youths, ages sixteen and seventeen, have already served, the plea argued, "many of whom have already born fatigues and withstood the dangers of a campaign with credit and honor." That month the governor sent his bodyguard of boys from the Arsenal in Columbia home.[29]

Many of these boy soldiers came from yeoman households from Upcountry districts such as Spartanburg and York. Yeoman farmers have seldom received sufficient attention. Few manuscript collections deal with yeoman families who had underage boys in the war. Fortunately, the Pursley family letters fill this vacuum. They are a window on a boy soldier, his family, his unit, and the community. They show the maturing of the youth and document a direct link between the home front and the battlefield. By 1850 York District was becoming an important cotton-growing region in the South Carolina Upcountry. Blacks formed a majority of the population by 1860. Yet, there were still pockets of yeoman farmers. The Pursley family worked a farm in the northern part of York, near the North Carolina border. They lived in New Center, located in a region not directly linked to the railroad. The white neighborhood was closely knit Scots-Irish. In addition to planting corn and wheat, the Pursleys raised hogs and sheep. Like most yeoman farmers, they owned no slaves and took their Presbyterian faith seriously.[30]

The patriarch William (1813–1879) was forty-eight years old in 1861; his wife Elizabeth J. Hemphill Pursley (1812–1886) was a year older. Their only son was James Warren Pursley (1845–1904), who enlisted in December 1861 at age sixteen. The older child, Mary Frances "Jane" (1837–1915), was twenty-four years old. She chose not to marry because of the freedom it afforded her and her devotion to her family. The war sealed her decision. Her work as a skilled weaver added to the family income, which became even more important as the war dragged on. A strong personality, she was the hub of the family. She corresponded with relatives who moved west to Texas and Arkansas. She helped raise Warren and her nine-year-old sister, Martha Tirzah (1852–1897). It was to his older sister Jane that the boy soldier confided his feelings, thoughts, and experiences at the front.[31]

As an only son, Warren represented the future of the family. He was their precious "Corn Seed." They feared the impact soldiering might have on such an impressionable lad. He had never traveled far from York District. His first tour of duty was in the Lowcountry just outside of Charleston; the experience was an eye-opener. Yorkville, he exclaimed, would hardly fill a city block in Charleston. Warren's family read the letters of a sixteen-year-old youngster seeking adventure. They clung to this illusion by promising him that they would keep his pet horse Mike out of the work fields and in the pasture. Jane, worrying about Warren's spiritual well-being, repeatedly lectured him on possible snares. The family wanted Warren and his cousins to be good boys and avoid bad company.[32]

Warren, however, saw going to war as an affirmation of his manhood. The veterans soon tested him. Shortly after he enlisted, two men challenged him while he was on guard duty. They tried to get his rifle but failed. His next test was harder to pass. As a teenage soldier, Warren had to come to grips with his own mortality. He had not yet been in battle. He confessed some of the angst he felt when he toured the battlefield at Secessionville. He saw men severely wounded and dead Yankee soldiers without heads. Warren was shaken by the experience. His self-doubt, however, fell on deaf ears. Sensing he was scared, Jane impressed upon him the need for godliness. She warned him he had better be good; he could get his head blown off, too! Jane no doubt offended his budding sense of manhood. Exposing her own inexperience, she asked him if the Yankees were ugly or good-looking. At that, Warren reminded his sister that the Yankees were dead for trying to take away their rights.[33]

Tirzah was the apple of the family's eye. Warren welcomed her letters, short as they were. But she spent her early teen years worrying about her brother, and later her father, when he, too, was sent off to war. After Warren departed for the front, the little girl decided to raise a lamb to welcome him back. When her father left with his reserve unit, she developed a headache. As the war continued and speculation spread, Tirzah sought ways to bring in money, too. She made a scarf to sell. Warren told her he would buy it himself for five dollars and encouraged her to put more time in her education. Tirzah's lost innocence, like the premature death of her pet lamb, showed how her family could not shield the child from the worldly impact and pressures of a nation at war.[34]

In 1862 an injury to William Pursley shook the family. He hurt himself plowing. By the time he healed, rain prevented him from completing his chores. In November he received orders to serve a ninety-day stint in the Lowcountry. He was a private in the First Corps of Reserves, Seventh Regiment. William's leaving raised anxieties. He worried about Tirzah's smallpox vaccination. He talked over the care of the farm with Elizabeth before he left. She reassured her husband that friends and neighbors would help with the killing of the hogs. William returned to keep the farm together as best as possible. Household income was supplemented by distilling whiskey. Warren himself had to engage in speculation to make ends meet and send money home.[35]

Women helped save the farm. Jane Pursley clipped sheep and wove yards of wool. Elizabeth Pursley participated in hog killings while Jane assisted her in the care of Tirzah. Both daughters did chores. As members of a small yeoman family, the women and girls acquired farming skills most naturally. Tirzah helped with seed planting. Jane bragged that their little sister could sow corn as fast as she could. When girlfriends visited, they all played a game of who could plow more rows. In 1863 Warren was delighted to learn that the neighborhood women and girls helped with the corn shucking at the Pursley barn. He missed the big event. Jane's ability to weave became increasingly more important as economic hard times set in with the continuation of the war. In May 1862 she boasted to Warren that she had woven more than one hundred yards of cloth since his last furlough home.[36]

Warren's parents had reasons to fear the evils of camp life on their son's moral well-being. Rumors spread in New Center about the antics of his chums and himself. Confronted by his sister about an alleged whiskey-drinking binge, Warren denied it. But here was a young boy growing up too quickly; he openly confided to his family very personal feelings about death, immorality, and debaucheries he witnessed in Richmond. He later confessed to Jane that he skipped a Sunday sermon on gambling. Instead he went for a walk and was lured into a game of throwing "Dixie," or dice. The family knew they could not keep the good-looking youth from pursuing young women. Pursley had an eye for girls. Sunday service offered him an opportunity to meet them. In March 1863, while worshipping near Wilmington, North Carolina, he described one soldier's wife as ugly as sin. On his way to Florida in 1864 he was smitten by a girl refugee from Jacksonville, "pretty as red shoes and smart as forty coons." In addition, her daddy was "rich as Dew." She fed him meals free of charge.[37]

When Warren enlisted in the Eighteenth Regiment, SCV, at Camp Hampton in December 1861, he had no idea that York's participation in the war would be more costly in terms of the percentage of dead white males than any other district. Nor could he ever imagine where the war would take him. Many York men enlisted in the SCV Infantry regiments that formed the brigade under the command of General Nathan "Shanks" Evans (1824–1868). The men became known as "The Tramp Brigade" because it was independent and went wherever it was needed. Besides participating in the defense of Charleston, these men fought at Second Bull Run, Antietam, Vicksburg, and the first Petersburg campaign. They helped stop the Union army under General B. F. Butler from making a breakthrough to Richmond in May 1864. Two months later the brigade suffered severe losses in the Battle of the Crater. Under the command of General William Henry Wallace, those remaining surrendered at Appomattox. By the war's end more than eight thousand men had served in the "Tramp Brigade."[38]

For yeoman youngsters, the army was an avenue of social mobility. Service in the Tramp Brigade allowed Warren to see much of the Deep South. He speculated about permanently moving to places where he might prosper as a farmer. His leadership qualities and support from the other enlisted men insured his rise up the ranks. In July 1862 he served as an acting orderly sergeant in General James Longstreet's division. By April 1863 he was a sergeant. Elected an officer by his fellow enlisted men, Warren studied and subsequently passed an examination to become a second lieutenant. In August 1864 he was promoted to first lieutenant. He was only nineteen. His father was thrilled and sent a fine sword for the occasion. A practical yeoman, the son asked his father for a less expensive replacement. He requested Jane to make his uniform.[39]

Despite her joy for Warren, the war inevitably hardened Jane. Neighborhood feuds, inflation, and the scarcity of food were draining events. She suffered the loss of kin and had to endure seeing a neighborly New Center turn fractious. Sometimes disputes among normally friendly neighbors escalated into ugly incidents that revealed economic and political fault lines. Jane counseled Warren that the boys at the front should not fight among themselves because of disputes between families at home. In June 1862 a Pursley uncle got into a heated row with a neighbor over a stray ewe. The neighbor hoped the North would defeat the Rebels. Deserters and runaway slaves terrified Jane. By 1864 they had become commonplace. After one deserter was shot through the face, the normally sanguine Jane said he got what he deserved.[40]

Warren's description of how he survived Antietam was coldly analytical. For himself as well as the Confederacy, the battle was a turning point. Hit by a shell to the left shoulder and afflicted with broken ribs, he lay down under a hail of fire. Locking arms with a fellow soldier whose fingers were cut off, the two men walked off the field. After resting at a Wayside Hospital, he was admitted to Chimborazo on October 4, 1862. He was moved to a hospital in Danville, Virginia. He returned to duty on November 3, 1862.[41]

In late 1862 and early 1863, the Pursley family was split over the issue of kin avoiding the war. They argued over whether William Pursley's brother-in-law, William Ervin, should be exempt from further service. William Pursley was ashamed, observing that other families were in equally bad fixes. Ervin's wife, Kate, however, began a petition campaign to keep him home on furlough. Gossips charged that Kate feigned sickness to achieve her goal. Elizabeth reminded her husband that Ervin was deaf. Warren simply counseled that if the man could not get a job as an overseer or shoemaker, he should return to his company without saying a word about the exemption attempt.[42]

Furloughs made it more difficult for Warren and others to adjust to returning to the war front. Writing to Jane was an outlet for him as he grew embittered. Through these letters the family learned about the boredom and hardships of camp life, the soaring inflation, and the increasing demoralization within the army. In February 1863, Warren complained that his company had become thieves, stealing hogs, potatoes, and anything else they could from the people living in Wilmington. Some men were even pilfering personal letters from their comrades.[43]

In May 1863 the regiment made ready to move toward Vicksburg, Mississippi, and at month's end it was in Jackson. Warren was convalescing from fever as the Vicksburg campaign reached its peak. Problems on the battlefield and at the home front came to a head. In May 1863 rust endangered the crops in New Center; Warren feared that the family would starve. He wanted to come home to help with the harvest. The morale of the enlisted men was sinking. The general opinion among the privates was that the Confederacy was doomed. In February 1864 the regiment was in Florida helping to prevent a Federal invasion. Next Warren and his comrades marched to Wilmington. After a brief stay in Charleston, the regiment was called to Virginia. At the Battle of the Bermuda Hundred (May 20, 1864), Warren lost an uncle. The troops then moved to the trenches at Petersburg.[44]

The Battle of the Crater was an unmitigated disaster for Warren's company and regiment. On July 30, 1864, whole companies of South Carolina regiments, including four from the Eighteenth Regiment, were blown up. Only 105 members of Warren's regiment, just nine from his company, survived. He helped dig for bodies. By August 1864 the soldiers were reduced to taking shoes, haversacks, and rations from dead Yankees. On January 31, 1865, writing from Petersburg, Warren noted that the men were deserting in large numbers. In March he predicted that their families would hate them for it. On March 24, the young lieutenant was hospitalized at Petersburg, apparently for aggravation of the wound he suffered at Antietam. Similarly, he was hospitalized at Greensboro, North Carolina, in early April 1865. In 1866 a friend tried to console the battle-weary veteran, who was now "a cripple."[45]

3

Childrearing

I n 1860, childrearing in South Carolina was in transition from premodern to modern. The society was undergoing anxieties caused by the transition. Confederate men and women still subscribed to the supposed Christian ideal of family life, which was patriarchal. Gender shaped all aspects of child-rearing. Girls were expected to be self-sacrificing and service-oriented; boys were encouraged to be aggressive. Thousands of men left their homes to fight in a war that lasted for years. This heightened anxieties, causing strain and instability in family households. How parents negotiated in dealing with child-rearing under these circumstances is revealed as this chapter discusses child-birth, naming patterns, teething and weaning, holidays, birthdays, discipline, play and recreation, disease and medicine, and children and death.

Newspapers and other sources presented the ideal of the Christian family. Confederate Jews shared a similar vision. In 1863, the Columbia *Confederate Baptist* published a poem written by a soldier in Micah Jenkins's Brigade. "The Soldier's Home" pictured a wife, in a cottage, talking about pa to their baby on her knee and weeping. The poem equated the absent father's soldierly duties with the protection of the hearth. The same ideal permeated letters to and from the home front. Although this vision was shared in the North, it had pro-founder resonance in the evangelical South. The poem was reprinted in other local papers including the Yorkville *Enquirer*. In 1864 Presbyterian officials decried the deviation from "the good old way." That ideal was the family assembling on Sunday (Sabbath) evenings for reading scripture, reciting the catechism, and singing hymns. The evangelical ministers blamed the deviations on "loose discipline . . . painful to contemplate" and the "indifference of many."[1]

One of the best ways of showing how the ideal completely permeated the culture is examining the subconscious. Jefferson Davis described "Dreams" as "our weakest thoughts." Soldiers took comfort in dreams that placed them back home with their loved ones. "See Her Still in My Dreams" was a song popular among Confederate soldiers. If some dreams offered a brief respite from war, others manifested a soldier's suppressed fears; both surrealistically coalesced in his psyche to increase his anxieties. Good dreams morphed into nightmares. Taken collectively, the dreams present a conflicted patriarch, torn between service to the country and duty to the family. Fathers' dreams expressed anxiety and guilt at being separated so long from their wives and children. The dreams also revealed how deeply entrenched patriarchal beliefs were in the men's subconscious. Male children often appeared in their dreams. In September 1861, J. W. Reid dreamed he was on his way home. It was night. He saw his child Irving and their dog hunting a possum. Irving profusely kissed his father, who then entered the house where his sisters also kissed him. But his wife would hardly talk to him. Her coldness woke him up, and he found himself alongside the Potomac, hundreds of miles from home.[2]

James B. Griffin worried about his son Claude, who was born with a club-foot. Griffin understood how cruel people could be. He wanted the boy operated on as soon as possible but knew his wife delayed because of his absence. In February 1862 he dreamed that the young boy was running with his twin brother Cally (Calhoun) about the house. Claude was the faster runner. Griffin wrote home urging his wife to proceed with the operation. In May 1862, Theodore Honour told his wife Becky that he had groaned in his sleep because young Theodore was "prostrated on a bed of sickness, looking pale." Despite greetings of "Howdy" to slaves at home and instructions about their tasks in these letters, blacks were conspicuously absent from Confederate dreams.[3]

Dreams grew more negative as furloughs became harder to obtain. As the war continued, the individual soldier found himself in a paradoxical situation where his loyalty to his family came at odds with his devotion to the cause. In March 1863, James Barr wrote to his wife Rebecca that although he did not know when he would be able to get a furlough, he visited her in his sleep. Guilt over abandoning wives and children persisted, especially when the men could not be present to celebrate wedding anniversaries, birthdays, holidays, and the arrival of a new baby. Not surprisingly these men dreamt their loved ones felt estranged from them. In September 1863, Honour dreamed that he returned home to find Becky ignoring him. During the Atlanta Campaign Ellison Capers had a nightmare in which his wife was dead. In June 1864 John N. Cumming, writing from a Virginia battlefield to his wife Carrie, revealed the surrealism of his dreams. One night he saw she and the children were well. The next night, however, he saw her dead and the children lost; the anxiety of this nightmare continued to plague him.

Full of anxieties almost to the breaking point, the women also suffered nightmares. When David Golightly Harris's return to his Spartanburg homestead was delayed by a railroad accident, Emily pictured her husband crushed and mangled, lying somewhere between York and Columbia. Fortunately, her fears were unwarranted.[4]

The Cheraw merchant Alonzo Vanderford was a prolific dreamer. In April 1863 he began having dreams about his wife Cynthia and their baby Sallie, an only child. During the Battle of Fort (Battery) Wagner (July 18–19, 1863), the officer faced death. His dreams became darker. Not having heard from Cynthia for quite awhile, his only contact with her was through sleep. In September 1863 he dreamed that she was sick. As the war worsened, so did Vanderford's dreams. In November 1863 he woke up thinking that Cynthia and he were about to get married but did not have enough time. In December he had a nightmare about her. Some dreams, however, were life-sustaining. His wife and he once had the same positive dream at roughly the same time. Such a coincidence raised his spirits. Later in his sleep he was home playing with "little Sallie."[5]

Despite being torn by the war, husbands and wives consciously raised their children within a patriarchal context. Theodore Honour was a private during the war, but both Becky and he came from elite families in Charleston. The birth of a new son caused him to question his own mortality; he feared he would not be able to exercise his paternal influence. In 1862 he felt he should reiterate to his wife specific guidelines about childrearing. Obedience and patience were "taught at the breast, and engrafted in their minds even in their cradle." He instructed Becky to teach the children how to pray, as well as to read books before giving them to the children, select their playmates, and avoid careless nurses. Watch for vanity, he continued, but do not check their joy. In 1863 Honour expressed the wish that his oldest son Theodore get a military education but left his wife to decide on the education of the other two children, John Henry and Eoline. This was the accommodation the couple had reached.[6]

South Carolina men uniformly preferred the birth of a male child, especially the firstborn. Men also welcomed a girl after a string of boys. Caught in a prolonged war, the birth of a healthy child was a happy time for a regiment. This was the case when Ellison Caper's second daughter was born on November 11, 1862. Alonzo Vanderford worshipped his only child Sallie. But in general the war reinforced the importance of male children. Alfred and Elisabeth Doby of Camden, South Carolina, convinced themselves that their first child would be a boy. Captain Alfred English Doby was an extreme example of how patriarchal absentee fathers could be. His determination to be a good father was reinforced by his own experiences as an orphan. Doby carried out his role as patriarch with thorough delight after Elisabeth announced she was pregnant in February 1862. A staff officer, he mounted a campaign, offering the mother-to-be incessant advice. He reminded his wife that her diet and exercise impacted the baby. A good mental state was also a necessity. He warned her not to lie on her stomach because it could injure the baby. His advice was intermingled with lavish romantic praise. Elisabeth adored the attention from her solicitous husband.[7]

Convinced that she carried a boy, Elisabeth Doby named the unborn baby Alfred. She must have felt some apprehension when her husband told her that she could mold "the embryo." The romantic warrior predicted that Alfred would be "a real patriot, a second Napoleon." He referred to the fetus as a "little soldier." In October 1862 Doby received news that his wife had given birth to an eight-and-one-half-pound bouncing baby girl. He named the child Elise. "Hope the little Darling is doing as well as when I left her," Doby wrote to his wife two months later. "Kiss her sweet little cheeks for her dear papa." On May 6, 1864, Captain Doby was killed by friendly fire at the Battle of the Wilderness. The widow wore black for the rest of her life.[8]

Alfred Doby may have tried to be a traditional patriarch because he had been an orphan. Others, such as Theodore Honour, were more modern or, at least, sensitive to the feelings of their wives by qualifying their strictures. After reminding Becky that she should not ride leisurely with any gentleman other than her father or brother, Honour added, "I did not marry a slave, or child to scold, but a companion coequal with myself, and having a mind capable of judging between right & wrong."[9]

Tensions between the traditional and modern occasionally appeared in the event of naming a child. The war precipitated or heightened these tensions. Sometimes a new baby went a long time before being named, a premodern custom. Parents would simply refer to "Baby." This might have been because so many children died as infants. Naming the child after the father took on added significance in wartime. William Box, Laurens District, was delighted when his wife Margaret wanted the new baby named after him. Fathers took particular interest in naming their male children, but when they deviated from family nomenclature and chose the names of Confederate generals, the women sometimes balked at such a break from patriarchal tradition. In July 1861 David Golightly Harris referred to his eighth child as Beauregard. His wife Emily demanded that the boy be named after the father. Harris nicknamed him little "Dixie."[10]

Some women were left the task of naming their children, especially after at least one male child had been born and his name selected. James Barr of Lexington could not decide on a name for one of his three sons. His wife Rebecca made the decision. Inheritance could hinge on the naming of a child. Theodore Honour told his wife that his father wanted the new boy named after himself, John Henry. Theodore feared the child would not be an heir. His brother might name his own son after the patriarch before they could. Ministers named their children after leading clerics. Thaddeus Stevens Boinest, a Lutheran minister stationed in Newberry District, named his son after his religious mentor, the well-known John Bachman of Charleston. One pretentious woman named her child after a character in a Dickens's novel.[11]

Teething and weaning, which had always presented a serious health threat for both the child and the mother, encouraged the practice of postponing the naming of a newborn. Theodore Honour was relieved to hear that his baby girl's teeth were coming out at last. Some husbands discouraged their wives from nursing their children too long. This was motivated by practical reasons, but love was surely a factor. Elijah ("Donie") Brown of Anderson, a private, told his wife to stop nursing Eloise. Her health was more important to him and the family than all the money in the land. James Barr similarly discouraged his wife. Furthermore, fearing that the birth of another child might have a detrimental effect on her health, he suggested that the couple should wait until after the war before having a daughter. Cynthia Vanderford wrote to her soldier husband that Sallie was sick with diarrhea. The mother associated it with her attempts to wean the child. Vanderford told her to tell Sallie she "could have not more titty." The father promised Sallie candy if she was good. Soon after, the little girl was weaned. Premodern notions lingered. In this case, the men were more practical, even stern, about practicing modern ways of childrearing. Some wives resorted to spanking their children to get them to stop. In May 1862, Margaret Box reported to her husband that their baby daughter was good. She had not whipped the girl since weaning.[12]

During this time of war and upheaval, parents put aside their childrearing differences to create a sense of cheerfulness and stability during the holidays and birthdays. But it was a difficult task. In 1863 the Yorkville *Enquirer* counseled its readers to let the "little ones have their Christmas." Children asked their parents about the absence of Santa Claus. In December 1862, David Golightly Harris reported that the Yankees caught Santa and took away his toys. During the war, Easter was particularly a time for healing and renewal. As in Europe and the North, youngsters believed that their good behavior would encourage rabbits to lay their eggs. Confederate boys and girls alike enjoyed Easter egg hunting. David Golightly Harris's children hunted turkey eggs in March 1863. As the war continued, boys in Charleston expressed a desire to celebrate the holiday at a later date when hens laid more eggs. The abundant vegetation also increased the amount and kind of "dye stuffs for their Easter eggs."[13]

Men's spirits were raised by good news about their children, particularly sons. They wanted to know when the baby first talked, crawled, walked, and wore pants. David Golightly Harris found everything about his baby boy interesting. The father rejoiced in seeing the baby crawling. In early April Harris beamed as his baby managed to stand by himself. Like many soldiers, Elijah Brown, writing from Virginia, told his wife to kiss the baby for him. He then lapsed into baby talk, telling her that baby should know Daddy was near "a great big Ribber," where sharks and porpoises as big as cows appeared. Girls were not neglected. Alonzo Vanderford doted on the antics of his baby Sallie.[14]

Despite the doting of these soldier fathers over their children, discipline was sometimes harsh, a legacy of the premodern period. Mary Chesnut equated such disciplinary measures with the patriarch and slavery. She hated the way parents arbitrarily disciplined their children. Male children were to be raised manly, but their spirits were not to be broken. Observing this, Chesnut disliked the machismo and supreme egoism bred in young males. In 1863 she had an encounter with such a future lord of the manor. The little boy was magnificently handsome with eyes that could melt any girl's heart. He was so agreeable, but when displeased, turned into a devil, fighting, kicking, and screaming. Chesnut thought she had met her match. The boy treated her with complete contempt. Drawing her attention to his fine legs, he pronounced them great.[15]

People in urban areas believed that the old ways of discipline were not productive. Progressive educators advocated a more compassionate approach. They were influenced by a view of childhood sweeping across Western Europe since 1750 that children were innocent and malleable. Newspapers reflected these trends from Europe. The Yorkville *Enquirer* had a column entitled "Children's Department," which offered advice to parents. The columnist urged them to inculcate into the children "self-government." This entailed more than physical discipline. If a child was passionate, show him by gentle and patient means to curb his temper. If greedy, cultivate liberality in him. The best thing to bestow to children was "the habit of overcoming their besetting sins." To elucidate modern ways to parents living in a rural backward environment was at times awkward for a small-town columnist. Dealing with "little ones" interrupting the conversations of adults, the writer counseled patience and asked parents to consider what it would be like to be dropped in a foreign country and not know the language.[16]

The discipline of children was a constant source of parental discussion and concern. The war highlighted the paradoxical conflict in the patriarch. Children were most likely to be "bad" when their fathers were not at home. Some men admired a certain spirit in their boys. They feared the maternal touch would make their sons less manly, a characteristic they needed to perform their duties as adults and to succeed when they left home for the wider world. In 1863 James Barr admitted to his wife that the children were out of hand, especially their son Jimmy. At the same time the father admitted the boy's smartness. Some girls challenged the authority of their mothers, who were vulnerable with so many male relatives at war. Occasionally a dispute between a mother and daughter became so destructive, the absentee father would have to send a missive ordering both to stop fighting.[17]

Like discipline, play and recreation activities were an extension of prewar practices. Although the war had an impact, it could not keep down the buoyancy of children at play. Some white and black children continued to play together. One ex-slave recalled playing with his master's son since they were little boys. When the young master went off to war, the black man acted as his bodyguard. Most black male children played such games as wrestling and marbles among themselves. Unwittingly they thought up games that prepared them for the whip. In "warm jacket," boys ripped branches from trees or bushes and flayed one another until the pain got too hot to bear. Sometimes a white adult male like the overseer would amuse himself by using his whip to play with the youngsters' shirttails. The whipping post was near by as a warning.[18]

Play remained gender-related to fit the children to fit into a patriarchal society that their fathers were defending. Male children, for instance, dominated marble playing, which socialized them into becoming more competitive. In 1861 fourteen-year-old Benjamin Tillman played marbles with his friends at Chester. The Yankee blockade put a crimp in their games. Fathers could not always keep their promises of sending marbles or other play items. Governor Bonham's son, Milledge, seven when the war started, already played marbles and cards, which usually appeared at a later age.[19]

Fishing and hunting were a common recreation for boys, especially among the elite who had the facilities. Their prey included rabbits, fox, possum, snakes, and even rats. Milledge was less than twelve when the war ended. The Edgefield boy recalled how the youngsters would trap partridges. He also hunted squirrels and possum. One of the most avid boy hunters was Langdon Cheves III. He was twelve or thirteen when the war broke out. The family took refuge in Flat Rock, North Carolina. Besides recording their travels as refugees, the boy kept account of his hunting activities. His chronicle illustrated how youngsters equated hunting with war and killing. Langdon noted: "Left Columbia February [1865] . . . just before Sherman's entry into Winnsboro that night." On the same page, he entered the names of some of the birds he killed in Abbeville, South Carolina, where the family sought haven in early March. The boy recorded the number of birds he killed or hunted between the years 1860 and 1865: sandpipers, ducks, partridges, larks, snipe, woodpeckers, pigeon doves, blackbirds, hawks, sparrows, and waterfowl. The talented young artist filled his account book with color sketches of various birds. On the very page Langdon listed the birds he killed, he drew sketches in pencil of Confederate soldiers in gray killing Yankees in blue.[20]

Dogs were associated with the manly defense of the household as well as with hunting and were considered appropriate gifts for boys. Theodore Honour promised to bring home a stray dog for his son. J. W. Reid reminded his son that possum season was coming. He told the boy to remind Bear to be good and not to bite anyone but Yankees and free blacks. David Golightly Harris liked to hear his young namesake say "Bubba" when referring to a puppy. Male dogs were often named after Confederate generals, such as Braxton Bragg and Robert E. Lee. Unfortunately, in rural areas they sometimes had to be put away when their aggressive behavior endangered the farm animals. But more searing to a child was when a Yankee shot a family pet for barking at him. On one occasion, when the mother asked the soldier to put the dog out of its misery, her thirteen-year-old daughter pleaded and prevailed. She nursed the dog, which lived for several years.[21]

While dogs and ponies were usually given to boys, girls received dolls as presents. One girl from the Upcountry made a "Dutch Doll." The Camden Archives and Museum has excellent examples of handkerchief baby dolls. Because supplies were scarce during the war, Carolina women made the playthings from men's handkerchiefs. The dolls were also called "Church Babies." They were probably more prevalent among the less affluent. Children could play with them without disturbing the service. Other dolls, made from hickory or gutta-percha, were dressed in homespun. Except for the rag doll made by her mother, one girl, using her imagination, created her own playthings and lived in a make-believe world. She envied her younger siblings, who had manufactured toys, including dolls. Children in wealthier families played with China dolls. Affluent officers, away for long periods of time, sent home exquisite China dolls and other expensive toys that came through the blockade.[22]

Horseback riding, especially for children on farms, was a necessary skill. Both the girls and boys in the Harris family could ride by themselves before the war. They wanted to name their new horse Roland, but their mother decided on Billy Buttons. In 1863 they were lucky to ride a donkey, given the military conscription of horses during the war. One youngster from Edgefield remembered that all the boys and girls could ride horses. Horse races were popular among the elite; some children raced mules. In the summer, to cool off after their rough games and chores, swimming in a nearby pond was a popular pastime.[23]

Riding and owning a horse was a step to becoming a man and a defender of the hearth. By age sixteen males were required to ride on slave patrols. James Achille DeCaradeuc gave his son Tonio a horse named after General Sidney Johnston. The boy, age seventeen, died in the war. It is no wonder that the Southern cavalry with its gentry was superior to its Northern counterpart at the beginning of the war. Southern cavalrymen provided their own horses. Those with money were in a better position to enter and stay in the cavalry as the war advanced. If they lost their horses, they could be detailed to the harsher rigors of infantry. It they were unable to ride, another man could take their place. In 1864, John Cumming of the Fifth South Carolina Calvary, fearing he could lose his horse because of his disability and be reassigned, lamented that a man's horse "don't belong to him and here they make him ride him if the owners is not able to go on him." Cavalry Major A. C. Haskell warned his brother and hunting friends that they could lose their horses to the impressment. Some families survived because of a trusty horse, especially if they had to become refugees.[24]

Despite the dearth of horses during the war, the socializing of young males into the masculine world through the horse continued. In fact the war high-lighted its importance and accelerated the training. Some fathers took their boys to school on horseback to prepare them for riding. Young boys ignored their school lessons to draw horses in their notebooks. The sight of cavalrymen riding off lured young boys to chase after them. Some became boy soldiers. In 1865, Confederate pickets in front of Sherman's troops let Rebecca Barr's young boy ride their horses in the yard.[25]

The crisis of war on children was felt in the areas of disease and death. Ante-bellum South Carolina children had succumbed to the croup, diphtheria, mea-sles, mumps, scarlet fever, and smallpox. The war dramatically increased the death toll from such diseases. Furthermore, the war added to this list other fatal "maladies," some unknown to medical men, according to the Charleston *Daily Courier*. Disease spread to and from the camps and homes. Measles was partic-ularly rife among young soldiers from rural districts. As early as the fall of 1861, both young and old soldiers were victims to various diseases. In December 1862, one soldier told his wife not to let his young boys visit a camp because they could catch the prevailing diseases. Some of the families who camped near the Twenty-fourth South Carolina Volunteers (SCV) were very poor. The coughing of their children confirmed the belief of those soldiers who did not allow their families to visit the camps. Refugees moving to the Upcountry added to the vulnerability of communities.[26]

Most elite families vaccinated their children. Vaccination was also becoming more common in the army. By 1864 newspapers spread the word to everybody. A Charleston newspaper believed vaccinations were necessary because of "the frequent removals of citizens and soldiers." Quinine was used for malaria. When it was not available, Peruvian or cherry bark was used as a substitute. In 1863 an article in a newspaper suggested using oil from dogs as a quinine substitute.[27]

Patent medicines filled the newspapers. In 1862 the makers of "The Southern Soothing Syrup for Children" advertised that their product could alleviate teething problems, bowel complaints, and other ailments. Folk medicine was still widely used, but the war pushed parents to resort to it even more. Charleston doctors had to put out warnings, such as that impure arrowroot could seriously hurt babies. Despite their admonitions, folk beliefs persisted. Soldier-merchant Alonzo Vanderford recommended crow soup for almost every ailment his child might face. A sixteen-year-old soldier was given pepper tea to help his sore throat. A Charleston lady professed the curing power of the following remedy: take a handful of alder root, dogwood root, and bark of persimmon; boil with pink vinegar down to half a pint; add a little water, plus a lump of alum, plus a little honey; then gargle.[28]

The war contributed to narcotic addiction. During the war, opium was popular at home and at the front. It was widely used for sick children. A Camden newspaper reported that a Georgia doctor suggested peaches as a cure for diarrhea "instead of opium." Cargoes arriving in Charleston contained opium and morphine. The ladies of Charleston, Colleton, and Beaufort districts were urged to cultivate poppies. The juice provided a valuable medicine for the army. Mothers were even encouraged to involve their children in the process. Such efforts sometimes offered additional income. With patriotic ardor these children helped their mothers in planting poppies. How many men, women, and children became addicted is difficult to estimate.[29]

Religious Carolinians accepted death. The high mortality rate in the Lowcountry was a fact of life. But nothing in their premodern experience prepared them for the fatality of this war. The scale of death was so great that authorities advocated changing the traditional custom of elaborate mourning dresses. A Yorkville newspaper suggested in 1863 that women should consider wearing something simpler. Perhaps a black ribbon or bonnet might be more appropriate. This would be better for morale and save money.[30]

Periodicals and newspapers, especially religious ones, had to address the issue of death to children, not just as a moral lesson, but to help them cope. Death took on a darker presence in time of war. At the start of the conflict the correspondent of the Children's Department of the Yorkville *Enquirer* enlisted in the army. In 1861, he saw the graves of many children in Richmond. He suggested that Yorkville children should be ready to go "to that beautiful world, where there is no change and blight." He added that he too could "in a few days . . . fill a soldier's grave." Although somewhat prepared, the children must have been upset when they learned that their good friend had died in 1862. A Methodist, he had taken "great interest in the Sunday School children, who loved him as a father." In 1863 a religious paper attempted to prepare children for the increasing number of soldiers dying. "Chosen in the Furnace" proclaimed that the soldiers had "fallen asleep in Jesus." Sunday school youngsters had to cope with the loss of friends who died on the battlefield shortly after they left. In a letter to the "Family Circle" section of the Columbia *Confederate Baptist*, a friend reported that a young man barely four weeks out of Sunday school had died. "The Destroyer" had invaded their "Eden." The analogy revealed how the war and death had intruded into the imaginary play world of these young people. The same journal printed the "Dying Soldier Boy," an ode to a wounded lad who knew he was going to die. The boy wanted his mother to know that he read his Testament. His heroism and devotion to Jesus was hailed for attracting other soldiers to God. An editorial proclaimed that the boy was not afraid to die; his example would give "nerve" to everybody facing the "next fierce struggle." Parents also prepared their children for the large number of disabled soldiers. Asked by her mother to pray for a soldier, a child begged "the Lord to give him a new leg."[31]

Male children were not reticent about talking with their father soldiers about death. They were particularly curious about their fathers' feelings about going into battle and being killed. Gallows humor sometimes came to the rescue of fathers besieged by such questions. In March 1863, John Cumming told his child he was not yet dead. Some children, especially girls, kept their emotions bottled up. Captain T. Sumter Brownfield suffered a slow death from diarrhea that lasted six months. "Little Brazilia" could not bear to hear his name mentioned. Questioned, she finally blurted out that she did have feelings for her Bubba. She cried for him in private.[32]

The terrible challenge women faced was dealing with mortally wounded husbands and deathly sick children. Rebecca Barr of Lexington experienced the worst nightmare. Accompanied by her brother, she went to pick up her husband's body while her infant was deathly sick. On June 11, 1864, James Barr had been mortally wounded at Trevilians Crossroad, about twenty-five miles from Charlottesville, Virginia. Before she left, she dressed the infant Charlie in clothes suitable for his funeral. Fortunately, the baby survived.[33]

Childcare for the well-to-do was eased by slave women, the stereotypical "Mammies." They became indispensable to nursing and raising children. Planters called a nursemaid *dah*, an African word for mother or older sister. Dahs no doubt applied African cultural patterns in raising the children, but some took vengeance on the masters' children. Emma Holmes related a chilling story about her cousin's infant. In July 1861 the nurse who took care of Nora Barnwell's children was considered "good." The Barnwell baby had been born several weeks after the firing on Fort Sumter. The elderly black maid allegedly made the baby swallow eleven pins. Some of them worked their way out of the baby's side. It is impossible to determine how truthful or accurate Emma's version of the incident is. However, such accounts, whether just anecdotes or rumors, expressed the deep fear that slaveholding communities harbored, especially the women.[34]

In families without servants, siblings helped. In the Pursley family, Jane made sacrifices and Warren, away at war, worried about their younger sister Tirzah. He sent money home and asked Jane to establish a school to further Tirzah's education. Young women got their start as schoolteachers by teaching their younger brothers and sisters at home during the war. The support of the extended family could make an important difference. Grandparents, uncles, and aunts could be counted on to give support. Unmarried women with wealth could also help. Emma Holmes was related to some of the best families of Charleston. Her father was a doctor but not wealthy. When he died, the mother was left to care for nine children. In 1862 Emma went to work as a teacher to assist her family. She also helped her married sister Caroline White care for baby Sims.[35]

Most white South Carolina families raised their children in a patriarchal system without the extensive resources of wealthy households. Husbands and wives were forced to negotiate how their offspring would be reared. They had little time to discuss the patriarchy in the abstract. The war just heightened these circumstances.

4

"Spilt Milk": Three Family Cameos

Southerners expected the war to bring a quick victory to the Confederacy. It did not, and as the war continued, a volunteer army became insufficient. The Conscription Act of 1862 was passed, requiring all men between the ages of eighteen and thirty to serve. Those ranging from eighteen and over thirty-five, already in the army, had to serve an additional ninety days. Two weeks after Antietam, in September 1862, the age limits were changed to seventeen and forty-five. The upper age limit was subsequently raised to fifty. Married men with children were caught in this expanding war net. David Golightly Harris, Alonzo Vanderford, and John Cumming were among them. These three men and their families were more prosperous than most, and they even owned slaves, but none had the resources of large planters (see Appendix A and Appendix B). They left letters or journals that probably mirrored what many white South Carolinians endured as the war dragged on.

These three family men upheld notions of manly honor. The patriarch's duty was to secure the economic viability of the household and protect it from threats mounted against it. Away at the war front for extended periods of time, they reluctantly left the operation of the farms or businesses to their wives. The three women, heavily burdened by growing responsibilities, saw the war through the prism of their neighborhood community, or the home front, specifically, a household without the patriarch to keep it stable. Daily confronted with the paradox of their men endangering their lives to protect the family, the women were more critical of the war. Both spouses came to realize that the prolonged conflict threatened their households and came to hate the war. Driven by a shared concern for their children, the couples developed strategies to cope with the "spilt milk."[1]

Harris Family

David Golightly Harris (1824–1875) and Emily Liles (1827–1899) married in 1845. At the beginning of the war they were living on a small farm in Spartanburg District, in a three-room house with their seven children: four boys (William, James, West, and D. G. Jr.) and three girls (Laura, Louella, and Mary).

Their ages ranged from fourteen to an infant. Although Harris owned ten slaves and employed an overseer, he was hardly a prosperous planter. On one hundred acres, he cultivated some cotton (enough for a yearly bale), but he relied mostly on foodstuffs such as corn, cabbage, and wheat for his livelihood. Ambitious, he worked hard to excel his planter father in providing a good life for his family. The war and its aftermath destroyed this dream.[2]

Until conscription came, Harris did not have to join the regular army. In March 1862 he was ordered into the state militia for ninety days. When men up to age forty-five were declared eligible for conscription, he served for six months. In July 1863 he volunteered shortly before he was to be drafted. After serving two months, he hired a substitute. In late 1864 he served in a cavalry unit on James Island in the Lowcountry until the war ended. He did not participate in any major battle.[3]

During the war, life was hectic for Emily, especially when David was gone. In addition to caring for their rambunctious children, she had to manage slaves, oversee the livestock and crops, and keep the household afloat in a period of inflation. The family farm journal paints a vivid picture of Emily's life with the seven children. The two older daughters, Laura and Louella, helped their mother update the journal when their father was absent. The strain of simultaneously managing the farm and the family was nerve-wracking. In November 1862 Emily found herself unilaterally deciding everything, including when and where the hogs were to be slaughtered. Troubles on the farm, events on the battlefield, and even the harsh weather coalesced to sap her energy. Learning of the shelling of Charleston, the distraught woman beseeched God to protect her soldier husband. She felt that everything rested on her. Even the seemingly endless flow of visitors added to the strain. Besides worrying about her husband, Emily was finding it more difficult to get the slaves to do their chores, especially with the news spreading about the Emancipation Proclamation. In January 1863 she lamented they were not doing much to earn their keep.[4]

With the war entering the fourth year, Emily felt nearly spent. Riddled with self-doubts, she blamed the deteriorating conditions of the homestead on herself; she believed herself to be a bad manager and a "wicked" person. On the other hand, she felt that there was no one on the place who had the well-being of the family at heart but herself. She began to hate herself, the war, and the Confederacy. In December 1864, the slaves seemingly conspired to feed and conceal Yankee soldiers. At times, she found the children as unmanageable as the slaves.[5]

In October 1864 the eldest daughter Laura captured her mother's distraught state of mind and probably her own in the entries she made in the journal. She was aware that because everything fell on her mother's shoulders, the older woman internalized mishaps. When the fattening of the hogs was beginning to show promise, someone killed and took the best. Laura worried that her mother might "go up the spout." Although the family succeeded in finding an overseer by December 1864, sixteen-year-old Louella Harris recognized that her mother's anxiety had not lessened. The teenager described the war as cruel, leaving people hopeless. The death of the men was taking its toll. Thousands of families in need did not know what to expect.[6]

David's tacit recognition of his wife's success in running the farm in his absence did not stop her from having bouts of depression. She herself admitted that she had become a good farmer, but at a heavy price. Her deep love for her children might have helped her keep her sanity. In February 1865 Emily seemed to have left space in the journal for one of the younger children to practice writing the ABCs. The youngster wrote the letters N–Z in pencil but left out the letter X. The child also attempted to copy the mother's handwriting of an entry date in the journal. Such efforts of penmanship by her child gave Emily solace and hope. Both David and she believed in the goodness of education.[7]

Many others in the society shared Emily's concerns about the future, especially women whose security was being compromised. "Every body seems to be distressed about the war," she wrote in November 1864. "The dark days have surely come." The prospects of emancipation and the aftermath threw her and untold others into deep anxiety. Imagine her reaction in January 1865 when one of the slaves, in her husband's absence, boldly demanded his freedom. Another nagging concern was what was going to happen to her family after the war. She did not want the children working in the fields. In 1863 she had rebuked David for encouraging the younger children to work in the fields. After half an hour, they had become sick and thirsty. After emancipation, she and the children, including the girls, worked harder than they ever had. Still the household suffered economically. Thousands of dollars had been lost when the slaves had been freed. David had to sell land to pay his taxes. In 1875 the patriarch died knowing he had not done better than his father. Emily, coming to a more peaceful resignation of her lost dreams, lived with her children until her death in 1899.[8]

Cumming Family

John and Caroline, or Carrie, Cumming resided with their three children in Colleton District in the Lowcountry, near Ridgeville. In 1860 the farmer's real estate was valued at $400, and his personal estate at $900. He was thirty-four, his wife twenty-seven. Their children were four-year-old Alice, two-year-old

Geneva, and six-month-old Mitty. The farmer owned six slaves. John probably volunteered when the upper age limit for conscription was raised from thirty to forty-five. By March 1863 he was a member of the Fifth South Carolina Cavalry. It defended the state's coast but later fought in some of the most brutal campaigns in Virginia, such as the Wilderness (May 1864) and Cold Harbor (June 1864). John's letters to Carrie begin when he was stationed at James Island near Charleston.[9]

The husband, concerned about the household, sent his wife detailed instructions on how to run the farm. Anxious, he barraged her with directives. On March 4, 1863, he told her to plan to get a good crop and attend to the stock, feed the hogs, and tell the slaves to do their best. He also wanted the children in school. Carrie was ill prepared to handle such a situation without sufficient support. She could not count on relatives or neighbors. John counseled her to compose herself and trust in God. He added that she should get a respectable woman to help with the three children. Later that month, Carrie and one of the children came down sick. Her spirits dropped accordingly. She worried that her husband would soon forget her. John assured her that he would be miserable without her and the children. He promised he would come home as soon as possible. A furlough in April 1863 did not alleviate the anxieties both felt. Carrie's illness worsened, and she was confined to bed. By June 1863, Cumming realized that his demands had pushed his wife to the verge of a breakdown. He told her to stop worrying about the crop or the slaves. The soldier considered going home without leave. In July he explained to Carrie his dilemma over honor and duty to both the army and his family. Realizing the conflict, he was determined to avoid an impending battle. He understood the consequences for his family if he was killed.[10]

Cumming's own state of health and mind deteriorated just as it appeared that Charleston might fall. In August 1863 failing health continued to plague him, especially fever and bowel problems. On September 7, 1863, confined to a Wayside Hospital, he hoped that God would help his wife and poor little ones. Soon afterward he was sent to the Ladies Hospital in Columbia, but the board refused to give him a furlough home. Feeling depressed about his situation, he complained how it was for the soldiers. Had he known the consequences of going to war, he would not have gone, but avoiding service would have disgraced the family. He concluded that it was too late to grieve over "spilt milk."[11]

In May 1864, Cumming's unit moved toward Richmond and a veritable meat grinder. A lame horse, little food, and concerns over his household and farm upset him. His anxieties began to consume him. Lack of letters since his furlough made him uneasy about the well-being of his family. He let his imagination get the best of him. On May 26, 1864, he related to his wife reports of

Yankee atrocities, especially to young women. The Yankee raiders destroyed
everything, leaving families only enough food for one meal. The lust of the
black Yankee raiders, who took white women into the woods and kept them
there until they were satisfied, enraged him. These accounts of Yankee brutality,
exaggerated or not, fortified his decision to remain at his post.[12]

Cumming experienced an adrenalin rush in battle that must have baffled his
wife. His exploits were scary yet exhilarating, a feeling that most women at
home did not experience firsthand. Outnumbered at one skirmish in 1864, the
soldier barely missed being captured. A ball went through his jacket without
even scratching him. Killing a Yankee sobered him; he did not have the heart
to take anything from the dead man. Between June and December 1864 his concerns remained essentially the same. Somehow the family survived the ordeal.[13]

Vanderford Family

Alonzo Vanderford, born in 1835, was an ambitious and successful Cheraw
merchant when the war began. As a youth he had joined the state militia, and
at the age of nineteen he was a second lieutenant. After a romantic courtship,
he married his sweetheart Cynthia in 1859. Daughter Sallie was born in February 1861. Vanderford, twenty-seven years old with business and family responsibilities, was full of hope and energy. In 1861 he became a lieutenant in Company
D, Twenty-first South Carolina Volunteers (SCV), Hagood's Regiment. He saw
action on James and John's islands and fought in the Battle of Fort Wagner
(July 1863), the Battle of Bermuda Hundred (May-June 1864), and Petersburg
(June 1864).[14]

When Vanderford left home for war, the dilemma of honor and duty to both
the army and his family began. He worried endlessly about the health of his
wife and child. When Sallie accidentally burned herself, Vanderford was beside
himself. At another time the little girl got sick; the father wanted to return
home. Furthermore, Cynthia's mental and physical well-being was fragile.
Breast-feeding Sallie for two years after her birth had jeopardized the young
mother's health. Brief furloughs only made Cynthia more despondent when her
husband had to leave again for the war.[15]

Cynthia sent Vanderford boxes of various items, including a bed quilt. Soldiers looked forward to receiving these boxes from home, especially around the
holidays. The merchant Vanderford and his family had great access to food and
other critical supplies. His family was never in want of food. In addition, Cynthia could count on her parents for help. On one occasion Vanderford
instructed her to send him fifteen pounds of bacon, potatoes, and a griddle in

a box. Two months later he requested a box with black peppers, red peppers, bacon, and muslin. Several of the items Cynthia sent he most likely bartered or sold. He was a shrewd bargainer. Stationed near a port, the merchant soldier was able to send his family much-needed and much-prized salt.[16]

By January 1863, Vanderford knew that his death was a real possibility. He asked Cynthia to add the child's name to his will; this only made her more anxious. On May 3, 1863, Vanderford reassured her that he would be fine. He mistakenly believed that he would remain on James Island, near Charleston. He hoped the war would be over by the end of the year. In July 1863, Vanderford was wounded at the Battle of Fort Wagner. Instead of his being lauded, questions were raised about his conduct. As the Yankees had approached, some of Vanderford's reserves had fallen back toward the rifle pits, leaving the enemy an opening. The lieutenant was blamed for the incident. He was subsequently court-martialed for neglect of duty. He counseled his wife to tell them he was not at fault if people asked about the matter. There is no evidence that he was ever convicted, but the dark shadow cast on his honor and character from this affair would compel a man of his inclinations to redeem himself.[17]

By August 1863 Vanderford was back in service at Fort Johnson, near Charleston. He returned to Fort Wagner by the end of the month. In early September he described the war as "wicked." In November he longed to be back home with little Sallie on his lap and his wife's arms around his neck. He professed, "I have thought of you so much that sometimes I imagine that I can see you." But "the dreadful war" prevented their permanent reunion. In December of that year he wrote that he wanted to come home, but duty kept him at the front. The war gradually wore the couple down. Three months earlier Vanderford had begged his wife to do her best and keep well. A few days later Sallie came down with diphtheria. The best he could do for his family was to advise his wife to seek assistance from her father and to hire a slave woman to help with the child and household chores. Despite his efforts, problems at home persisted.[18]

Like many South Carolinians, Vanderford agonized over his business and the family's financial security. He came not to trust the young clerk he had put in charge of his store before he left for the front. So he began involving Cynthia in the business. In November 1862 he told her his suspicion that the clerk drank too much. Gradually Cynthia took on additional business concerns. In July 1863 her husband wanted her to renew the insurance policy on the old house. He instructed her to put up the house for sale and to pay the war taxes with her father's help. When the house was sold, he reminded her to inform the insurance agent. Vanderford boasted that selling the house was one of the best deals he ever closed.[19]

The Cheraw merchant soldier became alarmed at the increasingly high prices of such items as flour. He thought people had become obsessed about money. However, his store offered a unique opportunity for him to make profits that would give his family financial security. Cynthia became his intermediary. He informed her that her mother could get rich by selling chickens in Charleston for three dollars apiece. With his misplaced optimism in a Confederate victory, he had sold his old house and invested heavily in Confederate bonds. Despite his fears of uncontrollable inflation, he still trusted his business instincts.[20]

In the meantime, Cynthia's fears for her husband especially after he was wounded at Fort Wagner and the stress of conducting the family business debilitated further her fragile health and state of mind. By February 1864 their clerk reached the draft age and had to leave for the service. Cynthia wrote about dying. Vanderford told her to stop talking about death. His uncharacteristic reaction to his wife's cry for help reflected his own fears. The businessman had gambled his own life and the welfare of his loved ones on a Confederate victory. He was betting that the war would end before 1865. On February 10, 1864, he had informed Cynthia that her mother, who was a weaver, should save all the cloth she had and try to get rich before the war ended. However, by March the merchant was distraught over the soaring inflation that threatened his family's economic well-being. The next month he dreamed that some one was choking him to get him to give up his money, but he did not have much. In May 1864 the newspapers mistakenly listed Vanderford as dead.[21]

Writing from the trenches of Petersburg in June, the soldier asked his wife to tell Sallie, "Pa wants to see her but Cant. Cheer up." Through Cynthia's letters, he learned that Sallie had weaned and was talking, jumping, and running about. Cynthia appealed to her husband's deep affection for their daughter to make him come home. In one letter she related to him that Sallie said, "I wish Pa would run away from them old yankees & come home."[22]

Alonzo Vanderford was severely wounded at Petersburg around June 22, 1864. His right leg was amputated. By July 8, his health seemed to be on the upswing. Cynthia wrote her sick husband that she wished she could bear the pain for him. On July 17, Vanderford told her to kiss Sallie for him. His health was deteriorating because he had dictated most of this letter to a nurse. Four days later, the patient's state worsened to the point that officials urged the wife to come to the hospital. Cynthia was stunned. She had been contemplating his safe return home. She had promised him that she would run and jump bushes for him so he would hardly miss the leg. Wanting to protect her, Cynthia's husband and father had discouraged her from going to the hospital. She respected their wishes, although she preferred to be by his side. She had submitted to the will of God. By July 24, Vanderford's wound was hemorrhaging; he was experiencing chills. He died on July 29, 1864. His burial service was held at the local St. David's Church five days later.[23]

All three families were caught up in the quagmire of a destructive and prolonged war that weakened the patriarchy. The patriotic call to defend their way of life had left many families like them in a shambles.

5   Education and
                      Nation Building

Confederate leaders in South Carolina had no master plan for education when their state abruptly seceded in December 1860. The ensuing war disrupted schools and drastically reduced the number of teachers; families scrambled to find ways to maintain local schools. Women tried to fill the gap, but their contributions did not resolve a worsening teacher shortage. Although many parents were primarily focused on their children learning the basics under trying and distracting circumstances, state educators were working with their counterparts throughout the Confederacy in a nation-building reform movement to end Yankee influence. Religious leaders played a pivotal role in this crusade.[1]

By 1864, South Carolina educators were on the cusp of creating a children's literature and textbook movement designed to prepare the young to take their places in the New Republic. Male academies and colleges would produce the elite cadre to serve as leaders of the New Republic, while female academies would educate the future mothers and teachers of a new generation of South Carolinians. Besides the divisions within the Confederacy, those educators had to overcome deep fissures and prejudices within their state. Religion was a central force to overcome these obstacles and to sustain the war momentum. God would save his children if they kept the faith. However, too many South Carolinians seemingly resorted to speculation, immorality, materialism, and selfishness, thereby tempting God's wrath. Children's literature, although mirroring societal divisions and prejudices, flourished after the war to perpetuate the Southern heritage and prepare the way for Redemption.

The task of nation building in South Carolina was made more difficult by an educational system that was premodern. In 1860 twenty thousand white pupils attended thirteen hundred schools. Only about five thousand pupils were in public schools. The early free schools in the cities were underfunded and carried a stigma. Rural parents taught their offspring a rudimentary education until they were old enough to attend school. Their labor was still needed on the farm. Three-month-long field schools were popular in rural areas. Youths went from the plow to field schools and back. According to veteran Harvey Hart of York District, schools were mostly opened by subscription and ran from two to ten months. They were decidedly traditional. Lessons in spelling and reading were punctuated with an occasional whipping. These schools often experienced discontinuity as teachers moved on. Also, they were dependent on the financial ability of the parents to sustain them.[2]

The disruption of schools began almost immediately as thousands of teachers and their charges enlisted. Schools were forced to close. Brief respites brought the reopening of some schools, but disruptions continued throughout the war as a major shortage of teachers loomed over the state. The Conscription Act of April 1862 exempted teachers in colleges, academies, schools, and theological seminaries with twenty or more students. The act was tightened in October 1862 to include only those who had been teaching two years prior to its passage. Between 1862 and December 1863 only 140 men received exemptions or details as teachers in South Carolina. On February 17, 1864, the Confederacy still retained exemptions for teachers. A year later the superintendent of conscription recorded 196 exemptions for the state. That number needs to be placed in perspective. In 1860 the "free schools" in Newberry District subsidized forty-two teachers (whose 547 students paid tuition with difficulty) while Charleston's public schools employed fifty-three teachers.[3]

Victories at Fort Sumter and Bull Run brought a brief period of relief. In the cities some schools were reopened by December 1861. The safety of the Upcountry lured many refugees. This in turn created an educational cottage industry in Camden. In 1862 town advertisements announced the reopening of the schools in early January. Mr. L. McCandless reopened his on January the first. Sessions would be for nine and one-half months. Another Camden teacher, L. McDonald, planned to open his school on the sixth. Similarly, Charles Peck reopened the Camden Male Academy. In 1863 the plucky Sisters of Mercy reopened their day school in Charleston, a "popular seminary for young ladies," and their boarding school in Sumter.[4]

Placing wounded veterans in schoolhouses seemed an ideal solution to the teaching shortage. The veterans might also have more success in handling boys hell-bent on joining the army. One soldier joked that his limp helped him more than his Latin. Retooling males disabled by the war as teachers did not fully succeed; it came too late. Moreover, disabled men were already serving in the State Reserves; in rural districts they got out the crops. In 1863, Baptist Sunday schools provided "the institute of primary education" for many children. In February 1864, educators sounded the alarm. A Baptist weekly feared that education would be short-changed "amid the excitement and tumble of war" and South Carolina would "reap the bitter fruits of negligence." Too many breadwinners were deceased or at the front. Many soldiers "from South Carolina could not write their names" on Confederate payrolls. By August 1864 neighbors of Lutheran Minister Thaddeus Boinest could no longer afford to send their children to his school in Newberry District. Also, the minister had presided over too many funerals of his parishioners to remain unaffected. So he closed his school, left his family in God's hands, and went off to the battlefield with the state militia. After the war, educators concluded that "in many parts of the country" students had been "deprived of their teachers."[5]

Most parents did not experience the kind of success that David Golightly Harris and his wife Emily had in keeping their children in school. The couple was tenacious. The Spartanburg farmer had an edge. An older man, he managed to stay out of the war for most of the period. As a small slaveowner, he had enough money to hire a substitute. Still, schooling for his children was touch and go. In June 1861 they were attending Mary Lanford's school. When the session ended in October, Harris complained how difficult it was to start a school. He worried that his younger children might grow up ignorant. In January 1862, neighborhood families attempted to organize a school for three female teachers. Harris completed the work on the schoolhouse, but his neighbors bickered with him over the staffing. The financial exigencies of the families often dictated how long these schools lasted. Their enrollments were fluid.[6]

In March 1862, Harris's children Laura, Willie, and James went to a Mr. Henry's school. Harris carried them to the place on horseback. In August 1862 his other children were again attending Miss May's school, but the father complained that it was too crowded; it had thirty-three students. In April 1863, Harris tried to get another teacher, Mary Walker, but her terms were too steep. That December he secured the services of Miss Virginia ("Jinnie") Moorman. Harris became the school's handyman; he hauled wood and made a "causeway" to keep the children from trekking through the mud. When it rained, Harris brought the children and teacher to the building. During the harvest in June, Miss Jinnie dismissed the children for several weeks. Near the end of December she took sick, and the school was closed.[7]

In March 1865 the Harris's children were no longer in school. They spent most of their time playing. Harris, who prized education as the most lasting gift he could give his children, feared that without it they would be lost in an ever-changing world. In July 1865 the children returned to school. Having the kids in school preserved their parents' sanity, especially as the war approached its catastrophic conclusion. Once when "the children [had been] confined to the house," the harassed father wrote, "Their noise and confusion and the trials that I see in the future have made me a miserable day. I have felt crazy. I could almost feel the wrinkles coming on my face and the hair turn gray on my head." He recalled his mother's observation that those "who raised the most children had the most trouble."[8]

Families with more modest means were equally determined to educate their children but were less successful than Harris. J. W. Reid was born no aristocrat. He worked in a cotton factory while his dad labored in a gristmill. Since Reid did not have the chance to go to school, he feared his fourteen-year-old son Irving would miss the opportunity because of the uncertainty of the war. In 1862 the soldier counseled his son to attend school and learn all he could. Despite Reid's admonition, when Irving turned seventeen, he enlisted in the same unit to be with his pa. His father anguished that the war had put his only child in harm's way. To send the youth to the battlefield was tantamount to manslaughter. When Reid was Officer of the Guard, Irving would sometimes call out, "Papa."[9]

The study of twenty-four petitions to the Confederate secretary of war and the governor of South Carolina suggests that getting teachers exempt or returned to the classroom was problematic. The Upcountry was hard-hit. Some applications were simply declined. Small schools in rural areas were ignored. Established schools with twenty or more students had the best chance at getting exemptions for their faculty. The South Carolina elite placed a high premium on keeping the male principals and teachers in their academies and colleges. In October 1861 the president of Newberry College and members of the Board of Trustees sought the discharge of the Rev. W. Eichelberger from the Second Virginia Regiment. He was principal of the Preparatory Department. School authorities pleaded: "It is all important that the education of the rising generation be attended to at this time. The youth of this Confederacy will soon be called upon to discharge the grave and responsible duties that now devolve upon men of mature years."[10]

As the war continued, even wounded soldiers faced obstacles in obtaining discharges or details to teach; the need for manpower at the front undermined efforts on their behalf. In early February 1863 a petition of citizens from Clarendon District, including the Trustees of Summerton Academy, asked that their former teacher, Rev. William Thomas, be detailed as their schoolmaster. He had headed an institution with nearly a hundred students until he volunteered for service. The patriotic preacher was seriously wounded at Second Bull Run. Former Wofford Professor M. C. Layton found it impossible to get discharged after he had volunteered. The entire faculty of the college supported his request. They argued that he was physically disabled and much needed at the school. Layton, a member of the Spartanburg Sharpshooters, finally gave up the effort. Soon thereafter he died of disease at Chattanooga, Tennessee.[11]

Female academies and their clientele were determined to keep their institutions open. It seems they were more successful, especially as the fears of the Yankees and runaway slaves increased. In February 1865, 132 persons at Due

West Female Academy signed a petition requesting that all their professors be exempt. A pencil notation suggests the teachers were detailed to guard duty. On February 3, 1865, S. W. Bookhart of Blythwood Female Academy, Fairfield District, sought to remain at his post as superintendent. He believed that without him the school would be closed and the education of the daughters of the Confederacy placed in jeopardy. Supporters praised him as a wealthy man who aided the families of the soldiers and the poor in his neighborhood. He was granted a thirty-day delay.[12]

Communities throughout the state tried to get teachers exempted, detailed at home, or discharged. In 1863 citizens from Barnwell District wanted J. S. Mixson exempt from conscription. He had been a teacher since 1857 but had joined the First South Carolina Regiment. When the company underwent reorganization, he retired and returned to teaching. In April 1863 citizens of Edgefield sought the discharge of a teacher who had taught thirty students. A month later "Citizens of Spartanburg" asked that James A. Dodd be discharged because he had conducted a school of twenty children before the war. The school was located in a "dense settlement of boys & girls. Some almost grown & can't get a teacher well qualified." On May 16, 1864, Edgefield District parents asked that Hezekiah Bennett, Seventh South Carolina Volunteers (SCV) Regiment, be detailed as a teacher. He had been in charge of twenty students in a "densely populated" neighborhood. "Having a great many children to be educated," the parents pleaded, "we find it impossible to procure a teacher."[13]

Teacher-starved communities turned to the governor for help in late 1864 and early 1865, when the state legislature gave him the power to grant exemptions and details. The war had played such unforeseen havoc on their families; the governor was sympathetic to the parents' circumstances and fears. On December 23, 1864, D. R. Shannon was teaching at Bull Swamp in Orangeburg District. He had begun teaching in 1860. He taught all grades. His pupils numbered twenty-six. His request for exemption was approved. On December 31, 1864, a petition signed by twenty-seven parents from Laurens District wanted their teacher, a shoemaker named Lemuel T. H. Daniel, retained. His school served between thirty and forty students; there was no other school in the vicinity for miles. The governor granted him a thirty-day detail. On January 27, 1865, W. H. Witherton, a teacher at Marion Academy in Mars Bluff, asked for exemption. He taught some forty scholars; he was the only teacher in the village. These appeals to the governor revealed the desperation of parents and their communities. Although the long war appeared to be nearly over, parents did not want the education of their children to stop, too. On February 2, 1865, a group requested the exemption of T. J. Wells, the principal of the prestigious Mt. Zion Institute, originally chartered in 1777. His school of forty students was the only one of its kind in Fairfield District. Appealing to the governor, the petitioners lamented, "[Our] sons will probably be deprived of all benefits of education as they attain sixteen years of age." Soon thereafter, Sherman occupied the institute, located in Winnsboro, as his headquarters. According to folklore, he had the building burned down on his departure.[14]

Chartered in 1785 as a college, Mt. Zion represented some of the revered educational institutions that existed in South Carolina before the war. Despite its premodern educational system and increasing teacher shortage, the state had a variety of public institutions of higher learning such as the College of Charleston, which served the Lowcountry, and South Carolina College in Columbia. Both concentrated on the humanities and the sciences. For those interested in a military career, there were the State Arsenal in Columbia and the Citadel in Charleston; both formed the South Carolina Military Academy. In addition, there were private colleges such as Baptist-oriented Furman in the Upcountry. A plethora of male academies also dotted the state's landscape. York District alone boasted three: Union Military Academy, the Yorkville Male Academy, and King's Mountain. Military academies became prep schools for the South Carolina Military Academy. Such schools instilled in their charges a warrior ethos reinforced by service on slave patrols and in the state militia. In 1861 the South possessed a superior military culture as manifested by the numerous military academies and schools in the region. This warrior ethos imbued the mindset of South Carolinians and abetted educators in their nation-building efforts.[15]

When the patriotic fever hit South Carolina, impatient young men abandoned their books and enlisted in the army. The senior class at the College of Charleston asked for a leave of absence to join the cause. The college limped along until the evacuation of the city became imminent. It closed its doors on December 19, 1864. South Carolina College traversed a briefer course. In 1861 the students successfully organized a company of a hundred officers and soldiers out of an enrollment of 143. They left for Charleston without the permission of college authorities. Arriving after the fall of Fort Sumter, they served three weeks on Sullivan's Island. Most returned to the college. The trustees tried to keep it open, but by June 1862 the buildings were needed as hospitals for the increasing war casualties. Efforts to reopen the college in 1863 failed with the Union's twin victories at Vicksburg and Gettysburg. The turmoil fermented by the closing of these institutions came to light in early April 1865 when the governor considered a program to "gather all the youths of the State, and establish a military camp for their discipline and education."[16]

Very early in the war, women recognized the opportunity opening up to them by the growing shortage of male teachers. In July 1861 Emma Holmes noted that many ministers, doctors, and schoolteachers had to join the state militia when the upper age limit was extended to sixty. Young women, who needed to support their families, looked for a "situation" or opened up their own schools. Thoughtful parents recognized that their girls would face a changed world after the war; their education became more critical. It enabled them to earn a living as teachers, with luck at a female academy.[17]

Such academies were founded before the war: Greenville (1819), Barhamville (1828), Fuller Institute in Greenwood (1848), Edgefield (1850), and Spartanburg (1851). Emanating from modern Europe, these academies provided a haven for girls of elite families when they were no longer expected to marry at an early age. These institutions were to turn out "graceful, highly educated and thoroughly accomplished girls" ready to perform their roles in a patriarchal society. Preparing them for courtship, marriage, and motherhood was a means of preserving the patriarchy. In 1859, William F. Nance of Newberry told his two sisters that they should study hard in order to do their duty and "move in your own spheres." However, these academies were more like finishing schools. Extended schooling led to prolonged childhood and dependency. Some of these institutions like the [Baptist] Greenville Female Academy took modern reform seriously by attempting to adapt it to fit their agenda; young women's faculties especially needed to be trained, disciplined, and developed to preserve a way of life in a changing world.[18]

Schools in the Upcountry offered a refuge from threatening Yankee invaders. When the Ursuline convent in Columbia was set on fire by Sherman's troops, South Carolinians perceived this atrocity as particularly sacrilegious since the holy place was the ultimate refuge for women and children. With such an impending threat more a reality, the education of women took on paramount importance as a vehicle to purify a morally complacent nation. Judicious women teachers would fill the depleted ranks and morally reform the society by educating the young in the right direction. In February 1865 a Yorkville newspaper, reporting on the latest meeting of the Confederate Educational Association, noted: "This cruel and unfortunate war has so sadly interrupted the education of our sons, that it becomes doubly important to educate our daughters. . . . [Let our] fair daughters cleanse the social and moral escutcheon of public sentiment and character, with the intelligence of mind and purity of character." One of the last acts of the association was in May 1865 when it called on women to fill "the vacant post" of teaching. This call appealed to women to bolster the weakened patriarchy by declaring, "Their fathers, husbands, lovers and other natural protectors have fallen by disease or in battle."[19]

These female academies were not the peaceful havens of learning that parents envisioned. While the younger girls were often homesick, the older ones became jaded and rebellious. In October 1863, Emma Holmes taught at the McCandless School in Camden. She remained until December 1864. Emma felt like a nun. The girls were divided into six classes. Emma taught fifth class, which included seven-, eight-, and eleven-year-old girls. She had fifty students. Her classes began with a prayer at 8:30 a.m. Until 11:00 a.m. she taught them history, vocabulary, grammar, and geography. Another teacher helped the girls with their arithmetic and composition. Emma then taught a class of twenty other students. They read *Paradise Lost* and translated Racine.[20]

In November 1863 Emma's probationary period ended. She was offered a yearly salary of $200. In January 1864 she dropped the fifth and sixth classes and took over a course devoted to the works of the noted British historian and statesman Thomas B. Macaulay. Such a course was a perfect vehicle to instill the aristocratic ethos of nation building. By February Emma was disillusioned. In March her pupils staged a revolt against Macaulay, whom they found boring. The twenty-one girls were defiant. They played every trick in the book to undermine her authority. The underlying causes might have been grades; the girls felt that Emma was too demanding. Most preferred spending their leisure time reading novels. Resentful of this intrusion on their extended girlhood, these independent-minded and pampered young ladies took their hostility out on their teacher of classical education.[21]

In contrast to these finishing schools, evangelical academies became centers of reform. The *Confederate Baptist* was the official organ for South Carolina Baptists. On August 31, 1864 a correspondent for the Christian weekly wrote an article entitled "Is Woman Equal to Man in Mental Power?" The answer was a resounding yes. The author refuted notions that women were "weak minded, that they [could not] go deep." Before the war, "dandies about towns were as plentiful as blackberries in June." The article suggested that women had the same mental capacity as men and should have the same opportunity for mental and physical improvement that boys had: "Let them drink deep at the spring of knowledge; teach them not to live for mere pleasure; for she that giveth for pleasure is dead while she liveth. They should be taught to recognize the exalted destiny assigned them by Heaven, that the mission of women is very important." They should not be taught "to dress and fish for admiration and . . . the attention of brainless fools."[22]

The reformers refused to assault the ultimate firewall of the patriarchy: the prohibition against women soldiers. Everyone had a prescribed place in a patriarchal society. The idea of women in uniform threatened the patriarchal concept of natural protectors just as emancipation given to blacks as a reward undermined the foundation of slavery. In 1863 a Columbia newspaper reported rumors that a woman intended to enter the city fair dressed in a military uniform. The paper predicted that she would be arrested for violating a statute prohibiting "the interchange of costumes, between the sexes." Holding such beliefs, South Carolinians took a voyeuristic interest in Northern women officers. In May 1864, state newspapers featured the story of Dr. Mary E. Walker, a surgeon with the Fifty-third Regiment, Ohio Volunteers. She was captured on horseback "on a man's saddle *one foot in each stirrup*" near a Confederate picket line and taken to Richmond. A newspaper predicted that people would turn out to see such a *rara avis* on horseback. Walker's example convinced Southerners that the North had lost its moral mooring.[23]

Educators saw education as a prerequisite for nation building. Prewar divisions plaguing the Confederacy and South Carolina compounded the difficulty of their task. Some South Carolinians saw the war through the perspective of localism and states' rights. In 1861 the ladies of Spartanburg were upset when the clothes they collected went to units from other states. C. G. Memminger, the secretary of the treasury, took time out of his busy schedule to answer their complaint. That same year, a member of Hampton's Legion compared Virginians to Yankees. Both, he claimed, did not hesitate to become wealthy on someone else's funds. They were not true gentlemen. The idea of being sent off to Virginia while Beaufort and Port Royal were invaded did not sit well with soldiers from the area. For them, patriotism began at home.[24]

Class divisions and antagonism evolved from prewar politics. Secession initially muffled the historical division between the Upcountry and the Lowcountry. Fiercely independent yeoman farmers in the Upcountry saw secession as the best way to preserve white independence and equality against Black Republicanism. But resentment of Lowcountry domination in state politics bubbled below the surface. In August 1861 a Unionville man argued that the upper part of the state was not represented at the recent convention that passed the tax law.[25]

Lowcountry aristocratic women bridled at the manners and ignorant pretensions of their less cultured sisters in the Upcountry. In December 1864, Emma Holmes became a governess in the country. She was hired by Mrs. John Mickles to teach her six boys and two girls. The children ranged in age from an infant to a seventeen-year-old. Emma was chagrined that none of them had read *Gulliver's Travels* and *Jack the Giant Killer*, her childhood favorites. She also found their manners appalling. They wiped their noses and faces on the tablecloth; dogs and cats were allowed to eat under the table, and the kids joined in with the pets. The older boy was misnamed Patrick Henry, an insult to the revolutionary leader. In the governess's opinion, they should all be wearing dunce caps.[26]

The flood of refugees from the Lowcountry to the Upcountry sparked serious contention. The urbane refugees looked down on the more rural Upcountry people. The Lowcountry display of entitlement and the aristocratic ethos were downright aggravating. Upcountry people thought they were "full of airs," and decided these newcomers were "ostentatious" and "purse-proud" persons bent on transforming the yeoman way of life into the more secular style of the coast. The Upcountry people felt free to take advantage of them.[27]

When sent to defend Charleston, Upcountry soldiers sometimes showed contempt for these Lowcountry aristocrats by mistreating their property. In 1862 Theodore Honour was horrified to see that country soldiers had destroyed a $400 billiard table on James Island. At least the Yankee officers would have saved it to play on, the Charlestonian surmised. "Don't let the Upcountry people boast any more of sending their men down to near the city to protect our property." But even small slaveholders in the Lowcountry were cautious and uncomfortable with the aristocratic elite, especially their ladies. While recuperating in the Ladies Hospital in Columbia, John Cumming of Colleton District was thankful for the help he received from these women but described them as "Big fish." Traveling to serve in the Lowcountry, William Pursley of York felt the haughtiness of the hospitality ladies on his stop in Columbia. As in all wars, humor was a vehicle for the soldiers to let off steam. In 1863 a Yorkville newspaper reprinted an account describing a young lady's visit to a hospital. She asked "a regular hospital rat" if he was keeping a diary. He replied: "Yes'um, I've had the *diree* [diarrhea] right . . . about six months."[28]

Upcountry soldiers, many of them experiencing the Lowcountry for the first time, had trouble adjusting and underwent patriotic disillusionment. They had a class and cultural ax to grind, especially against the aristocratic elite. They came to fight but at times were ordered to clean up the city trash while local dandies paraded the streets in their finery. After the great fire of Charleston in the fall of 1861, a Chester soldier stationed nearby had no sympathy for that city full of "scoundrels." Even the evangelicals of the Upcountry, who were devoted to promoting national unity, clashed with the seemingly more secular and aristocratic culture of Virginia and the Lowcountry. In 1863 the Richmond correspondent of the *Confederate Baptist* railed against the "military popinjays" with "enormous gold lace on their coat sleeves." When the *Palmetto State* was completed in 1862, it sunk at Marsh's Wharf in Charleston. The Baptist newspaper attributed its tragic sinking to God's displeasure at a woman's christening the new ironclad with "a bottle of choice old wine." This "travesty of the Sacrament of Christian profession" was prayed over by two prominent Charleston Divines. Three months later, the *Confederate Baptist* condemned "secular" obituaries with "the Romanish application *requiescat in pace*." Despite its assiduity, the weekly was criticized by "brethren," who thought it was being insufficiently "Baptist."[29]

The towing of the line by the *Confederate Baptist* was important to many South Carolinians who believed that religion played a pivotal role in the education of their children for the New Republic. Parents feared that their young soldiers, "torn from their mothers," would confront "temptations often too great even for men" and succumb without the underpinning of religion. Baptists hoped that older men would continue to give younger men in the army religious instruction and guidance. Bible reading in their spare time was highly encouraged. Sunday schools became a bulwark for patriotism. The Charleston *Daily Courier* praised Sunday schools and their teachers for their "sense of duty to the young; and their love and patriotism to their state . . . determined . . . to risk their all for their independence and freedom." As the Confederate Educational Association proclaimed in early 1865, "freedom and religion are the fundamental principles of nationality."[30]

Religion initially bolstered Confederate nationalism and lifted morale, but the war also spawned great moral greed and materialism. "Mammon" became a serious obstacle to Southern victory. The chaplain of the Seventh Regiment, SCV, noted that people grew complacent after the victory at Bull Run in July 1861. "Many people at home quit praying," he continued, "and went to speculating in the necessaries of life, coning money out of the sufferings of soldiers and people, and the demoralization soon extended to the camps." In June 1862 the Charleston *Daily Courier* claimed the evils of the war were caused by the people's transgressions. If the faithful kept God's will, he would deliver them, but the nation had to be purified to obtain God's deliverance. In November 1862 the *Confederate Baptist* counseled patience; the road to the Promised Land was long and weary. The people's sins brought God's chastisement. The tone became more frenetic after the twin defeats at Vicksburg and Gettysburg. The soldiers themselves echoed the message. Private Theodore Honour argued that if God had turned against South Carolina, it was because the people sinned. Similarly, James Barr told his wife how wicked the people were; they were obsessed with money. During the Gettysburg campaign, a reader asked the Baptist weekly what churches should do with members engaged in distilling when soldiers' families were paying as much as five dollars for a bushel of corn. Kick them out, one minister advised. Better yet, let the wives of our fighting men run these sinners out of the district with their broomsticks. By January 25, 1865, this religious organ of Confederate nationalism was near despair. Days of fasting were turned into bacchanalian excesses. Impurity was epidemic. Women, once the blessing of the Confederacy, were becoming its "bane." The cast of

evildoers described in the pages of the religious weekly included duelers, speculators, hoarders, extortionists, rich men getting out of the war, and croakers.[31]

Another obstacle to Confederate nationalism was Southern dependency on
Yankee schoolbooks, deemed "Yankee trash." Educators believed that Northern
books were like the proverbial Trojan horse; they could ultimately bring down
the Confederacy. By late 1862 the North Carolina Educational Association had
organized a committee to foster a Confederate textbook movement. In March
1863 a Teacher's Convention, held in Columbia, was seeking "proper Southern
schoolbooks." Women played a key role in the movement. Mary Ford, the wife
of a wealthy Georgetown planter, was so distressed about the situation that she
wrote schoolbooks for her own boys. Teacher Harriet Palmer was excited about
this educational reform movement. Writing from Columbia in 1863, she promised to send her sympathetic friend a copy of the minutes of the recent meeting
of the state association. The inaccuracies of the Yankee books had dire consequences for young minds ("as the twig is bent, so the tree is inclined"). Northerners intervened with their "intrusions and dictation to occupy and control
our school books, our school room, and all our formative institutions and
resources of education." The once highly touted *Webster's Speller* was condemned. A commentator wanted a Confederate equivalent to replace the
"Defunct Yankee book." He hoped to "make a bonfire of the obnoxious stuff,"
so children could "sing over the flames their songs of independence." In 1864
the *Confederate Baptist*, discussing "Sunday School Books," trumpeted the
"emancipation from the intellectual thralldom of our Northern foes."[32]

Charles E. Leverett's *The Southern Confederacy Arithmetic for Common
Schools* (1864) was highly acclaimed as one success of the reform movement.
The author capitalized on the fascination Fort Sumter held for children: "The
United States commander in Fort Sumter has 2 lb of bread per day for each
soldier, for ten days; but by private dispatches, learning that his government
would relieve him soon, he wishes to stave off surrender 15 days, to do that
what must be the daily allowance?" The book prepared youngsters for an economy plagued by inflation. Under "Barter," the question was asked: "How many
pounds of butter, at 22 cents per lb must be given for a chest of tea, containing
75 lbs, at 80 cents per lb?"[33]

It took time for textbooks to be written and published. Newspapers and religious periodicals filled the breach. The *Confederate Baptist* was a precursor of
Leverett's textbook in capitalizing on war to capture children's interest in arithmetic. On October 29, 1862 it used Yankee plunderers and extortionists to make
a point. "Two Yankees plundering the farmers of Virginia steal 6 turkeys and
two chickens, which they sold for $2 apiece. A Yankee stole from the other all
except 75 cents. How much did he steal?" The Yorkville *Enquirer*, which had

begun a progressive Children's Department in February 1861, used a softer approach. The column created patriotic puzzles for children:

> My first is what all the young ladies like
> My second is what they all are entitled to
> My whole is the name of a distinguished military commander,
> Whom all the ladies admire. [Answer: General Beauregard]

By May 1861 its writer had enlisted in the Fifth South Carolina Cavalry. "Our corporal" reported from Camp Beauregard on Sullivan's Island outside of Charleston. He promised that although he could not answer the children's letters individually, he would respond collectively. During his time on the island, he told the youngsters about the seashells, porpoises, and sharks he saw. In June 1861 he described Richmond's statues and monuments to heroes such as George Washington and Henry Clay. The column continued to educate children and give advice to parents throughout the war even after the death of the corporal.[34]

Children's literature, however, sometimes undermined the very unity the educators were seeking when the authors could not rise above regional divisions and prejudices. Mrs. M. B. Moore chaffed at the haughtiness of the South Carolina elite. Her *Geographical Reader for Dixie's Children* reflected a North Carolinian's disdain toward South Carolina: "Many persons blamed the South Carolinians for leaving the Union too soon." The "upper classes" of that state are educated, but "the poor are generally ignorant." They are "hardly so well treated as in North Carolina and Virginia."[35]

Confederate literature for juveniles espoused deeply held religious values at odds with undesirable practices generated by the war. The best example of such morality genre appeared under "Family Circle" in the Columbia *Confederate Baptist*. "Uncle Fabian" was the fictional authority who wrote stories dealing with young people and their problems in this turbulent world. The series began in late 1862 and was reprinted in several other newspapers, including the Atlanta *Intelligencer*. Tom Brown and little Nell were the central characters of his stories. Poor but proud, they faced spiritual snares generated by the war, including selfishness and materialism. The exemption of overseers and the Conscription Act of 1862 were prime targets for Uncle Fabian's pen. They revealed his class and regional bias. He was critical of wealthy planters who used exemptions of overseers to keep their sons safe at home. His brash young hero, Tom Brown, "thumbs" his nose at "one of the laggards or cowards, who are escaping military duty by acting as an overseer." Too many "skulkers" are getting out of harm's way "while old gray haired men" are called to camp. Tom wonders whether such young men will describe themselves as overseers at parties after the war. Negative public reaction to Tom's "plain talk" caused Uncle Fabian to clarify the boy's remarks. Tom was not referring to young men who had to take care of their "old mothers or their wives and children."[36]

Extortion lent itself to the moral wrath of Uncle Fabian. A little girl, Ella Lee, wrote to him that she shared the newspaper with one of her cousins, who commented on Tom Brown's dealings with extortionists. She had asked her mamma: Is "that the reason sister and brother and I have to go in the cold without any shoes, and I wonder if dear papa is away in Virginia in frost and snow without any shoes." Younger brother Johnnie chimed in: If papa knew this was going on, he would come home and let the Yankees take the extortionists. The little boy declared that if he lived in Columbia, he "would help Tom Brown brickbat their houses and head, too."[37]

Uncle Fabian sent Tom off to camp when the boy turned seventeen. The elder blessed the boy for his willingness to give up his life for his country. He also lectured the youth on swearing and liquor. He encouraged Tom to read the Bible and "strive to be a good soldier of Jesus Christ." The boy's mother gave him a pocket catechism. His sister made a Palmetto State cockade as a gift. His journey to his company brought the young man closer to Jesus. At camp Tom received guidance from Uncle William, who preached to the company. He received the older man's approval to go defend Charleston and asked the preacher to baptize him. "If I fall in battle," the youth declared, "I want to die a good soldier in our blessed Lord." The born-again Tom expressed sorrow for a young soldier who wanted to kill as many Yankees as he could after the Northerners had mistreated his mother and sister. Tom was not unsympathetic; under the same circumstances he might not have "any Christian feelings for them."[38]

Tom never fully reconciled himself to the insensitive rich and spoiled youngsters he met, including a girl who looked down on poor wounded soldiers on a train. By their clothes, she considered them "no account." Tom was furious because such men were the ones who were defending the girl and her home. Not the young dandy he saw when he took the train down to defend Charleston. In contrast to the behavior of the Arsenal cadets and other boy soldiers from Columbia, the skulker took up five seats on the car with his bags.[39]

Uncle Fabian followed gender conventions. If nineteenth-century boys were encouraged to embrace the world outside the home, girls were socialized to concern themselves with spiritual relationships. Little Nell illustrated the lack of familial guidance. A "gay mother who did not teach her anything about religion, or the dangers of whiskey" raised her playmate Kate. Despite such friends, Nell gradually groped toward conversion. The heroine had to witness the overseer Mr. Carter's being bitten by a snake before she seriously considered changing her ways. His brush with death shocked the girl, who became aware of her own mortality. Mr. Carter's wife shamed her into getting baptized. Whenever Nell faced death, she wanted to die in the arms of the blessed Lord.[40]

The "Uncle Fabian" stories reveal the problems the new nation was facing by relating how young people could overcome them through their religion. This religious framework provided a way for white South Carolinians to come to grips with a losing war and its heavy casualties. Although the writer could not control his dislike for the cultural pretensions of the Lowcountry elite, whom he considered part of the problem, his stories contributed to a Southern legacy of storytelling that kept a way of life from being forgotten. Such literature for children flourished after the war. Sallie Chapin used the war and Reconstruction as a vehicle for teaching Southern children about their heritage as well as reconciling them to a changed world. Her fictional teenage hero Fitzhugh St. Clair has to postpone marriage until he could find a situation or career. Needless to say, he stays true to his morals and succeeds.

6

"Something for the Girls": Marriage Customs and Girlhood

P ut a high price on yourself," a Southern newspaper warned girls wanting good husbands who could provide for them. In 1864 the impact of the war caused the Yorkville *Enquirer* to reprint this piece of counsel highlighted "Something for the Girls."

> Put off the ways of children. Your girlish days will soon be over. Be helpful to the marriage. Do not be too forward or anxious; exercise prudence and modesty, and avoid noisy or boisterous behavior that men do not like. Do not adorn yourselves with braided hair, or gold, or pearls, or costly array. Those too anxious to marry might as well hang out a sign. According to St. Paul, women should adorn themselves in modest apparel.

Again in spring 1865, the *Enquirer* offered tips on "Who Will Make a Good Wife." A good girl rises early, sets the table, and fixes her father's breakfast "cheerfully." She must have "a kind heart." If she drags herself out of bed at 9 a.m. and says how awful she feels, she must be "lazy and mopish." On the other hand, if she sweeps the floor or cleans the clothes, she is "industrious." If she has a novel in one hand and a fan in the other, shedding tears, she is "unfit for a wife."[1]

In nineteenth-century America, marriage became a milestone marking formally the end of childhood. Therefore, this stage of life was a time to cultivate in the psyches of girls the acceptance of appropriate marriage customs. New brides had to bear children, preferably males. Married women without children were scorned. Even other women held them in contempt. Mary Chesnut was the target of her father-in-law's barbs. One day in her presence, the old man told his wife that, unlike Mary, she was not useless; through her children, she had produced twenty-seven grandchildren, a veritable tribe.[2]

Even before the Civil War, the premodern and modern intertwined in South Carolina to extend the period of childhood, or at least to forestall early marriages. Traditional farmers wanted to keep their children home to maximize the output of a struggling household. As for elite Carolinians, taking their cues from modern Europe, they too began prolonging the childhood of their daughters, which resulted in an extension of girlhood. Both trends encouraged later first marriages. In 1860 the average age of couples starting on their first marriage in Edgefield District was twenty for women and twenty-five for men. As in modern Europe, young elite girls were cloistered in secular convents, called "female academies," under the assumption that such innocents needed protection from the dangers of the outside world while they were being properly educated to be useful members of society. Although locked up in metaphorical gardens of extended childhood, these girls were not protected from the consumerism of modern culture. As young women, they resisted traditional notions of morality, religion, and marriage. The instability of the war further encouraged their rebellion.[3]

The war made it more difficult for parents and educators to monitor the young, who were smitten with romantic patriotism. Younger girls were participating too early in courting and other premarital rituals. Some of them were merely thirteen or fourteen years old. Emma Holmes watched aspiring belles, only fifteen years old, engaged in activities that might have brought censure before the war. Sallie Bull enraged her somewhat stodgy older fiancé by performing in the scandalous round dance. Worse yet, *with someone else!* Sallie broke off the engagement and continued in her precocious ways. Even girls cloistered in private academies caught the war fever and its Byronic romanticism; they, too, wanted to break the bonds of girlhood. Sallie McDowall of Camden, for instance, wrote her first name in her notebook with the surnames of some twenty boys from elite families. She also drew a heart-shaped wreath with the inscription "Rise Sons of Carolina, Rise and Mount," the title of a poem that captured her romantic sentiments. Young girls who faithfully followed parental restraint wondered years later if they had done the right thing. One girl, declining a kiss from her fifteen-year-old beau, promised him one when he returned, but he died in an early battle.[4]

A cultural war prevailed between generations involving morality, marriage customs, and fashion. Adults thought the younger generation was going to hell in a handbasket (a refrain that began in America with the Puritans). Given the perspective of the twenty-first century, such fears seem more hysterical than apocalyptical, but youngsters were breaking taboos. The war encouraged lovemaking and courting. A soldier did more courting in one day during the war than he would have in ten years at home before the war. Such was the gossip among the older women. For their part, the youngsters were trying to come to grips with a society wracked by war. Although they saw their society through the prism of extended childhood, most were amazingly resilient and sometimes very creative in the responses they made. In the end, many made life-affirming choices in dealing with the stress imposed by the war.[5]

Adults were aware of the freedom extended childhood offered to their young people in these times of long-term warfare. Some elders catalogued degrees of forbidden behavior from the mildly scandalous to downright degrading. Older women believed that courtship for girls began with the onset of menarche at around age sixteen, sometimes earlier. In March 1865, Clara Dargan noted how a girl's sixteenth birthday proved a difficult milestone for her advancement to "womanhood," because eligible girls faced intense courting pressures resulting from the war. The more perceptive recognized that taking the hard line might be counterproductive. In 1862 one wise mother, when her daughter celebrated her fifteenth birthday, took the girl aside and gently counseled her on the responsibilities of womanhood.[6]

Proper conduct at parties, especially certain dances, became a bone of contention between young people and adults. Dances and recreation were a form of play that could lead to rebellious behavior. Girls who did not participate in round dances were ignored by the young men; younger belles were advised by the more experienced in such rituals. Other dances were equally verboten in the sacred garden. Men were willing partners in waltzes and polkas but forbade their younger sisters from doing the same. This just made the forbidden more alluring and fun to fifteen-year-olds.[7]

Some adults saw the phenomenon as a cultural virus emanating from the Yankee kingdom of iniquity. Such fears were not totally unwarranted. Mock or pretend weddings, which were popular in the North, worked their way to South Carolina. In 1862 an Episcopal minister officiated over one of them at a Christmas party in Charleston. According to gossips, possible mates shunned the pretend bride for four years afterward because they thought the mock wedding was binding. Journals used the "Y" word in urging boys and girls not to adopt "vulgar Yankee notions of private and personal correspondence and courtship." Newspapers warned parents to keep a vigilant eye on the courtship of the young. In 1864 Emma Holmes expressed her fears of the degradation women endured in the sinful North. In a flirt with fantasy, she depicted the newest Yankee dance craze in which a man harnessed two women and whipped them around the floor. However, not all examples of questionable conduct could be attributed to Yankee influence. That same year, the Big Creek Baptist Church, in Anderson District, expelled three girls for playing what was commonly called "twistification," music that upset their elders. A short time earlier, not far from Charleston, a boy soldier attended an entertainment, staged by the Washington Artillery, in which men, dressed as women, danced with other soldiers. Lowcountry ladies and gentlemen were also in the audience.[8]

Criticisms against the "fancy" during and immediately after the war became strident. It also exposed the fault lines between the mainly Episcopal Lowcountry and the evangelical Upcountry. Influential Baptist newspapers feared the disease was infecting the entire state. In 1863 the *Confederate Baptist* was "shocked" by the unseemly behavior of persons who were still mourning their dead. The paper excoriated women who attended balls "arrayed in dresses, [with] crape festoons [that] notified the gay throng, that they still mourned the loss of relatives, fallen on the field of battle." Women were slaves to fashion, "an imperious mistress." The evangelical paper criticized them for renouncing "their gentle nature."[9]

Although the war changed fashion in the South, the elite still took their models from Europe and New York. In February 1861 the Yorkville *Enquirer* listed such fashion sources as *Godey's Ladies Book*, *Harper's*, *Leslie's Illustrated Weeklies*, and the New York *Ledger*. Affluent young women, still in girlhood, had been avid consumers before the war. Chic was in. Early in the war the military style was the rage. Elite women, unable to serve in the army, vicariously identified with the soldiers by changing their hairstyle and dress. Like their Carthaginian predecessors, young women "shingled' their hair to look as "military as possible." Some sisters cut their hair short because they could not go to war with their brothers. The Garibaldi look became fashionable because in trying to establish a Republican Italy, the Italian hero was perceived as a kindred spirit to adulate. In 1862 ladies attended company drills with "a crape" on their Garibaldi hats. Emma Holmes and her friends made Garibaldi hats from cornhusk. A mother, asked by her little girl what to wear to church, suggested, "[Your] Pradi and Garibaldi." One woman appeared at a market with a Garibaldi shirt-waist and was offered a turkey for it by another. Infatuation with the Italian liberator was dampened by the Emancipation Proclamation and Garibaldi's letter to Lincoln, labeled by the *Confederate Baptist* as "blasphemy." The Italian patriot included Lincoln, John Brown, and Jesus in his pantheon of heroes. Garibaldi's "blasphemy" was upstaged by news of the capture of a Yankee woman surgeon, riding a horse like a man.[10]

"We've seen the Doctor! Yes, sir, we've seen her," observers exclaimed. People were fixated in Dr. Mary E. Walker's personage and the particulars of her hermaphroditic attire. "Twenty-eight or thirty summers old," the woman was five-foot six-inches tall, rather thin, "a little worn but still passably good looking" with her dark hair "gathered under a silk net." Her costume was a "Bloomer" of dark blue broadcloth trimmed with brass buttons. Cord tassels adorned her uniform hat, and she wore a surgeon's green silk sash over her right shoulder and across her breast, fastened on her left side. "Over her frock she wore a blue cloth military overcoat and cap." Observers caught her "plain calf skin boots over her pants, reaching to the bottom of her dress." Theodore Honour, riding on the same train to Richmond, wrote to his wife that the attractive doctor, who flirted with her guards, "dressed in style half man & half woman."[11]

Fashion consciousness remained late into the war. The Yorkville *Enquirer* reprinted an item on fashion trends emanating from Northern cities: "small bonnets, crimson raging color—hoops small, dresses fit tightly & mostly trail, buttons of color of dress used in great profusion." These fashion trends were also popular in Richmond. Such practices, infuriating plain folk, were a bone of contention. In 1864 the *Confederate Baptist* declared that women should not look to the decadent Parisian society for their cues. They should adopt the dress of the French peasantry. Reflecting its Jeffersonianism, the paper continued, "No shabby finery is to be found amongst them."[12]

"Shabby finery" was one step on a slippery slope to decadence that could culminate in the ultimate sin, miscegenation. Parents also feared for their sons who went off to war. Away from the moral constraints of their communities, Confederate soldiers indulged in sexual activities with black women. For the young, it might have been a rite of passage to manhood. The Emancipation Proclamation brought to the forefront a deep-seated taboo, white women living with black men, even marrying them and bearing their children. For white Carolinians it represented the logical outcome of abolition. In 1864 the Yorkville *Enquirer* berated the Republicans for "their wild love for the negro" and invoked mantras against intermarriage. Wholesale miscegenation was predicted. Such fears were more imaginary than real, but there were cases in which Carolinians, black and white, intermarried or lived together. Slave Kate Wilson was the common-law wife of rice planter William Harleston, who built a house for her in Charleston. She lived there with their eight children long after the war. According to the Southern Claims Commission, set up after the war, Ellender Horton, a seventy-year-old white woman from Beaufort District, had a "common law mulatto husband." The couple had four daughters, a large farm, and slaves. Her children worked alongside the slaves in the fields. The commission reimbursed the family for damages caused by Yankee troops. Whites in the community shunned the woman. In another case reported in 1867 a Freedmen's Bureau agent met two females, down on their luck, with mulatto children. One of the women had married the black father of her children. Disturbed by such an encounter, the Federal agent argued that the war deprived these women of their natural protectors, white men.[13]

At this time, the young were too caught up with their own emancipation and concerns to sympathize with their elders. The war brought on a series of elopements and secret engagements. A sixteen-year-old soldier excitedly recalled how his relatives thwarted the elopement attempt of an irate and desperate suitor to whisk away the boy's cousin. Some elite young women sneered at elopements (or premature marriages) and subdued weddings. They still cherished the grand wedding and the elaborate trousseau. Dismissing her friend's event as a premature marriage, a young Charleston lady decided to break off her own engagement to her soldier fiancé. Similarly, since an Allendale girl could not have the wedding gown and large celebration she desired, she chose to keep her engagement a secret until she could obtain her treasured dream. However, by 1862 elaborate weddings were less likely. This sad news was passed through the letter vine. A fifteen-year-old girl thus learned that a schoolmate had a skimpy wedding. Authorities encouraged this new fashion as wholesome. In 1864 a South Carolina newspaper reprinted an article on the wedding of a Virginia girl, entitled "A Bride Worth Having." Lucy F. Roller, the daughter of a wealthy planter, made her own bridal outfit from materials she spun and wove herself. Hardly poor, her gesture demonstrated how "independent Southern girls" were.[14]

Because the war gave young people more opportunities to make unilateral decisions regarding marriage, parents and children sometimes faced knockdown battles. Lawrence G. Glover's case is an extreme example of conflict between father and son over his manhood. He enlisted with his father's reluctant approval and chose to marry a woman of whom his father strongly disapproved. "From childhood, [the lad] has exhibited weakness of intellect," the father, Dr. Joseph E. Glover, claimed in his petition to get his son sent home under his care. He thought the boy suffered from brain disease. The seventeen-year-old youth had joined the Beaufort Artillery just before the Battle of Pocotaligo. It was rumored he married his sweetheart in Charleston. He escaped his father by transferring to the Twenty-seventh South Carolina Volunteer (SCV) Regiment. He was hospitalized in Virginia, taken prisoner at Petersburg on June 24, 1864, and finally sent to the prison at Elmira, New York. He was transferred for exchange four months later.[15]

Not knowing all the details, Dr. Glover feared that Lawrence might have taken an oath of allegiance to the Union to be released. He could be taken prisoner by the Confederates and executed as a deserter on the way back to South Carolina. The father pleaded: "God help me . . . this is my son whom I freely gave to my Country who has been twice refused to be given back to me when I found he was incapable of taking care of himself & instead of his being fortunate enough to be killed in defense of his Country, I am told if he comes back he may be hung before I know it." In February 1865 Lawrence deserted to the enemy and was imprisoned in Columbia, South Carolina. Eventually he was taken to New York, where he took the oath of allegiance to the Union.[16]

Even thoughtful young men seemed hell-bent on marriage. Emma Holmes's brother Willy had a reputation for not being impulsive. Nevertheless, he proposed marriage to a widow with several children. On learning the news, Willy's mother broke down, crying, while his sister pronounced it one of the weirdest matches of the war. Common people were more pragmatic and probably representative of the norm; most marriages did not involve agonizing turmoil. In August 1862 one South Carolina woman appealed to Jefferson Davis: "Jeems is willin,' I is willin,' his mammy says she is willin,' but Jeem's cpt, he ain't willin' . . . I think you might let up and let Jeems come."[17]

Some soldiers promised their undying love while shamelessly admitting marriage was merely a ticket home. A proposal of marriage in 1864 to Fannie Aiton included a plea that her consent would get the suitor a furlough. Her brother Thomas teased her about matrimonial blackmail. He mentioned that "girls" were beginning "to think they had better accept the first man that comes their way." Such teasing may tell us more about the young soldier's own fears. However, some girls were not inclined to marry someone they thought would be killed, maimed, or disfigured. This was the reason, according to James Barr, why there were no new engagements in his regiment in 1863.

On the other hand, women were acutely aware of the fickleness of some of their suitors, who professed to love them deeply. When rebuffed, these men quickly got themselves engaged to another. Few soldiers committed suicide. However, when they did, it likely involved a girl. In June 1863 a young officer in the Twenty-first Regiment stationed at Morris Island shot himself in the right temple because of a disappointed "love affair." He left a letter expressing his melancholy. Some officers decided to deny marriage furloughs. They reasoned getting married was simply an excuse for temporarily getting out of harm's way. Lack of patriotism did not prevent stay-at-homes from kneeling before the altar of marriage. Too many women seemed willing to marry slackers.[18]

Some historians have argued that because of the war, women could choose a more independent life. Teaching opportunities opened up for women. Some yeoman women who were artisan-weavers, such as Jane Pursley of York District, clearly enjoyed the independence their skilled jobs gave them. But how much choice did many young women really have, given the lack of personal security, changed economic circumstances, and the demographics? Jane Pursley did correspond with a York soldier who was killed early in the war. Emma Holmes had a terrible experience both teaching at the McCandless School and being a governess. Some women felt forced to break gender customs by advertising for husbands. In 1863 a twenty-year-old woman from Pleasant Hill placed in an Abbeville newspaper an advertisement seeking to initiate correspondence with a young gentleman interested in matrimony. Two persons replied, including a wounded veteran.[19]

For the elite, lavish weddings and elaborate dress were still part of the rites of passage. The "entire trousseau" of Sallie Chapin's fictional bride was made of silk. The young bride had "raised the worms, and spun the silk herself." Some hailed the decision to have an old-fashioned wedding. In January 1862 a brother complimented his sister, Mrs. Alfred Dobby, on her grand wedding. He noted that marriage had become too businesslike. Elaborate weddings never died out and remain in vogue today. As Sherman's troops were marching through the state, Joseph W. Brunson and Jane M. Carson entered connubial bliss in grand style. Joseph got a furlough to get married. The date was set for February 11, 1865. The event was so extravagant that even invitations were sent out. There were the customary bridesmaids and their male escorts, all dressed in their finery. The bride wore a white organdie dress trimmed with satin ribbon, and a long veil. Reverend Potter, Rector of Christ's Church, presided. The wedding party dined on cakes, chickens, roast pigs, salad, and other delicacies. The couple barely managed to leave the altar before Sherman swept through the state. After such galas, limited resources encouraged women to find pragmatic ways to recycle their wedding dresses, which, along with Confederate flags and other souvenirs, were made into quilts.[20]

The long-term impact of the war on women may be more difficult to measure. Some were very resilient, but others suffered from severe anxiety over not getting married. The war, shattering their chances for economic and physical security, rendered them poor. One young woman, for instance, was placed in the state insane asylum because she suffered from depression and anxiety of being murdered. She complained of not being able to get married, a situation that physicians attributed to the war and its aftermath. Newspapers probably heightened such fears of abandonment when they ran items dealing with bigamy. A South Carolina newspaper reported that North Carolina soldiers who already had wives were marrying girls in Virginia.[21]

The response by young women was hardly monolithic; their motives were more complex than meets the eye. Some thought it their patriotic duty to marry soldiers with serious disabilities, to help make these men feel whole. The loss of a limb challenged a man's image of himself as manly. One fifteen-year-old girl made the conscious choice to marry a college professor who had lost his leg at Gettysburg. A male friend, perhaps a former suitor, defended the impromptu marriage, praising the young bride for not marrying for money or a life of ease. The friend could not help but admire her decision, which was patriotic and liberating from customary social customs. It allowed the bride more freedom than she had at her parents' home. The war had broken down some of the traditional barriers young people were already questioning before the conflict.

As Reconstruction loomed, girl refugees, only sixteen years old, married older men.[22]

In the last analysis, young people were simply sick of the war. Suffering from war fatigue, they wanted to pursue their lives and dreams without out-of-date constraints. They used language inappropriate before the war; their linguistic rebellion was perceived as sacrilegious by adults and confirmed their worst fears of the hedonistic path the young had taken. In July 1865 Emma Holmes observed that weddings were as popular and widespread as they had been during the war. By October, Charleston stores were again selling *Godey's Ladies Book*, with "the usual beautiful fashion plates, dress and cloak patterns." In 1866 a bachelor complained to a friend who had married a much younger woman that a marriage epidemic was depleting the ranks of his fellows. Three years later, seeing older people getting married, the bachelor ridiculed the folly of old fools. Emma Holmes, also deploring the frenetic pursuit to be merry, condemned the large balls that were given shortly after the war. Her fears were overblown. Near the end of the war some youths simply decided to put it behind them as best they could; they left war talk to the older people. Most yeoman girls would have agreed with what a friend confided to Jane Pursley in 1877. How guilty the girls felt to be merry because their friends were dying. How often they thought of the dead and wounded. She thanked God the war and killing were over.[23]

As one Southerner described marriage today, he was looking for a partner with whom he could share his life. The war caused even the most independent women to reevaluate their stance. Clara Dargan, an accomplished writer from Columbia, was fiercely independent. Still, her subconscious suppressed a deep fear that she might never marry. In a nightmare she had on her birthday during the winter of 1865, she rode alongside two superb horsemen. One, who reminded her of her teenage suitor Jack Weatherly, was thrown off his horse and crushed to death. Weatherly had gone off to war in 1862. The dream morphed into a situation in which people were looking at a woman with a disfigured and bandaged face. Clara then dreamed that she had a baby in her arms and was delighted but felt compelled to throw it away. Overcome with remorse, she picked up the baby but it was dead. The lady concluded that she should marry.[24]

Young men also experienced nightmares over marriage. In April 1863 a Pendleton soldier dreamed about visiting his intended bride, who was a refugee from the Lowcountry living in the same district. As he approached her in the dream, she was alone. Her father lived in a blacksmith shop, where he was employed making fish baskets. Knocking on the door, they youth was shocked by the appearance of a decrepit and disheveled figure who turned out to be the father. Somehow the old man became naked, revealing the scabs and scales covering his dirty body. He invited the boy into his workshop where his daughter appeared on a trash heap, looking like an Indian maiden. The soldier was speechless.[25]

These dreams involved single persons with deep-seated concerns and conflicted feelings about getting married and abandoning their childhood or independence. The boy soldier's story was extremely contorted for he had never laid eyes on the girl. His romantic obsession with getting married was so extreme that he enlisted the support of his aunt and his fifteen-year-old cousin to help make the match. Just as in Europe, aunts and younger siblings acted as go-betweens. Yet, the suitor hampered their efforts by giving strict instructions not to mention him by name. Writing from Fredericksburg in February 1863, he asked his cousin to make the girl's acquaintance and requested a clipping of her hair. The object of his affection was probably not much older than his cousin. Much to the youth's chagrin, he learned in August that his intended was going to parties; however, the cousin was sure he would still prevail. In September the aunt made the girl's acquaintance and was pleased with her. The youth asked his aunt to put in a good word for him. Sadly, however, the soldier was killed at the Battle of Chickamauga; he was shot through the heart and buried by a young black servant. Friend advised the family not to open the coffin.[26]

Despite the turmoil and tragedies caused by a losing war, marriage did not go up the spout. It provided solace. However, by June 1863 many privates thought the Confederacy was going to blow up. A young York officer wrote to his sister to find out what the people back home thought about that question, as we will see.[27]

Confederate killing Yankee officer. Drawing by Langdon Cheves III (b. 1848).
(South Carolina Historical Society)

Yankees routed by confederates. Drawing by Langdon Cheves III (b. 1848).
(South Carolina Historical Society)

Drawing of horse by Willie Harth. *Below:* Confederate Home College, Charleston, S.C. (Both: South Caroliniana Library)

Sallie D. McDowall composition book; *left:* cover; *below:* valentine wreath below "Rise, Sons of Carolina, Rise and Mount," July 1861. (Southern Historical Collection, University of North Carolina, Chapel Hill)

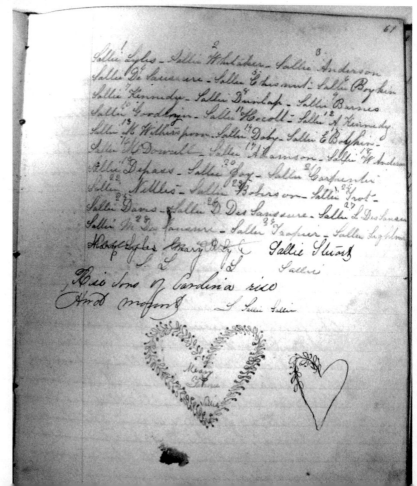

Mrs. Alfred English Doby in mourning attire, 1916. (South Caroliniana Library)

Joseph Hayes of Charlotte, N.C., as drummer boy of the Thirtieth North Carolina, of Mecklenberg County, Battle of Secessionville re-enactment, Boone Hall, Mt. Pleasant, S.C., November 11, 2006. (Photo by John Dunn)

7

"Going up the Spout": Converging Defeat on the Battlefield and Home Front

Perhaps the Civil War's greatest impact on children," Steven Mintz has noted, "was on family life." The widows, children, poor, and elderly of South Carolina paid dearly. South Carolina households went "up the spout" because the war drained their districts of doctors and skilled artisans vital to the smooth functioning of their communities. Men critically needed at home were swept up into the vortex of the battlefield; thousands died. Many more became sick and wounded. Morale at home sunk with shortages, inflation, and an ever-increasing list of casualties. Poor households suffered egregiously, while the economic viability of yeoman families hung in the balance. Refugees strained an already difficult situation. Life-threatening diseases struck the civilian population. Competition between the battlefield and home for supplies and skills encouraged demoralization, which spawned conspiracy theories. In the end, the state was broken long before Sherman left Atlanta for Savannah.[1]

Letters of appeal sent to the Confederate secretary of war from 1862 to 1865 offer a window on the economic hardships and suffering of fragile households and their surrounding neighborhoods. The letters from South Carolina show a growing number of widows and children unprotected, deteriorating conditions, and a sense of desperation as the war continued. These letters highlight the sacrifice made by the Upcountry where the mortality rate was most extreme (see Appendix A, Appendix B, and the tables throughout this chapter). Cameos and recollections are placed in a larger perspective.[2]

The most critical commodities for daily life were leather, flour, meat, salt, and cotton cards. In the face of shortages, prices skyrocketed. In December 1862 soldiers with a "moderately sized family" could not afford shoes, bread, and meat on their monthly pay of eleven dollars. Shoes became scarce and expensive as numerous leather products from saddles to boots were increasingly needed by the army. The prices of flour and salt jumped, especially in the cities. By December 1862, salt cost between $15 and $20 a bushel. That year some people had already given up eating meat; it was too expensive. Women found themselves hard pressed to feed their families. In March 1863 the *Confederate Baptist* feared the "cry of famishing children" would lead "unsexed" women to sack "granaries." At the end of 1864 woman teachers were barely able to purchase a calico dress, muslin, and a pair of shoes with a nine-month salary averaging $60 to $80 a month. Imagine the desperation of a family trying to live off a private's pay. In 1864 the cost of meat was so prohibitive, it was rumored dogs were being sold at auction for $250 apiece in Augusta. "Rather high for sausage meat," a Yorkville newspaper caustically quipped. Simultaneously, more physicians, blacksmiths, wheelwrights, shoemakers, tanners, millers, and overseers were being sent from the home front to the battlefield.[3]

The demand for physicians was greatest in the rural Upcountry where the mortality rate for soldiers was the highest (see Table 7.1). Between 1862 and late 1864, twenty-eight exemptions, discharges, and details for doctors reached the desk of the Confederate secretary of war (see Table 7.2). Eighteen (69.2 percent) were from the Upcountry, two (7.7 percent) from the Lowcountry, which had medical facilities in Charleston. In Upcountry districts, women and children felt the brunt. In July 1862 citizens of Fairfield District requested that Thomas B. McKinstry be sent back. The area, twenty miles long and fifteen miles wide, was "destitute" of medical help. In August 1862 a minister told Jefferson Davis that the doctor was "indispensable" to women, children, and slaves.[4]

Doctors in the Upcountry districts such as Abbeville and Lancaster were overwhelmed with work. They had to treat civilians and an increasing number of seriously sick and injured soldiers. In August 1862 citizens from Greenwood in Abbeville District complained that there was only one doctor within fifteen

Table 7.1
Physicians

Upcountry	18
Lowcountry	2
Other	6
Districts unknown	2
Total	28

Table 7.2
Total Requests for Select Exemptions, Discharges, and Details

Year	1862	1863	1864	1865	Category Totals
Physicians	13	10	5	0	28
Blacksmiths / wheelwrights	14	15	6	0	35
Shoemakers / tanners	14	8	5	0	27
Millers / millwrights	3	2	1	1	7
Overseers / agriculturalists	53	39	25	1	118
Year totals	97	74	42	2	215

miles. The district was "almost destitute" of physicians. Similarly, in February 1863 ninety citizens from Abbeville requested that Dr. William E. Link be sent home to take care of an area of fifteen by twenty miles. The section was subject to endemic diseases even before the war. When smallpox, the "scourge of the human family," broke out in April 1863, nearly two hundred citizens from Chesterfield and Lancaster districts asked that Dr. J. C. Blakeney be exempt to fight the epidemic, which was spread by the army.[5]

Crises on the battlefield brought repercussions at home. In the spring and summer of 1863 discharges or home details for physicians became almost impossible to obtain. In April 1863 seventy citizens of York asked that Dr. Richard G. Montgomery be detailed to help the sick at home, and in July Governor M. L. Bonham also appealed. But a notation on the file read: "The application for discharges to meet the demands for labor in the community professional as well as mechanics is very great—also to supply urgent want of families and neighborhoods. [However,] the country is not in a situation to allow discharges for the army for any one except the disability of the soldier." In December 1864 citizens were still trying to get Dr. Montgomery home.[6]

Refugees compounded the problem. Doctors in Barnwell District were inundated with patients from the Lowcountry who were escaping the dire situation in Charleston. In May 1862, J. F. Baggot was the only physician in Bamberg; another physician was six miles away. The city's regular doctors were in the service. In July 1862, Mrs. Martha Lease and about forty women in Barnwell District pointedly reminded the secretary of war that they had "cheerfully" parted with their sons and brothers in the army, but they sought Dr. Inabinett's exemption because there were no physicians for their families within eighteen miles of Cowpen Branch. Not all Lowcountry folks could afford to leave; there were pockets of extreme poverty where conditions deteriorated as the war progressed. In October 1863, Dr. Morton Waring was given a thirty-day detail to the Goosecreek area, where he was the only doctor "accessible to the poor class." Friends succeeded in getting the Charleston doctor another detail. In spring 1864 they attempted again, for he now served some six hundred women, children, and indigent soldiers.[7]

While the Lowcountry had a ready supply of slave artisans, Upcountry districts suffered greatly as their skilled artisans were called up for service. Twenty-one (or 60 percent) of thirty-four petitions seeking relief of blacksmiths and wheelwrights originated from the Upcountry (Table 7.3). Six petitions, nearly 17 percent, came from Spartanburg alone. Seventeen (or 63 percent) of the petitions for shoemaker-tanners came from the Upcountry. As early as May 1862 areas were without shoemakers, blacksmiths, and other essential artisans. James L. Carwill of Level Land in Fairfield District asked that blacksmith Christopher

Table 7.3
Blacksmiths and Wheelwrights

Upcountry	21 (60.00 percent)
Lowcountry	1 (2.86 percent)
Other	12 (34.28 percent)
Districts unknown	1 (2.86 percent)
Total	35 (100 percent)

Ellis, a member of the Sixth Regiment, South Carolina Militia, be kept home because he was "doing work for a great many destitute families whose husbands and sons [were] in the army."[8]

As Antietam approached in September 1862, more soldier artisans were sucked into the war effort, which took its toll on the home front. In October 1862, G. H. Caldwell had been a wheelwright in Edgefield District for eighteen years. His company commander noted that if he left, the community would be without one; also, the man had a large family dependent on him. That same month the residents of Jamison in Orangeburg District sought the discharge of J. D. Graves because the area had no other shoemakers. Petitioners pleaded, "Have mercy on the pore women & children." Moreover, Graves suffered from rheumatism and brain disease. Despite similar appeals and even the support of their local congressman, the citizens of Spartanburg were denied their blacksmith in November 1862 because the army was "not strong enough to bear details . . . asked for." The next year conditions did not improve. In April 1863 the citizens of Spartanburg this time asked for the discharge of two shoemaker brothers, William and John M. Nolen. Their father was aged, infirm, and incompetent. A notation on the letter cited the absolute necessity "for keeping our gallant army in the field." General Braxton Bragg's critical situation in 1863 rendered exemptions and details moot. As one official noted, "this is not a time when details can be spared from General Bragg's Army."[9]

Millers supplied flour for bread vital to the survival of families as the war and inflation abbreviated their diet. The well-being of some local neighborhoods hung in the balance. In December 1862 concerned citizens of Darlington and Sumter districts wanted John R. Pierson home. He had been wounded at Second Manassas (August 29–30, 1862). The proprietor of the local mill, James Tolson, was on the verge of closing it down because of his age and poor health. Pierson had served as his assistant. Tolson noted, "Their is several hundred women in this neighborhood who has no way of going a long distance to Mill." He added that "the familys of Soldiers and Widows" depended on his mill, and that he needed Pierson to feed them. In February 1863 the citizens of Chester

District requested a detail for millwright G. M. Wilfong to repair their mill. Taking millers from certain areas risked a backlash. In April 1864 a man from Taylor's Creek in York District predicted that if millers were taken out of public mills and sent into the army "great trouble" would result.[10]

The competition between the home front and the battlefield was fiercest over shoemakers (Table 7.4). In November 1863, as the Battle of Fredericksburg was shaping up, six thousand of General James L. Longstreet's men were without shoes. Less than a month later, shoemaker-soldier Marion Britton worried about his community as the winter season approached. Britton, an officer in the Tenth Regiment, South Carolina Volunteers (SCV), had been honorably discharged. But when conscription was instituted, he returned as a private in the Second Regiment, South Carolina Artillery. Citizens in Williamsburg District pleaded that he had been the sole source of shoes for their families. In March 1864 citizens in Chesterfield District, mostly women, thought they had a chance to get Alexander Johnson back home. Johnson, in his forties, had been discharged from the State Militia. Eligible for conscription, he volunteered for service in the Thirty-third South Carolina Cavalry. The ladies pleaded that he was "a practical tanner and the only one in the neighborhood who" tanned "for the public and that on very moderate terms." Without him the families of soldiers would "suffer for want of leather and for many other acts of kindness and attention." He headed a household of nine "dependent on him."[11]

Throughout 1864, shortages of skilled artisans hampered the efforts of local communities to be self-sufficient (Table 7.5). Blacksmith E. R. Goodman was

Table 7.4
Shoemakers and Tanners

Upcountry	17 (63 percent)
Lowcountry	2 (7 percent)
Other	7 (26 percent)
Districts unknown	1 (4 percent)
Total	27 (100 percent)

Table 7.5
Skilled Artisans by Region

Upcountry	60
Lowcountry	5
Other	26
Districts unknown	6
Total	97

detached from the Twenty-sixth Regiment, SCV, to work in a government workshop in Macon, Georgia. In January 1864 soldiers' wives and widows supported his return home. There was no blacksmith within twelve miles to service their needs. A month earlier, citizens of "Bachelor's Retreat" neighborhood in Pickens wanted H. M. Pitts detailed. His blacksmith shop, the only one within twelve miles, accommodated fifty to seventy-five farmers. The request was declined "for the usual reasons." In April 1864 nearly sixty residents of Holly Springs, including soldiers' wives and widows, demanded that Captain J. J. Neimeir, Thirteenth Regiment, SCV, be detailed. Their blacksmith had been in the military since 1861. His wife had recently died, leaving six children at home. Some artisans filled multiple community needs, making their loss especially hard to bear. In February 1864 persons in Edgefield asked that Joseph P. Terry be exempted; the wheelwright, an all-around mechanic, was "indispensable [to] a large surrounding community." In March 1864 the wives and widows of soldiers in Sumter District wanted their blacksmith detailed from the Twenty-third Regiment, SCV. Joseph H. Flemming fixed wagons and ploughs and furnished spinning wheels and cards so necessary for their livelihood.[12]

A security-conscious South Carolina preferred keeping the category of overseer exemptions in its own hands, but by April 1863 the Confederate government prevailed. One widow complained that exemptions from the state adjutant general had become "worthless." Poor slave control constituted a serious security problem, but special treatment for planters with twenty slaves smacked of favoritism. Those who held no slaves felt that their homesteads were just as important as the rich men's estates. They branded the act the "twenty-nigger law." The shortage of men to provide skills and protection to yeoman households and neighborhoods made the exemption of overseers a bone of class contention. The populist perception of favoritism had a basis in fact. From 1863 to 1865 the Confederate secretary of war received from South Carolina planters one hundred eighteen petitions regarding the need for overseers. Ninety-two of them (about 78 percent) requested relatives for relief (see Tables 7.6 and 7.7). Elite families preferred their own relatives as overseers. Despite Uncle Fabian's tirade against fops, it made good sense to seek exemptions and details for kinfolk who knew their needs firsthand. This was particularly valid for the elderly. In 1862 Wyatt Hames and his wife of Cold Springs were left without an overseer. In their seventies, the Edgefield couple had difficulty handling thirty-plus slaves. They asked for the return of their son William J. Hames. Emmanuel Allen of Spartanburg contributed three sons to the army. Between June and August 1862, he tried to get one of them discharged to oversee a large number of slaves. Cancer had eaten one side of the old man's face. In November 1862, the parents of A. D. Powers felt helpless when their overseer

Table 7.6
Overseers by Region

Upcountry	63 (53.4 percent)
Upper Piedmont	23 (36.5 percent)
Lower Piedmont	40 (63.5 percent)
Lowcountry	7 (5.9 percent)
Other	38 (32.2 percent)
Districts unknown	10 (8.5 percent)
Total	118 (100 percent)

Table 7.7
Petitions for Overseers from Planters and Their Relatives

Widows for sons / sons-in-law	25
Parents for sons / sons-in-law	31
Planters for themselves	20
Wives for husbands	7
Other Relatives	9
Total	92

was about to leave. The blind planter was seventy-five years old; his wife suffered from palsy. In July 1863, widow Martha Rogers of Jonesville, Union District, had no family member to help her. The sixty-two-year-old woman took care of a son described as an "idiot." She wanted her only other son, James, discharged as an overseer.[13]

South Carolina slaves were hardly passive observers in this war drama; they ran away and worked the situation to their own advantage. Antietam (September 17, 1862) was a turning point. First, the Yankee victory required the Confederacy to raise more men. On September 27, 1862, the upper age limit of draftees was raised to forty-five. Second, the preliminary issuance of the Emancipation Proclamation five days after Antietam increased the flow of runaways. These circumstances, coupled with the drain of white men from predominantly black neighborhoods, brought more crime and lawlessness. In late September 1862 memorials dealing with slave insurrections reached South Carolina's Executive Council. Half of the requests for overseers came between October 1862 and February 1863, when Lincoln's Proclamation became operational.[14]

In the early days of the war, South Carolina slaves, like those in North Carolina, had attempted to settle their differences with their masters in the context of a paternalism that had evolved decades before the war. However, events during the war shattered that framework. In May 1863, Robert Smalls seized the Confederate ship *Planter*. About a year later Harriet Tubman joined a Union raid on the Combahee River plantations, freeing several hundred slaves. Although an attempt to take Fort Wagner on Morris Island on July 18, 1863, failed, it sent shock waves across the state. The Fifty-fourth Massachusetts Regiment, led by Colonel Robert Gould Shaw, made the attack. The black regiment included men born in South Carolina. It symbolized blacks fighting for their emancipation, as President Lincoln had promised.

Elderly planters and widows found themselves in harm's way. Widows composed nearly half of those seeking the return of their sons as overseers. The case of Mrs. Mildred Thomson of Spartanburg District exemplifies how things began to unravel after Antietam. Life for the woman was deteriorating. One of her sons had lost a leg at the battle. "Unable to wait on himself," he required constant care. Another son, J. Bordon Thomson, had volunteered after Fort Sumter. When his father died, he had been furloughed sixty to ninety days to help get the family estate in order but then went back to his unit. The widow found herself living on a plantation with twenty-eight slaves without any able-bodied white males above the age of ten. In December 1862 Mrs. Thomson sought the discharge of her son J. B. from the Spartanburg Rifles.[15]

All of Adeline Dennis's sons were in the army from the start of the war. The Sumter District widow was left with two young daughters. In early December 1862, a petition on her behalf noted that all the white males in the neighborhood under age fifty were gone. Her plantation worked some sixty to seventy hands. Terrified by "Lincoln's Proclamation," the widow requested that her son, Private R. E. Dennis, Company D, Second Regiment, SCV be discharged to help her. Petitioner Ellen W. Wolfe of Orangeburg District complained on September 10, 1864, that blacks had burned down her smokehouse and killed her hogs; slave patrols were nearly nonexistent. "I do not consider it safe or prudent," she wrote, "for so helpless a family as my own to remain . . . on the plantation." Six grown girls "were dependent on me for protection." Some slaves achieved a form of de-facto autonomy on plantations where they were growing their own crops.[16]

Regulations allowed enterprising widows to collaborate to get overseers. In January 1863, two "helpless" widows from Barnwell District, Rebecca Bryan and Mary Roberts, joined together to get Mary's son-in-law, James Mallard, discharged. Their plantations were ten miles apart; together they owned thirty-two slaves. They lived in hearing distance of the enemy guns. Slaves were going over to the Yankees. In October 1863, Circuit Court Judge D. L. Wardlaw of Abbeville recorded that there were not many able white men within five miles to control the slaves; "half of them at home were either crippled or . . . invalid." The judge was struck by the number of widows in the area.[17]

The lifeblood of some neighborhoods hinged on the presence of sympathetic agriculturalists who felt compelled to join the army. The citizens of Lancaster District were chagrined to hear that John Gardner had enlisted. In May 1863, 204 friends and neighbors, including 170 women, sought his exemption. Gardner's house was a "depot and his crib a granary for the destitute and suffering." He charged $1 for a bushel of corn when he could have gotten $1.50. He sold shoes at $4 when the going prices were $6–$8. He brought salt to soldiers' families on relief and sent his milk cow to needy families. Finally, he represented the claims of twenty-one families to the Board of Relief. The petition was denied even though the enrolling officer hailed the man's generosity.[18]

These letters of appeal by soldiers, family members, neighbors, and congressmen indicated the desperation at the home front and battlefield while the Confederacy tried to keep fighting with dwindling forces and supplies. Of the 493 petitions for exemptions, discharges, and details, 63 described the physical disabilities of the soldiers mentioned (see Table 7.8). Some draftees sought exemptions but many others already in the army wanted to be detailed or discharged. More than half (that is, fifty-five) came from the Upcountry. Most of them, twenty-two, or 40 percent, lived in the Upper Piedmont, a section of the Upcountry with numerous yeomen. Pickens accounted for six, or nearly 10 percent, of all disability requests. As many petitions came from this Upcountry district as from the entire Lowcountry.[19]

To describe maladies, petitioners usually used general terms such as wounded, unfit for service, bad health, or sickness. Wounds headed the list. Rheumatism and heart, kidney, and lung ailments were constantly mentioned. Some appeals declared that these men faced certain death if they remained in the army. In November 1863 Marion District residents asked that John Turner, a spinning-wheel maker, be detailed. The soldier suffered from ascites (blood

Table 7.8
Physical Disabilities

Wounded	11
Kidney / liver	5
Rheumatism	4
Heart	2
Bronchitis	2
Lung	2
Misc.	11
General	26
Total	63

in the abdominal cavity). Doctors testified: "It really looks like cool murder to carry off such a man."[20]

Some young men suffering from kidney disorders since childhood landed up in the military. In June 1862, A. M. Folger Sr., a doctor living in Pickensville, requested that his son, Alonzo, be discharged from the militia. The boy had suffered before the war from diseases of the kidney, liver, and spinal cord. For three years, the youth had tried to make his living as a clerk in Spartanburg, but the work had been too much for his frail health. Serious kidney ailments were all too common. In November 1862, M. S. Strickland, Twentieth Regiment, SCV, sought a detail as a shoemaker because he suffered from kidney disease. In May 1863, Nancy Stalvy petitioned that her husband was "severely afflicted with the dropsy and an affliction of the kidneys." More often than not, physical problems were compounded by economic hardships at home. A petition in May 1863, noting that M. Pierce suffered from a kidney disorder, highlighted the serious situation at home. His wife Rebekah was extremely sick and nearly destitute. She feared their five children would "starve."[21]

Company commanders, such as Captain J. M. Moffet of Hampton's Legion, saw firsthand how difficult service was for family men between the ages of thirty-six and forty-seven. He proposed discharging them. But in July 1862 men as old as forty-five and fifty were supposed to serve an additional ninety days before being discharged, and some captains refused to let them go. Units experienced a generational rift, which further increased demoralization and anxieties among the older men. Those with large families mistrusted the judgment of the younger men.[22]

Older men with families were more likely to experience physical difficulties. In September 1862, A. W. Law of Lynchburg in Darlington District suffered from chronic bronchitis. His constitution was shattered. To add to his burden, the thirty-five-year-old man had the responsibility of an extended family that included a wife, two children, and an ailing mother who required care. Until October 1863, Newton E. Sistrunk had been allowed to remain at home as an agriculturalist. His plantation produced surpluses of corn. He took special care to help soldiers' families by giving them fair prices. By May 1864 he was in the Twentieth Regiment, SCV. Dr. W. C. Wolfe stated that Sistrunk's chronic bronchitis was such that if he should continue in active service, "it could probably terminate his life."[23]

But with the demand for soldiers ever increasing, Confederate authorities had to crack down on exemptions, details, and discharges for the physically unfit. In February 1863 General Order No. 22, issued by Adjutant Inspector General Samuel Cooper, indicated as much. Deafness must be "so excessive (which must be detailed in the monthly report) as to incapacitate a man for the duties of a sentinel." A doctor's certification was required. A speech impediment had to be of "a very aggravated character." Chronic heart disease that had been diagnosed as relatively "infrequent" should be monitored. However, the functional disturbance of the heart's action was "very common, not a valid ground for exemption." It could "generally be relieved by change to the life of the camp." Rheumatism (acute or chronic, articular or muscular) needed close scrutiny because it could be used "as a means of evasion." Epilepsy was "a disease being frequently simulated so as to impose upon a careless observer." It had to be confirmed by "nothing less than the observation of an actual paroxysm, or the affidavit of a responsible physician acquainted with the conscript." The loss of two fingers or an eye was insufficient for exemption.[24]

Severe wounds did not guarantee that a man would remain out of the conflict. Wounded soldiers discharged earlier in the war were drafted. John Blanton was so severely wounded at battles around Richmond that doctors despaired over whether he would ever survive from a shot through the face, neck, and right shoulder. He was not given a permanent disability. In late 1863, perhaps in response to the general order, petitions requesting discharges gave graphic details of the physical disabilities of the soldiers and the hardships their families were undergoing. In November Mrs. Morgan P. H. Poole and a number of petitioners noted how her husband was "badly ruptured" and physically unfit. Five of their sons were in the army. Four of the children at home were under seven years of age. The mother had no means of support. She herself was disabled.[25]

Families faced medical hardships compounded by the war. In 1862 John O. Tate of Union District was in the Thirty-seventh Regiment, South Carolina Militia. He had served in the Second Regiment, SCV, which was once part of the Thirty-seventh. Tate's wife had been suffering some twenty months with white swelling in the leg. A family physician pronounced her incurable. Tate himself was in bad health. Thirteen members from his regiment supported his discharge. In January 1863, Charles Bell sought a discharge to care for his father who suffered from paraplegia and hemiplegia, or stroke. Generations of the family had suffered from the same conditions. W. J. Bright's father was "a raving lunatic for the last four years." He was confined to a cell without his clothes. His "mania was of the furious kind. He meditated violence . . . against his wife and small children." All the sons "large enough to protect the family" were "in the Confederate service."[26]

Cancer remained a virulent killer. In January 1862 James D. Atkin's wife Mary Ann suffered from cancer on the head. She was the mother of three children with another one on the way. She had few friends in the neighborhood to help her. Without her husband at home, she feared the family would have to go to the poorhouse. In June 1862 Sarah Bates of Barnwell District desperately needed the assistance of her soldier-son Joseph. Her cancer had advanced to the point where she had lost the use of an arm. He was the only family she had. She prayed for his discharge or a furlough.[27]

There was no exemption specifically labeled "Family Hardship," but the concept existed. Many of the petitions that were based on equity, justice, public necessity, and community needs were reinforced by descriptions of desperate family situations that needed the man to come home. The appeal worked and some men got details. But increasing crises on the battlefield diminished their number. In February 1863 citizens of Barnwell District informed their Congressman Lewis M. Ayers that the family of Private D. A. Fender was in "a precarious condition." The household, including three children, depended on his wife but she was continuously having convulsions. According to a notation on the letter, "discharges on account of family bereavement, poverty, sickness & suffering have been to the number of hundreds and that the department has painfully continued to deny them all."[28]

Some households with extended families could not sustain the loss of the breadwinner. In August 1863 D. Zimmerman, a conscript from Spartanburg District, declared that his family was in "destitute condition." The thirty-three-year-old man was responsible not only for his wife and six children but also for his wife's mother and helpless grandmother. "[I am] willing to serve my country," he declared, "[but] I cannot hardly . . . think of the condition I have left my helpless children in." Four of his brothers were also serving in the Confederate army. Alfred W. Davis of Jonesville, Union District, was proud of his five sons in the army. But in September 1862, the wheelmaker wrote that the weight on his shoulders was too much. "I am a poor man," he explained, "and need one of them at home very much." The household consisted of seventeen children. He specifically requested the discharge of J. C. Davis, saying, "My son has a family at home." The attempt failed, but in March 1863 he tried to get another son, Patrick Jefferson Davis, detailed. Patrick, who made spinning wheels, was now one of six sons in the army. W. R. Sullivan, Greenville District, faced a quagmire. He entered the army as part of the State Troops in September 1863, but the regiment disbanded in early February 1864. He was required to enroll by February 20. In addition to losing his left eye, he had a wife and nine children. A tenth was on the way. His oldest son, eighteen years old, was already in the service. He owned a small tract of land but was very poor. A doctor and other witnesses agreed he would do more good for the public at home. But he had lost only one eye.[29]

Demoralization became widespread after Antietam. A committee, headed by the prominent Lowcountry secessionist John Townsend, addressed the people of South Carolina on the precariousness of the situation. One-fifth of the soldiers at Antietam fought barefooted; half were in rags. The group implored women not to give into the selfishness of the "speculator, monopolist, or the extortionist." But desperate to feed their children, some continued to sell goods on the open market. The discontent with governmental policies such as conscription and impressment reached a crescendo in 1863 after the twin defeats of Vicksburg and Gettysburg. At the same time desertions became a serious problem in Upcountry districts such as Pickens, Greenville, and Anderson. The knockdown battles in the east further disheartened the homeland. Yet in December 1863 a York officer still believed that the Yankees could not whip them if the men were given the supplies they needed. Despite his faith, by late 1864 an increasing number of residents in the Confederacy, including aliens, sought passports out of the country. Taken collectively, these indices indicate a sharp decline in morale (see Table 7.9).[30]

Deteriorating conditions were aggravated by conscription and impressment. No single issue upset South Carolinians more than conscription (see Appendix A and Appendix B), which came to symbolize the evils and inefficiencies of big government in a society that prided itself on localism and Jeffersonian idealism. From its inception in April 1862, conscription brought complaints. In May 1862 an anonymous letter from Anderson District charged that R. H. Anderson, an able-bodied man, was given an exemption because his relative was Congressman James L. Orr. The writer noted that many poor white men had to leave their fields and go off to war. Conversely, it did not escape the notice of ordinary South Carolinians that elites found safe havens in the partisan rangers. Such units were overenrolled.[31]

Conscription undermined any faith in the exemption and detail system. In Charleston members of Beauregard's staff were implicated in a profitable conscription scam. Some enrolling officers were accused of favoring certain soldiers with details against regulations at the same time when medical boards were passing unfit men for the army. In May 1864 more than one hundred Yorkville

Table 7.9
Indexes of Declining Morale

Year	Complaints	Desertions	Passports	Category Totals
1861	1	0	0	1
1862	7	2	6	15
1863	9	1	5	15
1864	20	7	23	50
1865	1	0	7	8
Year totals	38	10	41	89

citizens condemned the widespread practice of putting into service unfit men, ages seventeen to fifty. A Lancaster paper charged that numerous invalids were being sent into the army. According to a Sumter newspaper, one man, injured two years earlier, could barely walk. His past exemptions were discarded.[32]

With armies in the field insufficiently clothed and fed, and widows and children needing food and shelter, Confederate authorities began impressment. Farmers and other citizens were required to pay one-tenth of what they raised in kind. The Upcountry districts and others in the interior felt its sting the most. The policy had unforeseen consequences. In September 1863 an officeholder from Anderson District believed that the impressment of grain was starving the region; he predicted that thousands would suffer while grain was left rotting at depots.[33]

Impressment also raised the politically explosive issue of the inheritance rights of orphans. In December 1863 a South Carolina newspaper intoned, "Orphan children have rights under such authority." Confederate officers were warned that they might find themselves personally liable for their illegal attempts to violate state laws. Some agents were heavy-handed. Agent Tillman Watson's notice in an Edgefield paper required those butchering beef cattle to get a permit, or have their beef subject to seizure. They also had to make a monthly affidavit on the number of cattle butchered. One Lancaster man slaughtered the cattle for his own benefit after they were impressed. Other farmers and planters refused to accept the imposed price schedule; they could make more money on the market.[34]

Soldiers' Relief, designed to help starving families, was caught up in red tape and lacked sufficient funding to help the families. In August 1862 a South Carolinian's wife and five children could not get soldier's relief because the man was in a North Carolina regiment. On January 2, 1862, the Soldiers' Board of Relief for Newberry District levied a 25 percent general tax on the citizens of the region. The $6,087 raised took care of some 140 families, averaging one to four children, with a maximum amount of $2 a month. This relief applied only to children under the age thirteen unless they were disabled. Between May 1 and August 1, 1863, district authorities spent $2,759 for some 474 applicants, who received $6 a quarter. Such limited measures provoked resentment. Mary L. Cumming of Ridgeville in the Lowcountry resented supporting another soldier's wife when she had problems feeding her own six children. Volunteer efforts were not able to fill the gap. The wealthy were also feeling the economic pinch. In April 1864, elite women's efforts to establish a Wayside Hospital at Florence were hindered by lack of funds. "Our planters are patriotic," reported the secretary of the relief society in Charleston, "but their energies are tasked to the ultimate to pay their tithes, support their negroes and supply the families around them with provisions." Her appeal to the Secretary of War to purchase provisions from the government was denied.[35]

The resulting cacophony spawned conspiracy theories and scapegoats. Inflation in late 1862 and early 1863 caused South Carolinians to vent their antagonism toward mill owners whose profits seemed inordinate. Most mill owners were not extortionists, but they were perceived as such. Yielding to a crescendo of attacks, an exasperated James Gibbes finally sold his Saluda mill in 1862. Farmers such as David Golightly Harris were forced to speculate in cloth to support their families. Despite the necessity of these endeavors, his wife Emily found herself questioning her wickedness.[36]

Deteriorating conditions stirred a latent anti-Semitism. Efforts to convert Jews increased with the beginning of the war. Miriam Cohen rankled at such proselytism. According to Mary Chesnut, almost everyone included one or two Jews in their social circle. Despite such exceptions, "Jew" became synonymous with speculator and extortionist. In December 1863, there were complaints that poor people in Williamsburg District could not afford shoes because "Jews and Speculators who run about the county claiming to be foreigners do not allow any articles to remain in the hands of retail merchants except at such enormous prices." In Kingstree, located in Williamsburg District where the soldier mortality rate was high, anti-Semitic rhetoric was vitriolic. In 1864 forty-three petitioners decried, "We are infested with a set of Jews in Kingstree which are doing nothing but extorting." The secretary of war could at least "relieve us of the extortion of a Jew by the name of Swartz."[37]

The hatred for conscription and impressment officers blossomed into an all-out attack against the government. In September 1864 a "Citizen" complained to Jefferson Davis that too many men were absent without leave or detailed. In cities, towns, and villages were crowds of "healthy looking young men walking the streets & lounging about Hotels [and] drinking Shops as unconcerned as if we are at peace. They belonged to The Greater Master Commissary, or some other department of government." The writer wondered about the poor soldier "with a helpless wife and children." The letter also contained several highly critical newspaper clippings. One woman from Greenville, South Carolina, wrote an article entitled "Filling the Ranks." She feared that she would be "despised" and her conduct considered "unbecoming" because women "were not permitted to speak in public before the war." She volunteered to take the place of the young men detailed to the cities. Another clipping from a Richmond paper charged that enough men were absent from the army "to plant the Southern cross on the spire of Philadelphia." Men of the cloth were no longer beyond criticism. In January 1865 "Anonymous" slammed "speculating preachers." The rich should come out and fight, "or let the poor return to their homes." He predicted, "The poor will not stand it much longer." As for himself, he concluded: "I would not give my life for all the Blame negroes in the Confederacy." The writer signed his ominous missive, "Worn out in Camp & Hospitals."[38]

In districts bordering North Carolina, deserters were active. In some communities women and children acted as sentinels for such groups. In August 1863 Greenville citizens petitioned the secretary of war for help. Deserters in Greenville, Anderson, and Pickens threatened the stability of the region. Three hundred deserters congregated at Bott's Cove in Pickens District. An observer noted: "The gang has still and is now carrying on an extensive business from the produce stolen from helpless women and children." Most deserters, however, were not gang members; they were simply tired of the war and its impact on their families. Captain William H. Peronneau pleaded that mercy be given four men in his company scheduled to be shot for desertion. They had been stalwarts at the fierce Battle of Fort Wagner in July 1863. Like others, they had decided to make their own peace with the Union and go home.[39]

As early as April 1862, South Carolinians were seeking passports to leave the Confederacy. Their numbers jumped in January 1864. Women and children left the New Republic for safety in the North. In mid-March 1863, Mrs. Jane Bowly wanted to be with her husband and four children in Baltimore. He was originally from New York. She had been visiting Charleston but was now living in Greenville. In January 1864, Mrs. Catherine Eagan, a widow living in Leesville, asked to join her family and friends in Albany, New York. Her husband, John S. Eagan of the Palmetto Sharpshooters, had died of typhoid after being wounded at Gettysburg. In July 1864, Mrs. John A. Owens of Barnwell District lost her physician husband. Friends described the widow Mary Ann and her four children as completely destitute. She desired to go to Kansas where her husband and father had participated in the effort to keep Kansas a slave territory.[40]

As the war grew grislier, some noncitizens sought refuge in Canada, Europe, and the Bahamas. Instead of seeing them as providing support at the home front, some Southerners bitterly resented that aliens were not subjected to the draft. Others condemned them as speculators. In response, noncitizens turned to their home governments for help. William Henry Herme, a German, had been in the United States since 1857. In June 1863 he enlisted as a twelve-month substitute in the German Hussars, Third Regiment, South Carolina Cavalry. Herme sought the aid of the Prussian consul in Charleston to get him out. Others, such as Walter Lynch, a British subject, felt pressured to join the army against their will. In June 1864, the Prussian consulate in Charleston presented the secretary of war with a list of nine men who had been forced to enlist. The result was that South Carolina and the Confederacy lost a source of much-needed businessmen and artisans.[41]

As William T. Sherman's army left Atlanta afire in November 1864 and marched toward Savannah and the Carolinas, the Confederacy was already "up the spout." A month earlier, a Chester woman summarized the dire situation as seen from the vantage point of a planter's wife. All the men in the family, including her husband, were in service. A seventeen-year-old son had gone off to war with the older men. She asked Jefferson Davis as "a fond father" to his nation to allow her sixteen-year-old son an exemption as an overseer. He had recently departed with the state militia for the battlefield. Large plantations were left with only women and little children. Women were pressed to their limits spinning and weaving; thousands of them were invalids. The slaves made it clear they did "not intend to be ruled by women." Meanwhile, news would arrive of "a husband and father slain or a son or brother." She summarized: "We cannot fight without something to eat any more than we can fight without ammunition." Finally, the lady broached a topic that would have been considered treasonous in 1861. She concluded that the community would only survive if the government "put a portion of our negroes in service" to fight the Yankees and left "white men at home to oversee."[42]

8 Baptism by Fire

Between 1861 and 1865, South Carolina underwent a baptism by fire. In November 1861 the Great Fire of Charleston swept though the city. During a 587-day siege, Greek fire rained down on the population. On the morning of February 18, 1865, the fate of the city was sealed when the last Confederate troops left. An enormous explosion at the city's Northeastern Depot followed their departure. Caused by children playing, the disaster killed more than one hundred people and injured about an equal number. As Union soldiers entered the city, Confederates rushed to destroy the *Palmetto State*, the repaired ironclad that had been built by the donations of women and children.

That same day, Columbia, the capital now occupied by Sherman and his army, went up in flames. A collage emerges that shows how women and children responded to these catastrophes.[1]

Perhaps no other campaign has come to symbolize the victimization of South Carolina than Sherman's rampage through the state. "Sherman" became a general term to cover all Yankee misdeeds and atrocities. An eleven-year-old boy recalled later in life that Sherman and his army were synonymous with death and destruction. Given events in Georgia and the fall of Savannah, it was inevitable that South Carolinians would brace for the worst. In December 1864, Edgefield was "flooded . . . with Yankee officers who [had] escaped from a prison in Columbia." They were "making their way to Sherman's Army." The Upcountry was no longer secure from the fire of the general's wrath.[2]

In January 1865, a month before its impending disaster, Columbia seemed eerily oblivious. On the seventeenth, the ladies held a great "Bazaar" in the State Legislature to help wounded soldiers. Booths named for Confederate states were brimming with wartime luxuries. Coffee and other delicacies, previously hoarded, were in abundance. Some gifts had come through the blockade from Great Britain, among them a beautiful doll from Liverpool. More than three thousand individuals attended. The frivolity and luxuries created a surrealist aura of decadence. Partygoers forked over $350,000 in what would soon become worthless Confederate currency. Young people enjoyed dressing up and feasting. Some older citizens reverted to long-lost childhood. Romping with the children, they escaped the war but only momentarily. Play turned to bedlam. The boys got out of hand; a hundred of them, in packs of a dozen or less, rampaged through the fair.[3]

Ironically, the day after the bazaar, the *Confederate Baptist* issued an announcement of hope entitled "A Ray of Life." This Columbia weekly opined that the tales of horror emanating from Georgia were exaggerated. The religious organ surmised that Sherman, a husband and father, was not "a modern Blue-beard" uttering "fiendish sentiments." It cautioned, "Hatred and fear some-times transform an enemy into a demon and people turn pale at the exaggerated stories of his enormities." To substantiate its claims, the paper reprinted an editorial from the Mobile *Register*, which declared that those who had passed over Sherman's track through Sparta, Milledgeville, and Macon "saw fewer signs of devastation than . . . expected." Stories of "incredible wrong and outrage" were spread to frighten women and children, and to make them leave their homes. The Baptist paper, trying to calm its anxious readers, under-estimated the enemy at its gate.[4]

The gaiety of the Columbia Bazaar was more feigned than real. The people were near panic. Within days many rushed to the railroad depots to depart before the Federals came. This encouraged remaining Confederate troops to despoil vacant homes and loot stores. The shelling of the capital magnified the danger. "Women and children" were "running to escape the terrible missiles that were thrown by the vilest of foes." The city was ablaze. A number of factors made the burning of Columbia possible, but no historian has fully exonerated the Yankees for the fire or for what happened during the blaze. An officer on Sherman's staff saw drunken soldiers involved in arson and looting. He was moved by the sight of "men, women, and children huddled about a few articles of clothing and household wares . . . saved from their ruined homes." An Illi-nois soldier confessed that such campaigning corroded the discipline of the Union army.[5]

Parents were worried sick about their children. Mrs. Joseph LeConte was convinced the family home would be burned. She swaddled baby Carrie in a blanket and took her into the back garden where the family stayed most of the night. Sallie Chapin authored the best contemporary fictional narrative of events during the shelling and burning of Columbia. It was designed for chil-dren. The author wove accounts from various families into a credible story about the St. Clair family. Mrs. St. Clair did not believe that graduates of West Point, her husband's alma mater, would burn down a town populated by defenseless women and children. Thousands "of women, decrepit old men, and helpless children, with bundles of clothing or baskets of food, were flying wildly in every direction, not knowing where to go for safety and shelter." Pandemo-nium turned "into hell."[6]

Chapin made a direct and sentimental appeal to her young readers in her account of pillage and death. The St. Clair child, May, was "a darling little pet . . . timid as a bird." When the shells exploded, she closed her "soft blue" eyes and cried, "Bad! May, tell papa." A squad of soldiers forced Mrs. St. Clair to give up her wedding ring. Her teenage son Fitz-Hugh wanted to defend her, but the mother said it was not worth losing him over such an item. A "beautiful Afghan—relic of better days" was snatched off the ailing baby May. A second shawl was likewise taken. The child's cheeks "were crimson with fever, and her head was tossed restlessly from side to side. A family servant fell on his knees asking for God to send an angel to help them." One "ruffian" nearly tore the limbs off May, who was in Fitz-Hugh's arms. The shock killed the baby girl, who had never seen her father.[7]

The Hanoverian consul seconded Chapin's fictional account. While the fire raged across the city, pale nuns and "trembling school girls" escaped from a burning Ursuline convent. Terrified residents, some with children, lived a nightmare as they fled from raging fires and plunderers who tried to strip them of what possessions they had. Some poor victims were assaulted. By the time Sherman left the city, some 458 buildings had been destroyed, approximately one-third of those in the city. In July 1865, a Union chief quartermaster from the Army of Tennessee described the devastation as "just and righteous retribution."[8]

Sherman's troops had established a fairly set routine in Georgia that continued in South Carolina. They searched the houses for weapons and food. Homes faced several waves of invasions. Some men handled their duties with a sense of decency. Others were unnecessarily provocative. Still others, the so-called "bummers," were outright thieves. The more sadistic did bodily harm. Women were particularly vulnerable to the actions of the soldiers, who sexually intimidated them. The historian, George C. Rable, noted how Sherman's men systematically looted the homes. Beginning in the kitchens and pantries, they ended up in the bedrooms, rifling through personal items and destroying the children's playthings. But it was black women who suffered the most from physical abuse.[9]

Elite families developed ways to deal with Sherman, beginning in Georgia. They sought him out and requested that his officers provide guards for their homes. Women counted on good feelings, chivalry, and old service ties. One woman appealed to an old friend, Union General John Alexander Logan, who in turn was a longtime friend of Ulysses S. Grant. She received a detail of three soldiers who protected a cow the family needed for milk. The efficacy of a guard depended on the character of the individual soldier. The record is mixed but some won the admiration and gratitude of those they protected. In Anderson, at the request of Elijah Brown's wife for a guard, she received an eighteen-year-old youth, who conscientiously performed his duty. He died at a nearby battle and was buried at First Presbyterian Church. Molly Brown always had their children place a U.S. flag on his grave. In some instances, children could act as shields. One black servant suggested that his mistress protect herself and her children by hugging them as close to her body as she could.[10]

During the horrible night of the fire in Columbia, one woman appealed to Sherman for help. She was the niece of a friend who had served with Sherman in the prewar army. Her husband and the entire family spent the night near the State Lunatic Asylum. The next day they were delivered in an ambulance to Sherman's stately residence, where they had breakfast with the general. Breakfast was tense, especially after Sherman declared things were not nearly as bad as they seemed. Even worse, the general showed an interest in the children (he had lost a young son during the war). At the dining table, the general had the little ones sit with him while he prepared their plates, even cutting their food. Like prisoners of war, the family endured the meal in silence. They remained a second night. Sherman gave the family bags of rice, wheat, and flour.[11]

Other cities faced similar, if less deadly, versions of the Columbia burning. Camden was singled out, possibly because so many Lowcountry people had streamed there in search of safety. Eliza Fludd, a refugee from Charleston then living in Camden, complained that the Yankees used their bayonets to destroy her furniture and stab the family portraits. They took all the food, leaving her and her four grandchildren desolate. Other households suffered even more. According to Fludd's secondhand accounts, both white and African American women were sexually abused. The Yankees stripped two fair-skinned domestics and then spanked them around the room in front of their mistress. At another household, other soldiers "violated" several domestic servants leaving them "almost dead, unable to move." Near Charleston, an elderly white woman and her fourteen-year-old granddaughter were "violated" by black Union solders. Although Fludd believed that God had restrained the Union Army and that there were fewer rapes in South Carolina than in Georgia, her description of alleged threats and atrocities committed by the Yankees during the war and Reconstruction foreshadowed the depiction of this era in D. W. Griffith's 1915 film *The Birth of a Nation*.[12]

A young woman refugee in Anderson remembered the dread of waiting. She felt powerless. Her aunt had an infant only ten days old. The girl decided to take the small children to the safety of her aunt's room, but a Yankee was already waiting on the top step. One of the little girls trembled at the sight of the soldier. Another Yankee threatened to kill some of the people if they did not hand over gold watches. Soldiers carried the girl's sixty-two-year-old uncle into her mother's room and nearly hanged him three times. The women heard his voice, followed by a shot. They thought he was dead, but he survived. However, his ordeal was not over. The soldier hit him on the face with a shovel. They slammed his head against the wall. Realizing he was about to be killed, the old man finally gave them the watch. A little girl from Winnsboro recalled how the Yankees sadistically destroyed what little food they had. The Federal soldiers mixed soap in the family's molasses, rice, flour, meal, corn, and coffee. They slit open the preserves and pickle jars and spat into them.

The very young were not always aware that the incoming soldiers were Yankees; some embraced them as playmates. The Daniel Brown home in Lancaster became the headquarters for General Hugh Judson Kilpatrick. The family had to stay in one bedroom. This allowed the five-year-old daughter the opportunity to spend time dining with the Yankees in the adjutant general's mess. One young officer hoisted her up on his shoulders; he became her human horse as he ran down the piazza. She soaked up the attention.[13]

How children reacted to Sherman and the Yankees is difficult to recreate. As the children matured after the war, some were not exactly sure what they had seen. One adult confessed she could no longer distinguish what she saw as a child from what people told her subsequently about the incidents. Her memory became a blur of what she thought she had seen with the adult conversations she had overheard. Rumors of Sherman's approaching troops did not deter boys from playing. Some were fearless and reveled in the excitement of war. Years later they vividly recalled their experiences, which for some were the highlights of their lives. Thomas McMichael remembered how as a five-year-old, he charmed Yankees into giving him money and breakfast. Other youngsters, usually girls, took atrocity stories to heart. They acted out their fears in play. Julia wanted to play the game of Sherman with her friend Fannie, who then bit the head off a doll. She also destroyed the other dolls and toys in the pretty play house. A James Island girl, later a refugee in Sumter, was stricken with anxiety that the Yankees were after her dolls. She quickly hid them in a box with their clothes. She was in such a panic that she could never find where she had buried them. Sallie Parker Truesdale was about nine when she buried her little dolls in a small box with a silver thimble. For years afterward Sallie and other children grew up playing at war by hiding things from the enemy soldiers. Perhaps such activities served as a safety valve to release posttraumatic anxieties, shared by their mothers. Several years later, in one such game of "play Yankees," Miss Sallie lost her precious silver thimble. The girls' fears were warranted. Union soldiers did pilfer dolls and other toys from children. These cherished items were not just little handmade playthings. Some were expensive European imports obtained at great effort by their fathers. But sometimes decency prevailed. One young soldier grabbed May Snowden's elaborate china-head doll, but another returned it to her.[14]

Accounts of how the Yankees had invaded household pantries and despoiled the precious food, leaving the families desolate, scarred the psyche of one Camden girl. She was terrified when a Union soldier offered her mother coffee and cream. She was afraid the coffee was poisoned. But the soldier was simply returning a favor; the mother had offered him some Confederate coffee earlier. Generally, though, children took their cues from their mothers. Sarah Bryce was determined to save all she could from Sherman. Her actions did not go unnoticed by her young daughter Mamie, who took as many small bags as she could as she left the house. She, too, had to save something from those bad Yankees. Another girl recalled how the children were given belts to wear so they could carry combs, towels, brushes, and pots and pans.[15]

Sherman's march through South Carolina left women and girls with nightmares that lingered into their memories. Boys shared these experiences and fears but their behavior at such events as the Columbia Bazaar revealed that war brought them exhilarating freedom. One Fairfield citizen, reminiscing to a local newspaper reporter many years later, recalled the war years as idyllic. The neighborhood boys were free from school to play war, collect Confederate buttons to wear, and even once get close to a skirmish without being detected. Sherman, with his striking red hair and uniform, riding a black stallion followed by his entourage, was the most handsome personage they had ever seen. Girls with their dolls and boys with their souvenirs played war in their own way.

Women felt differently and blamed Sherman for their vulnerability. Grace B. Elmore best summarized such sentiments. Recalling the horrors of Sherman's march into Columbia, she branded his troops as devils and children killers. She prayed that their wives and families would endure similar abuse.[16]

Charleston faced continual crises, beginning in late 1861 when the blockade began. Rumors of impending dangers alarmed its citizens. In August, stores on King Street were closed by 2:00 p.m. so that men between the ages of sixteen and sixty could drill. On November 7, Union Commodore Samuel F. DuPont seized forts Walker and Beauregard in Port Royal Harbor. Most of the Sea Islands fell into Yankee hands, including some of the state's richest cotton-producing areas. Charleston was now within striking distance. Panic swept through the city. One month later, the port was struck by an inferno, inadvertently started by black refugees. The blaze, swept by gale winds through the downtown area, covered 540 acres and destroyed 575 private homes. The homeless included both rich and poor. Their children were especially vulnerable. "Little children . . . had been snatched from their beds, with only their night garments to cover them from the cold." Such reports brought help throughout the South. A Nashville resident donated money for "the relief of such little ones as may be suffering from the effects of the late disastrous fire." The Ladies Aid Association of Camden sent clothing for the destitute, particularly those poor little ones. The refugee children of Charleston presently living in Greenville sent their "pocket money" to help. The area, known as "the burnt district," drew looters. A few months later, police arrested thieves taking iron from the neighborhood.[17]

With the Union fleet threatening Charleston, the city established a commission "for the removal of Negroes and other Noncombatants." In late January 1862 the commission suggested moving some five thousand persons out of harm's way. Depots would be set up in Columbia and other Upstate urban centers to handle them. Railroads would make arrangements to accommodate the mass exodus. By April members of the commission called for removing ten thousand persons to Summerville. A month later martial law was declared. In June all residents, including women, children, and servants, were issued certificates to allow them to travel on railroads at half-fare. Estimates were revised upward. Some fifteen thousand Charlestonians might have to be moved, mostly women and children. Rev. A. Toomer Porter recognized that the evacuation plans were inadequate because they ignored the destitute who could not be moved "except by Military Force." Moreover, many residents, "especially women and children," who were not already destitute would become so after the move.[18]

In 1862 Charleston braced for attack from land and sea. In June more than seven thousand Federal troops arrived on James Island. Union General Quincy A. Gillmore postponed operations, but in his absence, subordinate commander H. W. Bentham launched an ill-considered attack on June 16 against fortifications at Secessionville. The Rebel soldiers, led by General Nathan G. Evans, routed the Union forces, temporarily saving Charleston. In August 1862 the streets were deserted. With the shelling on the lower parts of the city, some affluent citizens moved to the safer upper wards of the city; others left for Camden.[19]

While things were going badly for the Confederates at Gettysburg and Vicksburg in 1863, the situation in Charleston stabilized. In April, the fleet of Admiral DuPont failed miserably in its attempt to seize the harbor. In July Confederates at Fort Wagner repulsed two attacks. The last one was by the Fifty-fourth Massachusetts, led by Colonel Robert Shaw. Charleston settled down for a projected siege of 587 days. The defense against DuPont was successful, but the city faced continued bombardment and evacuations.[20]

On August 21, General Gillmore demanded the evacuation of Fort Sumter and Morris Island in four hours; if not, he threatened to commence firing on Charleston. This triggered charges and countercharges on the "barbarity" of the intended shelling. Women and children became a central issue. General P. G. T. Beauregard, wanting at least three days to remove the noncombatants, informed Gillmore, "You now resort to the novel measure of turning your guns against old men, the women and children and the hospitals of a sleeping city." The British consul in the city supported Beauregard's assertion. He emphasized the danger posed to British subjects, especially women and children. Gillmore, who thought that the city had already been evacuated, granted it a brief reprieve.[21]

Bombardment began in late August 1863 with Greek fire from the infamous "Swamp Angel." The sound and fury of artillery was dreadful. Susan Forest Nelson, a slave child, held out "her arms for someone to hold her." A shell, crashing through the small house, just passed over the head of her sleeping father. In a separate incident, another child also miraculously escaped death. A shell went through a roof into a room on the second floor, "tearing away the bed from under [the] little child," and landed in the basement. Others were not so lucky. A Confederate report, covering August 21, 1863, to January 5, 1864, described the death of several individuals. Mrs. Hawthorne was wounded by a shell in the side of her body. She died six weeks later. Another woman at the corner of Market and Meeting streets lost her right leg. She died four days later. For safety reasons, the children of the Charleston Orphan House were evacuated to Orangeburg.[22]

Christening such a terrifying weapon an "Angel" seemed unnecessarily cruel, if not fiendish. Shells bombed indiscriminately. Women and children scrambled to leave the upper part of the city for the outer upper wards. A second great bombardment began in late October 1863, lasting forty-one days. The heaviest shelling occurred on Christmas Day, 1863. By March 1864, Charlestonians began abandoning their houses, especially in districts susceptible to shelling. This left many homes unprotected. A Charleston newspaper urged absentee owners to visit their homes because army prowlers were breaking into them. School-aged boys joined in the looting. The newspaper added: "We regret to see more boys thus prowling who should be at school or at some desk or branch of apprenticeship."[23]

In time the Swamp Angel blew up. But even after that, the shelling remained horrific. One Parrott gun alone fired 4,615 rounds into the city. In June, Confederate General Roswell S. Ripley told his Union counterpart that prisoners of war, five Yankee generals and forty-five field officers, would be placed in areas of the city where noncombatants lived, especially women and children. Union

General A. Schimmelfennig justified the bombardment by claiming the military goal to destroy the arsenals and foundries that provided three ironclads for the Confederacy. The Confederate authorities replied that the barrage was "promiscuously" killing "women and children quietly sleeping in their accustomed beds." Perceptive citizens such as Porter estimated that the Yankee assault of the city achieved little military purpose. The Episcopal minister condemned a "senseless bombardment [that] killed some eight inoffensive old people, men and women." For South Carolinians, the bombardment confirmed their perception of Sherman's march through their state as a war on women and children.[24]

On Wednesday, June 8, 1864, a sea captain presented the city of Charleston with an impressive tribute to Confederate courage. It was a statue of General Thomas J. "Stonewall" Jackson. The monument, over nine feet tall, had been fashioned in Nassau from "the most tasteful and elaborate shell work" by a North Carolinian and a Canadian. City authorities decided that the most fitting place to exhibit the gift was at the Charleston Orphan House. General Jackson's concern for children was well known; the Christian warrior had been a teacher. Next to the monument was placed a contribution box for sick and wounded soldiers. Hundreds of citizens came to admire it and read the inscription, which offered solace for a nation in jeopardy: "Do Your Duty and leave the rest to Providence. All is right."[25]

Gradually the bulk of the population managed to go on about its business. Some evacuees returned. Those who remained took pride in their ability to survive. The siege of the city had already lasted longer than that of Vicksburg. Children had miraculously defeated death. For them, war became a game. The "little" ones laughed and defiantly clapped their hands as they saw the missiles fail to hit their targets. The world of play allowed children and their families a respite from the impending doom. In late January 1865, one Lowcountry toddler played hoop and hide (hide and seek) with his aunt and other family members. As they played, the fall of Charleston was imminent. During the night of February 17, and the following morning, the last Confederate forces evacuated the city. The Twenty-first U.S. Colored Troops prepared to enter the city and occupy it.[26]

In the meantime, crowds of people, black and white, thronged the Northeastern Depot in search of food and whatever else they could take. Some simply engaged in plunder. Unfortunately, the depot was the storage area for about two hundred kegs of gunpowder. Small boys rejoiced in scooping up handfuls of the powder and tossing it on cotton bales that departing Confederate soldiers had set afire. In their merriment, the boys left behind a trickle of the deadly substance, which soon ignited. Their escapade did more killing than the Swamp

Angel. An explosion rocked the city. More than a hundred people were killed; an equal number wounded. Death records confirm the carnage. Many died from burns, including a thirty-year-old white woman named Ann Beslow, a German-born man, a ninety-one-year-old black male called Ishmael, and Affy, a twenty-two-year-old black female. The blast caused the loss of millions of dollars in property as the fire spread to some of the richest districts. The same day, the *Palmetto State* went up in flames, and women whose fundraising made the gunboat possible watched in dismay. Observers thought the last plume of smoke formed a palmetto tree. The sight of black troops occupying the city unnerved white women. Boys, ranging in ages from ten to fourteen, helped elderly ladies, carried water for young girls, and ran errands for those women who dreaded going downtown.[27]

In March 1865 the Northern press painted a rosy picture of the city's recovery. Business had returned to King Street. The South Carolina Railroad was operational. Federal authorities assisted those taking a loyalty oath. Prominent Charlestonians, such as Dr. Albert J. Mackey and William A. Courtenay, were cooperating to curtail random violence. But some South Carolinians pledged, "Their names will not be fragrant hereafter in the nostrils of patriots." School-children seemed better able to cope with the new era than their parents. In May 1865 white children, attending the city's public schools, went aboard *General Hooker* for an excursion around the harbor, including a visit to Fort Sumter. Union General John P. Hatch, who was in charge of the occupation of the city, sponsored the trip. The children were "delighted."[28]

During the summer of 1865, the children of the Charleston Orphan House, who had been evacuated to Orangeburg, returned, another sign of hope. But by now the number of widows and orphans had increased to such a great number as to pose a threatening social problem.

9

Beginning in July 1861, Magnolia Cemetery became an integral part of Confederate folklore. Charleston nearly shut down as growing crowds watched a procession transport the dead soldiers of Bull Run from the train station to St. Paul's Church. The procession culminated in a ceremony at Magnolia, where there is now a Confederate section. Ten years later, on Confederate Memorial Day, six thousand people hailed the return of dozens of South Carolinians who had fallen at Gettysburg. They were reinterred at the cemetery. The Rev. John L. Girardeau passionately urged the gathering: "Afflicted Carolina, rise in thy mourning weeds, and receive thy returning children to their maternal breast." Widows and other women relatives led private efforts to claim, honor, and rebury their dead.

The funeral of General Micah Jenkins struck a chord with white South Carolinians, especially adolescents. The South Carolina general died in May 1863 at the Battle of the Wilderness. Cadets from the South Carolina Military School (the Arsenal) escorted his body from Columbia to Summerville. Women from the village brought wreaths and flowers. Disabled soldiers participated in the procession. The coffin was draped with a Confederate flag. The beloved general was buried in Charleston's Magnolia Cemetery. Born on Edisto Island, he had graduated from the South Carolina Military Academy (The Citadel), and had helped found King's Mountain Military Academy. He had taken seriously the education of the youth of the state and profoundly affected many by his example. Newspapers emphasized that his "young widow and orphaned children were left without their natural protector."[1]

Carolina, following a custom that dated back to medieval London, defined an orphan as anyone who had lost one parent. By this definition, the war produced a staggering number of orphans. No one had to tell ordinary Confederates how devastating the loss of a father was. Fragments of a shell at Second Bull Run wounded Hodgin Fant of Chester District in 1862. The twenty-four-year-old soldier lingered for twelve days. His obituary read, "He left a devoted wife, upon whom this affliction falls with crushing power; and little Eddie is an orphan—too young to know his irreparable loss."[2]

The number of orphans began ballooning by the summer of 1862. In July a Charleston newspaper, relying on reports from the Orphan House, predicted it would have "a large accession to the family, already large from the desolated homes . . . in the track of war." To address the issue of educating these orphans throughout the state, reformer Sallie Chapin worked with Richard Yeadon (a lawyer and an editor of the Charleston *Courier*) to establish the Soldiers' Orphan Education Institute in April 1863. John L. Branch, a friend of the Institute, believed that an endowment of $675,000 would be necessary based on the following logic. In September 1862 South Carolina had 42,973 men in the field, an average of 1,432 per district (the state consisted of thirty districts). One-third of the men (477) were married. Branch estimated that 119 husbands died per district, or 3,570 for the state at large. Since the war might continue, he increased his estimate to 150 dead husbands per district, or 4,500. If each man fathered three children, there would be 13,500 orphans needing the aid of the Institute. The estimated number of orphans per district was made before the trench warfare of 1864. Even with victories came "the wail of the widow and the orphan."[3]

Baptist minister Basil Manly Jr. was another citizen deeply concerned about the orphans. He had dedicated much of his life to children and their families. His *Little Lessons for Little People* (issued in 1864) was used by South Carolina schoolchildren. In September 1864, Manly estimated that 525 families (2,120) persons in Abbeville District and 825 families (2,700 persons) in Anderson District needed support. Of these 1,350 families, "about 4,000 persons resided within the limits of the Saluda Baptist Association." Twenty-eight hundred were under twelve years old. Six hundred were orphans; a third of them were of school age. Manly predicted the children would swell the ranks of illiterate adults. He concluded they "might as well have been born before reading was invented." In 1866 Freedmen Bureau's officials offered similar estimates. One agent believed there were four hundred soldiers' widows in Greenville District and six hundred in Pickens. He could only imagine the number of orphans. The Survivors' Association of the State of South Carolina met in Charleston in 1869. The group professed that they must help many widows and orphans "left for destitute by the death of their husbands and fathers during the war."[4]

In both cases, widows with orphans, or orphans without parents, were mostly absorbed by their extended families. Women's kinship ties were crucial; grandmothers filled in as surrogates when necessary. Alfred Doby had been particularly solicitous of his daughter because he had been an orphan himself. His widow had the support of the extended family in raising their daughter. Ten years after the war, Elise's grandmother showed her the room where her Papa was born. Some orphans resided with elderly widows who were heads of households. Even those widows with extended kinship networks struggled; households became pressure cookers. Take the case of Lucy Williams of Union

District. The household of this seventy-six-year-old widow certainly had the makings of an extended family by anyone's estimate. She was the mother and grandmother of 140 children. The elderly widow had several of her grandchildren as well as their widowed mothers living with her. The matriarch had four sons and many grandsons in the service; she wanted her youngest son, W. F. M. Williams, discharged from the Fifth South Carolina Regiment to help her "needy family."[5]

Generous farmers did what they could to help. Colonel Ellerbe Bogan Cash, a general in the state militia, provided needy families with thousands of bushels of corn and other produce. He sold it in Confederate currency at antebellum prices. After the war, he cancelled all notes, claims, and mortgages he held on estates of soldiers. He gave $5,000 to one widow with a small family whose father had been killed in his regiment. Despite such aid, the unscrupulous, preying on widows, bought up their lands during the war in depreciated Confederate currency. After the war, white as well as black children were apprenticed.[6]

Other concerned citizens tried to organize associations and institutions to aid widows and orphans. Sallie Chapin was uniquely qualified for such work. She came from evangelical Methodists who had an abiding commitment to assist the poor. Sallie was born around 1830 in Charleston. Her father was a Methodist minister whose parents had come from Ulster. Her mother hailed from Rhode Island Huguenot ancestry. Their daughter was educated at Cokesbury Academy in Abbeville District. In 1847 she married Leonard Chapin, a businessman and philanthropist from Massachusetts. He helped establish the Charleston branch of the Young Men's Christian Association. Both husband and wife had a strong sense of noblesse oblige. Sallie was active in the Sunday School Movement and served as president of the Soldiers' Relief Society in Charleston. The concern she felt for orphans was heightened by the fact that the couple had adopted her brother's daughter when his wife died. Her husband, a member of the Fifth South Carolina Cavalry, was wounded in October 1864; this just highlighted to her the gravity of the crisis posed by war widows and orphans. Fitz-Hugh St. Clair, the hero of her children's novel, was orphaned during the war.[7]

Major cities in South Carolina had orphanages before the war, including the Camden Orphan Society (1776) and the Ladies' Benevolent Society for Orphans and Destitute Children in Columbia (1839). Charleston's Orphan House (1790) was the first municipal orphanage organized in the United States. Some were religiously affiliated. Charleston had the Hebrew Orphan Society (1850) and the Catholic Sisters of Mercy. Unfortunately, the Sisters of Mercy house was destroyed in 1862, forcing the nuns to move out "with their little flock of orphan children." By 1869 their new house had sixty-eight children, male and female. These long-established orphanages had difficulty coping with the exigencies of war. The Columbia Ladies' Benevolent Society was hard put to manage the crisis. It was designed for girls, aged one to ten. In September 1864 it had a list of about twelve children. The society's constitution was amended to take in boys, but in October 1865 it had to close its doors because of the "utter inability of the ladies to meet the wants of the Orphan House."[8]

The Charleston Orphan House was not established to deal with the flood of orphans. The war did not radically change the way the institution functioned until 1863 when the children were required to leave the city for their safety. Discipline was pervasive. Violations such as disrespect could lead to expulsion. Some of the children were rebellious, oblivious to the benevolence proffered them. In 1862 a twelve-year-old boy attempted to burn down the Orphan House. Banished from Charleston, the culprit was placed aboard a ship bound for other ports. Two other accomplices were locked in a closet for ten days and subsisted on only bread and water.[9]

Between April 12, 1861, and December 31, 1876, approximately 588 children were admitted to the Charleston Orphan House. Of them, 106 came during the war (1861–65), while 232 entered right after the war (1866–68) and the remaining 250 came from 1869 to 1876. Of the total admitted from 1861 to 1876, fifty-five appeared to have had a male parent in the war and were almost evenly divided by gender; only seven were admitted during the war. These fifty-five were between the ages of one and twelve, most between four and nine. Twenty-three were sent back to their mothers; twelve were indentured. Most orphans managed to survive their ordeal. Catherine Reilly Brown's two children, James and Michael, were admitted in 1866. Their father James Reilly, a Roman Catholic, had volunteered in June 1861 with a company raised by Captain Edward McCrady. Reilly died from wounds at Antietam. The children were eventually sent to live with their stepfather.[10]

Some Northern soldiers abandoned their Southern-born offspring. William Zehe sent his niece, Annie, to the Charleston Orphan House in 1870. The girl was born in 1864 in Gillisonville, South Carolina. The unnamed mother had married a German. When he absconded with all she had, she soon died, leaving three children including Annie. Similarly, Ann Elmore, a Confederate widow, married a Yankee shortly after the city was evacuated. When his unit was ordered home, she followed him to New York, where she discovered he already had a wife. Ann's son, three-year-old Michael Joseph, was accepted into the city orphanage on February 7, 1867. The distraught mother was to be confined to a hospital. In 1878 the child was returned to her.[11]

Only forty-seven of the Charleston Orphan House children were admitted with their mother's name given. Only twelve applications listed a father's name. Susan Boyd's husband had "died in the army in Virginia." Their two children, Andrew, age six, and Caroline, age ten, were admitted in 1866. Caroline returned to her mother on February 2, 1871, while Andrew was indentured to Thomas Holloway in August 1876. Mildred Ballantine's girls, Frances, age nine, and Susan, eight, were both admitted on June 28, 1867. Their father was described as "a Confederate soldier killed during the war." They had been living at No. 681 King Street. The younger girl was "a cripple." The two were returned to their mother in 1874.[12]

Mrs. Ballantine's children were Baptists, but most of the children came from the Catholic poor. For example, the Cross family were Roman Catholics. They lived at No. 216 Meeting Street. Catherine Cross was born in Ireland. Her husband Robert had served in the army and had been captured twice. He had spent considerable time in prison at Fort Delaware and Fort Lafayette. In 1867, just sixteen months after returning home, he died from war-related injuries. Their children, Josephine, age five, and the twins, Lilla and William, age eight, were admitted on February 16, 1871.[13]

New associations sprang up but were not equipped to help substantially the poorest families. May Anne Buie began her work with wounded soldiers during the war. With the help of Governor James L. Orr and Wade Hampton, she began raising funds to educate the orphans of Confederate soldiers. She succeeded in establishing an institute, named after her, in Edgefield. She later moved the institute to Whiteville. Former Confederate General Joseph E. Johnston was her main financial backer. In 1867 the Episcopal minister A. Toomer Porter established a home school in Charleston for needy white orphan boys. It was later called Porter Military Academy. One of the most successful endeavors was the work of black Baptist minister Daniel J. Jenkins, who established an orphanage and industrial school in Charleston to cope with the ballooning number of destitute black orphans.[14]

Just a year after the war, Amarinthia Snowden and her sister mortgaged the only real asset they had, their own home, to open up the Home for Mothers, Widows, and Daughters in Charleston. Its initial charter applied to relatives of deceased soldiers, but its literature stressed the need to preserve the elite families and the best of prewar Southern culture. Soon "deceased" was dropped from the constitution. In 1868, fifty-eight students, mothers, and widows were living in the house. An increasing student population encouraged Snowden to open up a school for the girls. The Confederate Home College came to be located on Broad Street. The tuition remained $100 per student between 1867 and 1884. The attendance rose from thirteen in the school year 1867–1868 to 118 in 1909–1910.[15]

The Catholics solicited aid from the North. In 1866 a Charleston newspaper reported that "The Ladies' Fair for Destitute Children of Charleston" was held in New York "for the benefit of the school, poor, and orphans of the S.C. under Bishop Lynch." Poverty had always existed in Charleston, but aid for the poor was not extensive. In January 1862, Maria Walsh, unable to care for her infant child, left the baby at the corner of Wentworth and Rutledge streets. Charleston police arrested the poor woman. That year fifteen hundred people had to receive help from public and private sources to survive. In the last four months of 1864 and the first month and a half of 1865, thirty-six people were accepted in the Charleston Alms House. Nearly four hundred sought outdoor relief. For the year 1866 the number admitted to the Alms House rose to 211. Fifty-nine of these were foreign born; most of them came from Ireland. In 1867 the City Council tried to make a distinction between the respectable and the undeserving poor. The latter went to the city poor house, basically a "house of correction." Crime had compelled the city to open the old workhouse. Designed to morally benefit the inmates and help the city, the workhouse demanded strenuous labor. Those who did not measure up were given only bread and water. It was the place of last resort for women who had no other place to turn for help. By 1869 there were ten blacks (two women and eight children) in the Alms House. Whites numbered one hundred. How many poor were without aid is impossible to determine.[16]

The rhetoric of those involved in benevolent work was heartrending, but it obscured a basic truth. Many families and orphans survived by the dint of their own efforts. State aid was slow in coming for those who suffered during and after the war. It was not until 1923 that South Carolina offered pensions to Confederate veterans and their widows. The turmoil caused by the Civil War would continue to play itself out during Reconstruction. Children, not as fragile as Victorian America assumed, were involved in that struggle.[17]

10

Reconstruction and Redemption: The Civil War, Part II

Bishop Benjamin Tanner, active in the African Methodist Episcopal Church in South Carolina, denounced the deification of the evangelical Confederate General Thomas J. Jackson: "The prayers of Stonewall Jackson were as refreshing to Beelzebub as a draught of ice water." Tanner knew the canonizing of Confederate heroes could endanger the opportunities for blacks and their progeny wrought by the war. He was convinced that Congressional Reconstruction (1867–1876) heralded the beginning of a New World. Black ministers, such as Tanner, offered a millennial interpretation of the war, climaxing in "The Promised Land" of a multiracial democracy.[1]

For African Americans, Reconstruction brought the abolition of slavery and the restoring of their family life on a more permanent basis. The war liberated black children in ways their parents and grandparents could never have imagined. Black men and women were better able to shape their family and religious life. They eagerly sought education, especially for their children. Black schools proliferated with the aid of the Freedmen's Bureau and various missionary societies in the North. Congressional (or Radical) Reconstruction allowed them to shape South Carolina politics. Out of some 487 men elected to office during this era, more than half were black. These black officeholders and their constituency shaped a liberationist version of history. An annual Emancipation Day Parade still marks this pivotal era of black liberation.[2]

In contrast to this millennial interpretation of the war, Episcopal minister A. Toomer Porter could not help juxtaposing "the stirring scenes" of the past with the bitter defeat of the Confederacy. Expressing the doubts and emotions whirling in other white South Carolinians, he questioned a God who would allow the failure of good Christian soldiers such as Robert E. Lee and Thomas J. Jackson. God seemed to have abandoned His chosen people. Uttering the words of a shared despair, the minister "wished to die" but was saved by a vision of his dead seven-year-old son when he visited the child's grave at Magnolia Cemetery. Recalling his poor boy, Porter feared for the education and economic prospects of South Carolina's white children. A voice told him to establish a school to educate the orphans.[3]

In 1866 a Baptist journal mirrored Porter's concern: "Our children are nearly all the treasures left to us." With black and white Republicans controlling the state, the reality of Black Republicanism nurtured the gnawing fear that the Confederate legacy would be lost. These "treasures [our children] must be taught their fathers and brothers did not die in vain. The deaths of so many men required that their sacrifice be honored for generations." In 1869 Edward McCrady Jr., president of the Survivors' Association, told the gathering, "Only we can collect and preserve our transactions." Likewise, Wade Hampton claimed it was up to South Carolina's "surviving children to vindicate the great principles for which she fought." Generations of white children might forget or misinterpret their ancestors' heroic actions.[4]

Despite the gains of Congressional Reconstruction for black families, the Civil War was a lingering catastrophe for South Carolina's children. Caught up in the secession fever of December 1860, state leaders recklessly gambled away the future of generations of children. By the summer of 1865 the state's economy was in a shambles. Planters went up the spout, losing millions of dollars in slave capital. White yeoman farmers found themselves competing with blacks as landowners, renters, sharecroppers, and laborers. The advent of black suffrage in 1867 resulted in a multiracial democracy in a state with a black majority. The new alliance of white and black Republican, however, was unable to bring peace, prosperity, and security to the state. Disaffected whites attributed the failed situation solely to widespread corruption fostered by carpetbaggers and scalawags in collaboration with black officeholders rather than to the severe national economic downturn. The North, tired of the war, had turned its interest and resources westward in a journey of manifest destiny. In 1870 smoldering discontent erupted into an insurgency movement in the Upcountry, which threatened to spread and set back the gains of former slaves. It pitted the children of the war, white and black, against one another, in what one historian has described as part 2 of the Civil War.[5]

Death on a massive scale was one of the chief legacies of the war. As early as June 1863 a teacher of the State Arsenal Academy worried about the thousands of "killed and mangled human beings" for a cause criticized by the enlightened Western world. The thought haunted mothers, aunts, sisters, and the elderly that the deaths of their men might have been in vain. Confederate Congressman William Porcher Miles, consoling an elite Lowcountry mother for the death of her youngest and oldest sons, pointedly declared their loss was not in vain. The mother had witnessed the excruciating agony of the oldest, who had expired at home. Other "Sons of Privilege" also died in droves. No company better epitomized them than the "Charleston Light Dragoons." Their Byronic sense of noblesse oblige and bravery commingled with combat inexperience ultimately led to their decimation; not many survived untouched by the scourge of war. A few resorted to barbaric activities their loved ones thought only the Yankees did.[6]

In the end, thousands of South Carolinians died; many more were wounded. Some were seriously maimed. Between 1867 and 1907 there were more than twelve hundred applications for artificial limbs. Little children, their treasures, provided the best therapy for some veterans. Two boys helped their father overcome the trauma of losing much of his leg. The trio played horse with the four-year-old mounted on the veteran's healthy leg and the two-year-old on the amputated one. The father provided the locomotion and a song that rhymed with the sounds of a horse's hoofs. Still, the net impact on many families was extreme as men returned home physically and mentally debilitated, only to face daunting economic problems. Just how many South Carolina soldiers experienced posttraumatic stress disorder (PTSD) is problematic. Economic and physical problems often accompanied complicated mental ones. In October 1865, an impoverished veteran was admitted to the state asylum. His insanity was caused by measles and exposure as a soldier. A farmer-carpenter was admitted as a pauper on July 4, 1866. He had been suffering for two years since the death of his brothers in battle. One married man, a father, might have been paranoid. Exposure and hardship during the war and loss of property pushed him to the breaking point. In another instance, a dentist was admitted for suffering from ill treatment as a prisoner of war. He had once tried to commit suicide.[7]

Women were also casualties of the war, as revealed by the records of the state lunatic asylum. Some came from nearby states but almost all had connections in South Carolina. The prolonged war triggered long-standing emotional problems. In 1862, a single woman from Charleston, age thirty-seven, was diagnosed as insane. Victimized "by the excitement of war," she wanted to be shot. She had relied on morphine to ease her depression. In 1863 a forty-five-year-old woman, who had been married for twenty-two years, was admitted to the asylum. She had a long history of mental illness, but doctors believed her most recent episode was precipitated by the death of her soldier-son. Another married woman, age thirty-four, who had raised five children, was admitted in February 1865. Her first attack of fever had been caused by sleep deprivation resulting from nursing her wounded son. She called herself "Eliza the son of God." In March 1864 a widow, only twenty-two years old, with two children, became a patient for trying to burn herself. Her psychosis was brought on by the death of her soldier-husband. A twenty-five-year-old woman from Pickens District entered in February 1866 because she could no longer contain her distress over her husband's death. The people admitted into the state asylum just give a glimmer of the continued suffering caused by a destructive war.[8]

Military failures brought bitter recriminations; some were aimed at the soldiers themselves. In May 1865 Pauline DeCaradeuc Heyward refused to delude herself further about the valor of the soldiers; she branded them as cowards and deserters. Most hatred was directed toward Northerners, some of whom had been in South Carolina before the war. One Confederate soldier from Horry District lost a leg at the Battle of the Wilderness. Nine years later, he married a local girl. Her mother never forgave her son-in-law for having been born in New Hampshire. His wife concluded that her mother held a deep resentment toward the North for their tribulations.[9]

For Manson Jolly of Anderson in the Upcountry, the war turned into a vendetta. Jolly joined the Confederate army in February 1861. More than six feet tall, the redheaded farmer enlisted at Pendleton in Company H., First South Carolina Infantry Regiment. Later he was a scout in Company F, First South Carolina Cavalry. His five brothers died in the war. Black soldiers allegedly killed his baby brother. According to Confederate folklore, Jolly set a quota of Yankees he would kill for their deaths. The estimate ranged from fifteen to one hundred for his five brothers. Whatever it was, he met his quota. When Jolly returned home, Union soldiers had occupied Anderson. The Yankee-hater moved to Texas, where he died in 1869. His fame was heralded in a ballad made popular in South Carolina. Among the young, he became a legend.[10]

Adding to the mental anguish of dealing with the deaths of so many loved ones, families were undergoing an economic crisis that cut across political, class, and racial lines. Between 1866 and 1870 South Carolinians experienced some of the worst poverty in the nation. Nearly a hundred thousand were in danger of starving as severe drought hit the state in 1866 and 1867. Children, black and white, suffered. A Charleston newspaper declared, "Children are eating all sorts of things they can get hold of, and their appearance betokens great destitution." Conditions began improving in spring 1869, but the national depression of 1873 plunged the state into the doldrums. Unable to pay their taxes, small farmers and workers lost their land. During the year 270,000 acres fell under the auction block; shortly thereafter the number doubled. The violence associated with the election of 1876 just worsened economic conditions. Rather than blame the unfavorable climate of the national economy, many whites attributed their collective misfortune to losing the war and resulting Republican corruption; scapegoating the Yankees and their black cohorts was a way of venting the frustrations and bitterness that had been building up for a long time. As for the blacks, many became disillusioned by the deteriorating situation. Some considered making peace with the Democrats.[11]

South Carolina's elite found themselves without some of the assets they enjoyed before the war. The Rev. and Mrs. Paul Trapier had invested all their money in Confederate securities and currency. General M. C. Butler joked that all he got out of the war was one leg, a wife and three children, and a mountain of debt. Like the rest, the Rev. A. Toomer Porter was left penniless. Thomas B. Chaplin returned to the Lowcountry an old man without power and fortune. He survived by teaching at a school for blacks. The ex-soldier suffered from a severe opium addiction that might have begun during the war. Chaplin, obsessed with getting back his plantation, called Tombee, became engaged in an exhausting and extended legal struggle. Tombee became his again in 1890 after the Democrats came to power. Amarinthia Snowden and her sister lost most of their money and other assets except for the family home. Others depended on kin in the North.[12]

Children of the elite had to acquire new "situations" and skills. The struggles of Sallie Chapin's fictional hero, Fitz-Hugh St. Clair, mirrored the hardships of the elite youth. General St. Clair, the patriarch, had died in the war. Bereft of the family fortune, the youth worked at odd jobs. He departed for New York to seek a "situation" to support his little brother and sisters as well as his widowed mother. He was falsely accused of stealing but was saved by the intervention of Mr. Winthrop, the president of a bank and former college roommate of the boy's father. Winthrop had lost his entire inheritance in speculation. General St. Clair had loaned him money to get back on his feet. Not only did Winthrop shower money on the youth, he offered the lad his daughter's hand in marriage. Her father had named her Lucie in honor of Fitz-Hugh's mother. Chapin, using her hero as an example, predicted that the South would rise "like a Phoenix from her ashes."[13]

The elite had its resources. Right after the war, during Presidential Reconstruction (1865–1866), when only whites could vote, some survived on patronage. Many allied themselves with railroad, factory, and merchant business interests. Railroads especially provided job opportunities for the elite lacking assets and other means of employment. Richard H. Anderson, a former Confederate general, worked as a laborer for the South Carolina Railroad. John Glenn of Newberry, the son of a doctor, came back from the war after he was twice wounded and imprisoned by the Yankees. Governor James Orr helped him get on as a conductor on the Greenville and Columbia Railroad. In Newberry District his case was typical. Confederate children as they grew up readily found employment on the railroads when the Democrats (Redeemers) again controlled the state. According to C. Vann Woodward, from those malleable to make these connections evolved the *Origins of the New South*.[14]

Formerly prosperous families, such as the Palmers of the Santee River and the Bryces of Columbia, had difficulty surviving in a changed world. Louis P. Towles, the historian of the Palmer family, titles their story *The World Turned*

Upside Down. In 1869 Edward G. Palmer placed his daughter Harriet in the state insane asylum. The directors of the Charlotte and South Carolina Railroad, in appreciation for his past services, voted an annuity of $250 for her benefit. The stigma was probably great, but at least she was not on the pauper list. The Bryce family of Columbia weathered the war, but not the hardships that followed, even though the plantation was intact. When the family patriarch died in 1867, he left a large debt. The war had irreparably damaged his son John, who suffered from alcohol and drug abuse. He could not make the adjustment to peace and became a mercenary. The young women in the family survived through judicious marriages.[15]

Enterprising women pulled their families through hard times. Pauline DeCaradeuc was born in 1843 into a large planter family. Her brothers and sisters included Francois ("Frank"), John Antonio ("Toni"), Margaret Ann ("Mannie"), and St. Julien Raoul. Her bright prospects were darkened by the war, especially when both Frank and Toni were killed. Toni was only sixteen when he had enlisted; he was the family favorite. Rejecting his death for a while, she saw him in her dreams. She felt desolate and lost but realizing her mother's growing sadness as the death toll of young men in their neighborhood rose, she turned to the responsibilities added to her by the war. As the older sister, she tutored St. Julien when she could capture him from his outdoor activities and cared for Mannie who was not robust. In July 1865, Mannie, a teenager, had all her teeth extracted and replaced with dentures. This painful operation hurt her chances for marrying well.[16]

After an elegant courtship, Pauline married Guerard Heyward in November 1866. Despite financial difficulties, her family willingly made the sacrifice to hold an elaborate wedding ceremony and reception. Besides a magnificent wedding gown of white silk with a long train, the beautiful young bride had a bountiful trousseau. The bridegroom's family had roots in the Lowcountry elite; Thomas Heyward had signed the Declaration of Independence. During the war Guerard's family had trouble making ends meet while both the patriarch and the scion were at the front. The war was a debilitating experience for the young man. A first lieutenant, he was captured on Morris Island in July 1863 and subsequently imprisoned at Fort Delaware. He was not released until June 12, 1865.

Gruerard and his father attempted to recoup their losses by planting cotton near Bluffton. Their efforts proved fruitless. Pauline's father had given up to work for the railroad and later relocated his family to Charleston. When George Heyward, the patriarch, died, Guerard had two families under his care. In 1868 the young man quit planting to become a bookkeeper in Savannah. He was able to find clerical positions for his younger brothers. By 1876 he had established a partnership with a successful cotton and rice factor. Pauline had borne nine children; five survived. When her husband died in 1888, she was determined to keep her family intact. Within a week after his death, the widow had turned their home into a boardinghouse.[17]

Even families with powerful patrons suffered from the war. Eliza Fludd's life (1808–1887) was a panorama of scenes from a prewar life of comfort turning into a refugee existence to the difficult return home and adjustment of living impoverished in a city now occupied by the enemy. Her travails were not unique, giving insight into the hardships elite women and their families endured in the transition to peace. In the winter of 1866, a federal official noted that upper-class women were without shoes, food, light, and heating. He appealed to New Yorkers to send care packages for the needy. Eliza was the daughter of Kinsey Burden, one of the state's wealthiest planters. Her sister Portia Ashe had married Charles Louis Trenholm (1809–1865), a Charleston merchant whose brother George made a fortune as a financier in the Mercantile House during the war. Charles had left $300,000 in the hands of his brother. But when George departed to serve as the Confederate secretary of the treasury, his partners squandered his brother's money. When Charles died in September 1865, his real-estate holdings were considerable but produced little liquid cash. George did what he could to provide the widow and her family with the necessities but their lifestyle took a plunge. The situation caused tensions between the Trenholm families. Charles's funeral was held in Eliza Fludd's residence on Spring Street in Charleston and the burial was at Magnolia Cemetery.

Eliza herself was in financial straits. Her husband, John M. Fludd, had died before the war. She was left with a grown son, John S. Fludd, and a married daughter. The widow was devoted to her daughter, Mary Portia, and cared deeply for her grandchildren, one of whom was called "little" Charles. By the end of the war, Mary and her husband James D. Mitchell had four sons, all less than six years old, and a six-month-old daughter. The war had left Mitchell penniless and unemployed. Adding to the family tribulations was the death of Julius, the third boy, in October 1865. Seeking solace, Eliza related the ordeals of the family through her correspondence with her Philadelphia confidant and fellow evangelist, Mrs. A. P. Jolliffe, whom she endearingly called "Sister."

Eliza, a radical evangelical, had come to believe that God had called her to enlighten the people of Charleston who had become haughty after the early Confederate victories of 1861. God told her to move to the small town of Gowansville in the northwestern corner of the state to avoid divine retribution on the city. Friends and family ridiculed her. People derisively referred to her as "The Prophetess." But her daughter and son-in-law, who refused to emigrate to the wilds of the Upcountry, agreed to join her in Columbia. Mary was several months pregnant with her third child. In December 1861 the Great Fire consumed Charleston. The Circular Congregational Church, which Eliza had attended, went up in flames. Besieged by a Yankee army and armada, many who once had laughed at the Prophetess also fled to Columbia. In July 1862 Eliza moved to Gowansville, where her daughter and grandchildren joined her while Mitchell returned to the port city to carry on his business. Visiting Charleston in late 1864, she was prevented from returning to Gowansville by a monster storm. Early February 1865 she was staying in Camden, soon to be invaded by the very Yankees she had tried to avoid. Ten days after she arrived in Camden, Columbia was on fire. An inferno shook the capital after its surrender. As the Prophetess had warned, God's anger manifested itself by a baptism in fire.

The family, living in Camden, was in crisis. Sarah was pregnant with her fifth child. The children as well as their mother were constantly sick. The children battled with whooping cough. Their grandmother worked from five in the morning to ten in the evening daily to keep the family afloat. When they returned to Charleston, their situation did not improve. Although able to do some household duties, Mary had not fully recovered. Eliza bore much of the responsibility for taking care of her sick grandchildren. Difficulties did not lessen; the family's financial situation was dire. The head of the household, James Mitchell, an accountant, could find only temporary work. Eliza's three houses in the city did not provide much economic relief. The Freedmen's Bureau had seized two of them. One was turned over to blacks; the other was rented to an Irish family. The Fludd family home was stripped bare; Eliza's fine clothes were gone. She had to borrow a bed to sleep on. The widow used her buried silver to buy bread but most of this asset was eaten up by taxes. Once that was gone, the family was without income and servants. In November, family members, having only one change of clothing each, suffered through the cold nights. Sometimes there was no food in the house. When the children asked for sweet potatoes or bread because they were hungry, they could not understand why their parents could not get the food for them. To Eliza, the family's descent seemed surreal. She bewailed the taking of their property without compensation and other mistreatment by their oppressors who left them destitute while their enemies took such pleasure in their misfortunes. She especially anguished over the sufferings of her daughter, whom she had pampered and protected from "the insolence" of blacks. Despairing, the old woman cried out, "Is there no righteous God to avenge these wrongs?"

In March 1866, Eliza's faith reached the breaking point. Her beloved daughter, suffering from a prolonged depression, contemplated suicide. To make things worse, Mitchell's prospects for a permanent post were dim. Business was at a standstill, with hundreds of men looking for work. The family vegetable garden was no longer providing food. They seldom ate meat. The oldest boy had a fever. A doctor blamed the declining health of the entire family on the lack of good food. Eliza herself had become sick for want of food; she did not even have sheets for her bed. Comparing her lot to Job's, she sewed for pay. The new year found the baby girl having trouble teething. Eliza's nerves were wracked. By the summer of 1867 both Mitchell and Eliza were worn out. Confined in bed with an infant, Mary was a basket case. She was probably undergoing postpartum depression aggravated by poor diet, stress, and liver problems.

Congressional Reconstruction did not significantly improve the family situation. In July 1867, Fludd successfully managed to get food rations from an officer in the Freedmen's Bureau, but subsequent efforts failed. Blacks distributing the rations refused to give any aid to a white Rebel. One officer told her she had to sell her house first. On January 27, 1868, Eliza had to pay $200 in taxes on her home or lose it. She concluded that if she did not have a suffering family who sorely depended upon her, she might ask God to take her. Meanwhile, her close correspondent Mrs. Jolliffe had died. The woman's letters and boxes of gifts, including money, had bolstered Eliza's spirits. According to a source, the Northerner in her will had left her Charleston friend some money. Blessed by such goodness, Eliza called on her faith for endurance. As an evangelical Christian, she viewed Congressional Reconstruction in apocalyptic terms. The Prophetess predicted that Christ would crush the Dragon. The Republican Black Party of the Devil and its reign of corruption would end in violence. From the ashes of violence, a new Phoenix would arise, and once again the South would become a refuge for the godly. The widow's faith was affirmed when her daughter gave birth to a son in 1867 and a girl named Eliza Fludd in 1871. The evangelist lived to see the redemption of her state under the leadership of General Wade Hampton, a first cousin of her husband. Eliza died in May 1887, and her funeral was held at the rebuilt Circular Congregational Church. She was buried at Magnolia Cemetery near her dear friend Charles Trenholm.[18]

The suffering of the elite paled in comparison with the lot of most white Carolinians. The former aristocrats might have complained that their houses were confiscated, but most of these were returned. To economically distressed whites in the Upcountry, still dealing with the death of their men, Republicans with black allies and the black militia symbolized all that they hated most. Racism was an important factor in keeping ordinary whites in the Democratic Party. The Republicans also failed because their party did not do enough to help everyday people. White laborers, sharecroppers, and tenants found themselves competing with the emancipated slaves. Except for creating a state system of public education, Republicans failed to offer a platform that would sustain a coalition of poor whites, yeomen, and blacks. Such an alliance never fully materialized to make possible a viable multiracial democracy. In 1876 a Congressional Committee asked a black Republican "if poor white men work much." He replied that poor whites and blacks in Abbeville District worked "nobly," but the poor whites were "a heap harder on the colored people than the other white men."[19]

With conditions deteriorating further, blacks and whites became embroiled in a Klan-induced "Reign of Terror" during 1870–1871. The Ku Klux Klan was most active in the Upper Piedmont of the Upcountry counties (formerly districts), mainly in Chesterfield, Fairfield, Lancaster, Laurens, Newberry, Spartanburg, Union, and York. The Klan was unable to prevent a Republican victory in the 1868 elections. But it was fully operational by 1870 and led by prominent members of the communities. Physician J. Rufus Bratton of York was involved in the lynching of James Williams (also called Jim Rainey), a captain of the black militia in the county. Merchant James Avery, a former Confederate major, organized the York Klan in 1868. Both men escaped to Canada. The membership came from all segments of the society. Lou Falkner Williams concluded that the leaders were planters and professional men who had served in the Confederate military. "Ordinary Klansmen" were often poor whites, some as illiterate as their black victims. Williams has documented the Klan's war on black women and children.[20]

Black children had images of Klan violence permanently seared on their psyches. Millie Bates remembered the day the Klansmen came to Spartanburg. The children were playing in the house when the man they sought tried to get out of a window. Millie was scared to death and hid under the bed. The victim was shot in the head and fell to the floor but lived long enough to be hanged. She concluded: "Dem Day wuz worse worse'n de war." Alice Duke, an ex-slave from Union, was in bed when the Klan whipped her father. She covered her head and remained completely silent. Lina Anne Pendergrass also of Union recalled: "The Ku Klux Klan she scairt me. They took my daddy; my brother was too young. . . . Us nebber did see pa no mo'." Jane Wilson, born in Newberry, saw a Klansman kill a storekeeper. She explained. "I was a little girl and saw it. Some little children were standing out in front."[21]

In terrifying black families, Klansmen conveyed a message to their fathers and brothers: See us or else your family will suffer. In March 1871 the Klan broke into the home of John and Mary Robertson. The family lived near Chester. Mary wept, "One of the men gave my little baby boy two cuts." On a subsequent visit the Klansmen burst in unexpectedly. Mary refused to tell them where her husband was, only to have a pistol waved in her face. The hooded man promised to blow her brains out; another threatened her with a knife. Four of them whipped her five times each.[22]

The Ku Klux Klan appeared in York County in March 1868. It was particularly vicious. A Federal officer estimated that of the 2,300 males in the county eligible to vote, 1,800 were Klansmen. Three hundred persons were whipped and six murdered. Seventy-five percent of the black population was forced to live in the woods for safety. Klansmen stormed the home of Amzi Rainey in York County. Amzi hid in a box while his wife tried to delay the invaders. The men gave her four or five "licks" before they even interrogated her. Asked where her husband was, she denied his whereabouts. "I smell him," said one Klansman. Finding Amzi in the box, they again threatened to kill his wife. A little girl begged, "Don't kill my pappy." They threatened to kill her, too. The party shot several volleys over the couple's head. The daughter discovered her hands full of blood; a ball had glanced off her head. There were also allegations that the Klansmen raped another daughter in front of the other children in another room. Amzi Rainey was allowed to flee after he promised never to vote for the Radical Republicans.[23]

On several occasions the Klan visited Harriet Simril's husband Sam Simmons. The family also lived in York County. The first time the Klan came they whipped Sam. On the second visit his wife told them he was not present. They spit at her face and threw dirt in her eyes, momentarily blinding her. They dragged her onto the road and "ravished" her. Later asked about her condition by a Congressional Committee, she responded: "I had no sense for a long time. I laid there." At last she was able to get up and take the children out into the woods where they joined her husband for four nights. The family's home was subsequently burned. What the Klan specifically did to Harriet Simril was deemed "too obscene" for the Congressional Committee to publish.[24]

The Klan also victimized Minister Isaac Postle's family. They lived in eastern York County near Rock Hill. Isaac and Harriet Postle had six children; the oldest was fourteen. Awakening them at night, a Klansman yelled for the minister. Harriet, seven or eight months pregnant, was unable to put on her clothes. The fourteen-year-old boy hid under the bed but was discovered. Mrs. Postle screamed, "It is my child." One man stuck a pistol in the boy's neck; another gouged "a piece of skin [out of him] as big as [her] hand." She denied that her husband was present. They put a rope around her neck; she fell. A man put his foot on her body. Her pregnancy could have been terminated. She identified Dr. Edward T. Avery as the one who put the rope around her neck.[25]

In 1871 President U.S. Grant placed nine South Carolina counties under martial law. Federal authorities and marshals rounded up more than 600 men between 1871 and 1873. Of this total, 220 were indicted and 53 pleaded guilty. Five were tried and convicted by black juries. The trials began in the state capital during November 1871 but were moved to Charleston in April 1872. By the end of the year most Klan prosecutions had been concluded. Although a substantial number of Klansmen had been arrested in the nine counties, prosecutors concentrated on York and Spartanburg, where the violence was noticeably prevalent. The Enforcement Act of 1870 was used because the crimes were committed before the Ku Klux Klan Act became operative. Federal prosecutors also employed an innovative use of the Fourteenth and Fifteenth Amendments. In an eleven-count indictment, they argued the attack on black women and their children violated the constitutional protection of life, liberty, and property. Invasions of the homes of black men constituted an attack on their voting rights.[26]

The Constitution of the Ku Klux Klan required that members be at least eighteen years old; many were in their twenties. Some were children of the war. Judging from the thirty-one who pleaded guilty by January 1871, most of the rank and file were farmers. They were illiterate and dirt-poor. Lewis Henderson was described as "so ignorant that he seemed incapable of understanding the simplest English or expressing himself with any coherence." Another Klansman spoke so incomprehensibly that he needed a fellow Klansman to interpret his testimony. William Ramsay of Spartanburg, age twenty-five, pleaded, "I was but a poor, ignorant man, and did not know better." He further reasoned, "It seems to me that men who had good learning and knowledge ought to have teached us better." Asked if people were poor in his area, John Burnett, age twenty-one, replied, "Yes, sir, very." Most claimed they were intimidated into joining. Some feared for their safety or being shunned by the community. Verbal intimidation was common, including death threats. Whipping was the most common physical threat. Such Klan sadism, which had cowered some to join, had its impact on white Republicans. All over the Upcountry they withdrew from the party after the nightriders visited them.[27]

The trials provided a window on how the postwar judicial system defined manhood. Prosecutors, Southern and Northern alike, viewed night raids as dishonorable and unmanly. Manhood entailed maturity and responsibility; it could be lost. This challenged the idea that participation in the Klan constituted a rite of male passage. Since the most prominent Klan leaders fled, the judges and lawyers on both sides urged leniency for the rank and file on the grounds of youth, ignorance, poverty, and immaturity. Court officials put Southern slavery on trial. Judge H. L. Bond, a Republican from Maryland, noted that the young men, mostly illiterate, were raised in a society based on slavery and the whip.[28]

The judges considered youth, illiteracy, and other extenuating circumstances. Nineteen-year-old Melvin Blackwood was an illiterate hired laborer. He was probably around fifteen years old when the war ended. Judge George S.

Bryan, a Democrat from South Carolina, sentenced him to jail for only two months because of his "extreme youth." James Wall, an illiterate farmer with a wife and children, was allowed to go home to plant the spring crop. But Judge Bryan sentenced twenty-year-old day laborer Monroe Scruggs, who had been around sixteen when the war ended, to prison for six months. The Lowcountry judge conceded that prominent men and public sentiment had led Scruggs astray. However, using Scruggs as an example, he pointed out: "Whether these enormities have been committed on men,—still more on women—they were wholly unmanly, and let me say, utterly un-South Carolinian."[29]

The judges were harshest on older men with standing in the community. Judge Bond excoriated Samuel Brown of York for leading young and ignorant men to their downfall. Brown, a former magistrate, was in his sixties. The defense pleaded that he had stopped one raid. Bond observed that this was "one instance of a return in manhood." It was not enough to mitigate his transgressions. Brown was fined one thousand dollars and sentenced to five years in prison. Whatever their circumstances and final sentencing, the convicted were judged to have forfeited their manhood.[30]

Most of the rank and file received a fine and/or three to six months in jail. Those accused of more egregious crimes, such as the attack on the Amzi Rainey family and the lynching of James Williams, were sentenced to a year and a half in jail. In April 1872 the court tried additional cases involving murder. One man was sentenced to ten years in prison. More than a thousand other cases were pending trial. In the summer of 1873 Grant, wanting to end all this nasty, emotionally draining business, granted clemency for Klansmen awaiting trials. He pardoned those already in jail.

In assessing the ultimate impact of the Klan, scholar Jerry West notes that these men would come to participate in another movement that would end Republican rule in South Carolina. Red shirts would replace white robes. Wade Hampton, an icon of the old order, would make this transition possible.[31]

Recognizing how Federal intervention had broken the Ku Klux Klan, the opponents of Reconstruction changed their tactics for the gubernatorial election of 1876. Hampton with ties to the Lowcountry would take the "high road," promising blacks he would preserve their right to vote and attend public schools while Martin Gary from the Upcountry would use the force and intimidation of 290 rifle clubs with 14,356 members. Both men, former Confederate generals, would lead a campaign of Redemption. Some ex-slaves saw no difference between the Klan and the Red Shirts. Hampton supporters had to rein in Gary because too much violence could bring massive federal intervention. The flannel Red Shirt became a symbol of the Hampton campaign. Supporters wore them in Hampton's processions through various cities. Five hundred to two or three thousand men, many in Red Shirts, riding behind Hampton, created a spectacle. Hampton's strategists were brilliant in orchestrating the campaign.[32]

Hundreds of women and children participated in these political rallies. Younger women joined their mothers in stitching thousands of Red Shirts. They also decorated the platforms and made flags. On each occasion as their Redeemer reached the podium, they waved flags and joined with the men on horseback, shouting "Hurrah for Hampton!" Young ladies threw flowers in the general's path. They did everything but "jine the cavalry." Doushka Pickens Dugas, the daughter of Governor Francis Pickens, rode at the front of fifteen hundred Red Shirts as they entered Edgefield. She became known in Confederate folklore as Carolina's Joan of Arc. The campaign of 1876 was an important highlight in the life of many young people, including seven-year-old W. W. Ball of Laurens. His experience revealed how the women in his family taught him his heritage. Fear of the Radical Republicans had already left a deep impression in his psyche. When his grandmother made him a Red Shirt (thought not of flannel), he was elated, especially wearing it to see a Hampton parade with her. Attired in a Red Shirt while marching in a Hampton procession, particularly on horseback, was a new generation's rite of passage. In Newberry "the Town boys were also in the saddle, conspicuous in their red jackets." Young men, who were disappointed at not being able to serve during the war, wanted an opportunity to prove themselves to their older male kin, needless to say, many of whom were veterans. Some overly eager youths posed a danger to the Hampton campaign; they were all too willing to employ violence even at the cost of bringing more federal troops into the state. Veterans had to restrain these mere boys, who did a lot of the work.[33]

Many South Carolinians looked at the election of 1876 through the prism of a newly minted Confederate nationalism. From the ashes of the Civil War and Reconstruction rose a new Confederate Phoenix. The unity so lacking in the last two years of the Civil War blossomed in a later nationalism that eluded the historic Confederacy. Hampton's campaign and subsequent victory overcame many old divisions; the general offered a soothing and nostalgic view of the past and the road to recovery. Conscription, inflation, impressment, speculation, and desertion were no longer relevant, and the sacrifices of the dying and the maimed had been redeemed, given new meaning. The harsh reality of the war, if not erased, was cleansed by a righteous cause, home rule, led by a redeemer, "a gentleman and an officer" steeped in planter paternalism and the Southern code of honor. The Upcountry and Lowcountry united on the necessity of a Hampton victory. Class antagonisms were temporarily shelved or redirected against Republicans. Economic hardship, coupled with the failure of Republicans to help them, caused some blacks to reevaluate their situation. In appealing to these conservative blacks, Hampton blunted charges that the Democrats or Redeemers were antiblack. Hundreds supported him; many joined his processions, sporting Red Shirts, some on horseback. Their presence helped forestall federal intervention until late in the campaign.[34]

Hampton's victory meant that the state's patronage was firmly back in the hands of the Democrats, but his promise to blacks barely survived his two terms. A younger generation, children of the war, who were more in tune with hardliners such as Gary, would triumph over the paternalists during the agrarian revolt of the 1890s. How the Confederate legacy of white children and the deferred dream of the Promised Land for black children played themselves out is the subject of the next chapter.

11

The Last Phoenix: Conflicting Legacies, 1890–2007

S ince the 1890s, two conflicting legacies of the Civil War and Reconstruction have competed for hegemony in South Carolina. More than any organization, the United Daughters of the Confederacy (UDC) realized that children were central in preserving "Confederate Culture." Racial Radicals who eviscerated Hampton's paternalism abetted them. The blow to the rights blacks had gained under Congressional Reconstruction became final when the general departed to serve in the U.S. Senate. D. W. Griffith's *Birth of a Nation*, based on Thomas Dixon's *The Clansmen*, captured in 1915 the racist mindset of the period.[1]

Ironically, Racial Radicalism, by establishing Jim Crow segregation, nurtured the growth of a black professional class, including undertakers, physicians, and ministers, who provided the leadership to establish the South Carolina Chapter of the National Association for the Advancement of Colored People (NAACP). This black middle class, whose livelihood depended on a black clientele, fostered the dream of a promised land where multiracial democracy thrived. The NAACP prepared the way for toppling separate and unequal education in 1954. In the 1960s young people became the cutting edge of the civil rights movement.

The specter of white and black children attending school together (with miscegenation lurking in the background) provoked a backlash by whites. Their champion in 1948 was South Carolina Governor J. Strom Thurmond of Edgefield County. In the 1970s and 1980s, Thurmond and likeminded conservatives blunted the forward thrust of the civil rights movement. Hostile to affirmative action and the intervention of big government on their way of life, some conservatives welcomed a revival of a Confederate Phoenix in the 1990s. For most blacks, the Confederate flag flying over the state capitol did not symbolize states' rights but the oppression of the past and the hovering possibility of another setback in civil rights. The issue precipitated a nasty debate about the legacy and what the flag should mean to future generations of the state's children.

The present conflict evolved out of the triumph of Racial Radicalism in South Carolina. It could not have happened without the support of the yeoman children of the war. White farmers and renters, hard-pressed by the severe agricultural depression gripping the state, elected Benjamin R. Tillman governor of South Carolina in 1890. Sallie Chapin saw him as the embodiment of her fictional young gentleman, Fitz-Hugh St. Clair. The reformer urged Tillman, "Take Fitz Dear Boy as your model for your State sadly needs such men grown from such boys." Uncomfortable when General Hampton's people reminded him that he had not shouldered a rifle during the war, the Edgefield farmer used his Red Shirt activities as a young man to legitimize his military connections to the "Lost Cause." He proudly boasted of stuffing ballot boxes and murdering Republicans.[2]

In 1890 subterfuges to disfranchise blacks caused legislation to be introduced in Congress by Henry Cabot Lodge of Massachusetts to supervise federal elections. White South Carolinians feared national Republicans would force another black Reconstruction on the state; Tillman and his lieutenants assuaged their fears by bashing blacks. The state constitution of 1898 severely limited the black franchise; the stringent requirements also led to a dramatic decline in the number of poor whites voting. Whether or not Tillman was a populist, a shill for business interests, or an opportunist is problematic. He failed to address the economic ills of the white farmers and renters who supported him. Antiblack rhetoric became the staple of successful gubernatorial campaigns; lynching flourished. Of the 173 lynchings in South Carolina between 1882 and 1950, 141 (81.5 percent) took place between 1882 and 1913.[3]

The Phoenix Riot of 1898 spread terror in the Upcountry. Riders carrying rifles murdered Republican organizers in that town. Blacks left the area in droves. One group of riders connected with the riot terrorized Benjamin Mays, barely five years old, and his father. The future civil rights leader noted that the mob remained his first memory of childhood. Racial Radicalism seared the psyche of children, white and black, throughout the state. In the Lowcountry, Mamie Garvin Fields remembered that black and white children playing together in her neighborhood abruptly ended their friendships. Children who once played marbles together now used them as missiles against each other. When Tillman left for the U.S. Senate, Coleman ("Cole") Blease continued the legacy of Racial Radicalism in his quest for power. He was proud that he too had worn the Red Shirt as a child. Elected governor in 1910 and 1914, he expanded Tillman's base to include mill workers. In 1911 he attacked Benedict College, a private black Baptist school in Columbia, for employing white female teachers from the North. Blease was appalled that one of them, not bad looking, walked freely hand in hand with her black students, boys and girls, on campus. The Upcountry politician found Benedict foul and disgusting.[4]

While Racial Radicals were gaining the upper hand in South Carolina, the cultural pillars of the Confederate legacy were being built: the United Confederate Veterans (1889), the United Daughters of the Confederacy (1894), and the Sons of the Confederacy (1896). The *Confederate Veteran* became the official organ of these three associations. The Daughters' involvement as an extension of their nurturing role as mothers, wives, and sisters was crucial in sustaining the vitality of their Confederate heritage. They ensured that generations of children would remember the idealism and sacrifice of their forebears. UDC President General Cornelia Branch Stone of Texas (1907–1909) and Historian General Mildred Lewis Rutherford of Georgia (1910–1915) were pioneers in children's educational activities. Between 1894 and 1919, the Daughters organized Children of the Confederacy (CC) chapters on the state and divisional level. The ages of members ranged from infancy to twenty years. In 1917 the CC became an official auxiliary of the UDC. In 1955 the CC held its first annual convention in Atlanta, Georgia.[5]

In providing symbols and rituals that children could embrace, the UDC resembled the Roman Catholic Church with its catechism, relics, saints, holy days, processions, and emphasis on orthodoxy and education. Women were active in preserving and donating family memorabilia and papers to state depositories. In a sense, these archives became temples of their testaments to the "Lost Cause." A prime example of their efforts is the Palmer Family Papers, housed in the South Caroliniana Library on the campus of the University of South Carolina in Columbia. The Roman Catholic metaphor also holds for the proper education of children, particularly young men. During the Civil War, educators had proselytized the importance of instilling Confederate values in the future leaders and defenders of the New Republic. On the eve of the war, the Lancaster *Ledger* had published a series entitled "A Constitutional Catechism for Smart Boys." In July 1861 the Charleston *Daily Courier* had announced the publication of "a short and easy catechism, designed for the use of Sunday Schools in the Confederate States of America." The paper had perceived the catechism as part of an essential movement to cleanse the South of "teachings against our institutions."[6]

Continuing this tradition, UDC state divisions, by the turn of the century, began compiling catechisms. In 1904, three years before she became president general, Cornelia Branch Stone authored a UDC Confederate Catechism for Children. In 1919 Mrs. John Alison Lawton, from James Island, South Carolina, published a catechism dealing with the state. Decca Lamar West of Texas revised and enlarged Stone's catechism in 1926. The following year the *Confederate Veteran* ran the final compilation in serial form. In October 1954, Mrs. Henry Allen Davis, from Memphis, Tennessee, compiled the *Catechism on the History of the Confederate States of American.* Despite additions and revisions between 1927 and 1990, the content of these catechisms remained similar. Slavery in the South had been benign; the Northern states had annulled the rights of the Southern people, forcing them to secede. Their ancestors had fought in the War Between the States for a just cause.[7]

Victorian attitudes and gender conventions influenced the content of the catechism. Few Southern white women had experienced battles themselves. Therefore, the Daughters presented an interpretation of the "Lost Cause" that glorified war. This was especially appropriate during the era of World War I. What was missing from their catechisms was probably as instructive as what they contained. Divisions in society were ignored. As decades passed, generations of children, depending on their elders for war stories, were told nothing about the wicked side of the war or the ghastly way so many men were killed and crippled. Instead, under the guidance of the Daughters, they learned to honor the bravery of their forebears in famous battles as well as leading generals and the First Family of the Confederacy. Jefferson Davis's daughter, Varina Anne ("Winnie"), who was born in the Confederate White House, became an icon for young women through the assiduous efforts of the Daughters. Winnie, living figuratively in a gilded cage, never married and died in 1898 at an early age. The Daughters, appealing to boys, held up for admiration the heroics of young soldiers like Sam Davis, who was hanged in Pulaski, Tennessee, as a Confederate spy. He had refused to divulge his source of information. In 1900 the proceeds of a card game based on Confederate heroes was donated to the Sam Davis Monument Fund.[8]

The Daughters saw themselves as educational reformers. Mildred Lewis Rutherford was the UDC Historian General in 1911. The Georgian was originally from Camden, South Carolina, where the abuse of citizens by Sherman's soldiers was still white hot in the folk memory. Understandably she denounced "The [Northern] Textbook Trust." Her mission was to purge the schools of anti-Southern textbooks. It was Charleston's Poppenheim sisters, Mary and Louise, who extended the work of Rutherford to a wider women's network and consequently expanded the role of the Southern woman in the public sphere. The sisters were children of the war. Their father, C. P. Poppenheim, had served as a sergeant in Hampton's Legion. Their youngest brother, J. H. Bouknight, had been a cadet at the Citadel. Mary graduated from Vassar in 1888. Active in the UDC, she rose from president of the South Carolina Division to the rank of President General. Both sisters were also involved in the General Confederation of Women's Clubs. Mary established the *Keystone* in 1899, a monthly publication designed for the women's clubs. Louisa was its manager. It served as the official organ of the UDC in Virginia, North Carolina, and South Carolina. Unlike Mildred Rutherford, Mary Poppenheim supported women's suffrage.[9]

Sometimes the women deviated from Southern gender orthodoxy, especially a younger generation raised on the glories of the "Lost Cause" and exposed to liberating ideas in college. Between 1907 and 1909 veterans protested against the Daughters' adopting military terms such as colonel, general, and division to cement their organization. Some veterans found the illustration of an all-girl Confederate choir offensive. The veterans had no problem with pretty young women attending their reunions, but they were affronted seeing these girls in gray uniforms wearing pants. The old soldiers objected when they were asked to address the leaders as lieutenant or captain. In at least one case, college girls sported toy rifles. Even for some women, these girls went too far playing soldiers. One irate South Carolina woman branded such practices a deviation from the values of the old South.[10]

Such behavior did not reflect what was happening in most chapters. The minutes (1910–1915) of the UDC Black Oak Chapter of Pinopolis, South Carolina, exemplified how the guidance from the home office was carried out at the grassroots level. The Pinopolis ladies insured that their public schools would teach a Confederate-oriented history, which honored fallen soldiers. Many young men from such small towns had died in the Spanish American War. In 1911 the superintendent of education handed out leaflets to the children encouraging them to collect money for an Arlington monument. On Confederate Memorial Day (April 26), the youngsters laid laurel wreathes at the cemetery and viewed relics such as a palmetto feather from Fort Sumter, cockades, and a homemade ring from James Island. The Daughters distributed leaflets on Robert E. Lee's birthday. At one meeting a paper on the Confederate flag was read. The chapter was not wealthy. However, its members supported girls who wanted to further their education by sponsoring scholarships to Winthrop College for Women in Rock Hill and the Confederate Home College in Charleston. On the campus of the all-men Clemson Agricultural College, they had a drinking fountain erected as a tribute to Confederate soldiers.[11]

Children were always prominent in UDC processions. In June 1914 the Black Oak Chapter staged a ceremony to honor those who died in World War I by bestowing on them posthumously the Cross of Military Service. The presentation began with a procession of children filing into the hall. They escorted veterans to their chairs while the boys' choir sang "Bonnie Blue Flag" along with "Maryland, My Maryland!" and "S'wanee River." The meeting began with a prayer by a minister, followed by addresses and then a dinner. The climactic ending was a roaring rendition of "Dixie."[12]

The efforts of the Daughters of South Carolina, such as the Pinopolis women, ensured that generations of children would grow up surrounded by more than two hundred Confederate monuments and markers to help them not forget their Confederate legacy. Many of these memorials were completed by 1919. In 1906 Lucy Calvert Thompson counseled an audience at a dedication ceremony in Abbeville to "protect and honor this monument, teach your children and children's children to cherish and revere the memory of those who knew their rights and dared to maintain them." In 1908 the Samuel D. Barron Chapter of the UDC erected the Confederate Soldiers' Monument in Ebenezer, York County. Barron had entered the army at age fifteen, rejoined at sixteen, and was eventually captured and imprisoned Point Lookout, Maryland. The monument's inscription read, "Remembering How They Resisted Oppression And Injustice." In 1911 Camden schoolchildren donated their pennies toward a drinking fountain honoring boy-soldier Richard Kirkland. "Christlike," he risked his life to bring water to a wounded Union soldier.[13]

Condemnation of Congressional Reconstruction remained a cardinal principle for the Daughters and other proponents of the "Lost Cause." Born in Pulaski, Tennessee, the birthplace of the national Ku Klux Klan, Laura Martin Rose argued that such a vigilante organization was necessary to preserve Law and Order and White Supremacy. In 1913 the UDC officially endorsed her primer for schoolchildren, *The Ku Klux Klan or Invisible Empire*. Succeeding Rutherford as Historian General in 1916, Rose lauded D. W. Griffith's *Birth of a Nation* as instructive for those who wished to understand the importance of the Klan to the South.[14]

Griffith captured on film the white Southern collective memory of Congressional Reconstruction in a storyline that used the appeal of young love and innocence to win the hearts of a national audience. The film emerged from Thomas Dixon Jr.'s books *The Leopard's Spots* (1902) and *The Clansman: An Historical Romance of the Ku Klux Klan* (1905). The Baptist preacher had received his training at the Southern Baptist Theological Seminary in Greenville, South Carolina. In 1905 Dixon turned *The Klansman* into a stage play. Then, in 1912 he attempted to make the book into a movie but failed. A year later he sold the film rights to Griffith. Dixon wrote the script for the photoplay.[15]

The evolution of the man's works revealed the various modifications of his storyline to discover what worked best in justifying the activities of the Klan. Children and young people played key roles just as they did in the stories of Sallie Chapin and Uncle Fabian. Without them the humanizing appeal of the story would be lost. In his script for Griffith, the author finally found the right balance between the love story of a Confederate boy Ben Cameron and a Yankee girl Elsie Stoneman, on one hand, and the injustices of Congressional Reconstruction, which almost destroyed their young love. The story took place in Upcountry South Carolina, where the corruption of black Republican politicians and the brutality of the black state militia were rampant. Elsie's youngest sister jumped off a cliff to escape the lust of a black militia leader. To make things worse, the black lieutenant governor tried to force Elsie to marry him. The Klan saved the day by routing the blacks and restoring law and order and white supremacy. Their triumph over black rule and ruin was the beginning of a new American nation.[16]

The film was an instant hit in South Carolina. David D. Wallace, the dean of South Carolinian historians, urged all Americans to see it. The Wofford professor vowed to take his baby daughter when she was old enough. In *The Clansman* Dixon praised the children who kept silent about Klan activities and the women who made over 400,000 disguises for the Klan.[17]

Racial Radicalism had within it the seeds of its own destruction. In arguing that education was harmful to blacks and placing all blacks in one category, the Racial Radicals unwittingly precipitated the emergence of a challenge to their system from within the black community. Segregation led to the rise of a professional class of black doctors, preachers, and educators with its own constituency. They were living proof of the limitations of Booker T. Washington's version of self-help; despite their success, they were not accepted into white society. Out of this group came the leaders of the first phase of the modern civil rights movement. The Charleston chapter of the NAACP was organized in 1917, the same year W. E. B. DuBois visited the city. The education of black children became its main mission. The group was determined to make a better world for black children. In 1919, the chapter and former Congressman Thomas E. Miller successfully undertook a petition campaign to put black teachers in the city's black public schools.[18]

By the mid-1930s higher education came under scrutiny. Precedents during Congressional Reconstruction haunted conservatives. In 1936 the University of South Carolina Alumni Association decided to award the oldest living graduate a "gold headed walking stick." Much to the white members' chagrin, the cane went to Alonzo G. Townsend, a black who attended South Carolina College during Radical Reconstruction. The Charleston *News and Courier* was most concerned that school officials had given a whiff of legitimacy to an era when "aliens, carpet baggers, scalawags, the scum of the earth, bad negroes and many deluded negroes took over the state." In 1938, Charles B. Bailey, a black man, applied for admission to the law school at the university. During the 1940s James Hinton of Columbia led the state NAACP's drive to insure that South Carolina would get a black law school. He also headed the campaign to mandate equal pay with whites for black public-school teachers. Simultaneously, Governor James Byrnes feverishly pumped more money into black schools to preserve segregation.[19]

The legal efforts of the NAACP in South Carolina found a sympathetic ear in Federal Judge J. Waties Waring. In 1948 the Charlestonian struck down the state's whites-only primary. Two years later he headed a three-judge panel that upheld the segregation of schools. In his dissent, he urged the NAACP counsel Thurgood Marshall to make segregation rather than separate-but-equal the main issue in a Clarendon County school case. Marshall appealed the case to the United States Supreme Court, one of several challenging segregation. The Court chose a Kansas case, *Brown v. Board of Education of Topeka*, to make its 1954 decision outlawing segregation in public education. In 1955 Robert F. Morrison, a former president of the Charleston NAACP, explained: "We older Negroes know that the only way for the future Negro children to get a chance to get an education equal to whites in this atomic age is for us to go to the same schools that teach the same things." He concluded, "The Supreme Court and all well-thinking people realize that the separate but equal law has been given a 60 year test and failed."[20]

In the 1960s a younger generation reenergized the civil rights movement to help bring about the Civil Rights Act and the Voting Rights Act of 1965. They were part of a worldwide "Youthquake." Civil rights leaders agonized over using children in the movement, but their presence was crucial. In Birmingham, Martin Luther King reluctantly agreed to limit participation to children over the age of fourteen. Nevertheless children became foot soldiers in the movement. A children's crusade engulfed Birmingham. Hundreds of youths were arrested; the authorities used hoses and dogs on them. In September 1963 white supremacists exploded a bomb in Birmingham's Sixteenth Street Baptist Church, killing four little girls. Their deaths triggered a national revulsion.[21]

Benjamin Mays aptly described youngsters who took the lead in the desegregation of public accommodations as "Young Warriors." In 1960, South Carolina student sit-ins began in Greenville and Rock Hill, and then spread across the state. Lunch counters were the primary targets. That same year, the Charleston movement to desegregate the city was propelled by youngsters. They defied their parents and school authorities in boycotting schools, so they could join protest demonstrations. Charleston teacher Ruby Cornwell acknowledged the lead the youngsters played: "In '63 I only joined in their demonstrations." That year public school segregation ended in Charleston as students and their families braved crank phone calls at home and bomb scares at school.[22]

The United States was being torn apart by the Vietnam War in 1968; campuses were in turmoil. This was the national political background when on the evening of February 8, 1968, police shot into a crowd of twenty-eight young people attending a protest on the South Carolina State University campus. The issue involved the desegregation of a local bowling alley. Three students were killed. Two of those wounded were only high school youths: Harvey Miller, fifteen, and Ernest Shuler, sixteen. The explosive incident became known as the Orangeburg Massacre. In a sense, Governor Robert McNair and other state authorities were unable to diffuse the situation because events on the ground moved so quickly; the students had lost faith in both these officials and their traditional black leaders. The civil rights movement in South Carolina reached a peak in 1969 when poorly paid black women at the Medical College in Charleston staged a successful 113-day strike. High-school students were prominent in the protest; they flooded the city's picturesque Battery. The strike brought a partial victory and an upsurge in the registration of black voters in Charleston, which resulted in the election of reform Democrat Joseph Riley as mayor in 1975.[23]

Led by Strom Thurmond, "the white folks" fought back. As early as 1948 Strom embodied white South Carolina's resistance to civil rights for blacks. His ancestors had migrated from Virginia to Edgefield District in 1784. His grandfather, George Tillman (d. 1904), lost an arm in the Civil War. He came home broke. In 1894 Strom's father Will was elected to the South Carolina Assembly. He nominated Benjamin Tillman for U.S. Senator and became Tillman's personal lawyer and campaign manager. Strom's childhood memories go back to the days of Tillman and Blease. The father took his six-year-old boy to visit Tillman. Strom remembered being impressed as a boy by a fiery stump speech Cole Blease gave in 1912.[24]

Thirty-four years later, in 1946, Strom Thurmond was elected governor. The South Carolinian attracted national recognition when he bolted the Democratic Party to run for President as a Dixiecrat in 1948. During the campaign he railed against race mixing, and six years later was elected U.S. Senator in a write-in ballot. Thurmond's opposition to the Supreme Court's decision for desegregating education struck a responsive chord among a broad swath of white South Carolinians. In 1956 the Grand Dragon of the Ku Klux Klan in South Carolina threatened, "The day the Negro steps into a white South Carolina School as a student will be the day we pick up our weapons." White Citizens' Councils with a more affluent membership effectively managed to delay desegregation. The UDC immediately acted to insure the proper education of its members' children. The Confederate catechism was reissued, and in 1955 the Children of the Confederacy held its first annual convention. Today its organization mirrors the UDC, with a home page and national officers including a president general.[25]

In 1964 Strom Thurmond became a Republican and supported Barry Goldwater for president. Thurmond paved the way for the party's Southern strategy. In 1968 he aided Richard Nixon in dealing with the third-party challenge of

Alabama's George C. Wallace. Subsequently, Thurmond helped turn the Supreme Court in a more conservative direction. His political instincts served him well. He recognized that the black vote was hardly monolithic; Republicans needed a sizeable percentage of it in order to remain in power. He also knew how to disarm his critics. In 1974 the Senator appointed civil rights leader Matthew J. Perry to the United States Court of Military Appeals. Perry became a judge of the District Court of South Carolina and later the chief judge. Similarly, he added blacks to his staff and voted to strengthen and extend the Voting Rights Act. Thurmond's actions led the way for conservatives to accept blacks in the political system and thus remain powerbrokers. His career presages the Last Phoenix.[26]

A fire severely damaged the Confederate monument of Abbeville in 1991. This was the same memorial that Lucy Calvert Thompson had presented to the town and its children in 1906. On December 14, 1996, a refurbished monument was unveiled at a gala affair that included schoolchildren. An Abbeville school band played, and Phil Turner recited one of his own poems, aptly entitled "Phoenix Stones." During the Civil War, Abbeville County had suffered one of the highest death rates of white males in the state. Echoing on this occasion was Thompson's exhortation to "revere the memory of those who knew their rights and dared to maintain them." The political milieu provided the impetus toward another "Phoenix." The fall of the Berlin Wall and the collapse of the Soviet Union witnessed the rise of nationalism throughout the world. Some Southerners saw themselves as an ethnic group victimized by a tyrannical federal government. In 1994 the League of the South (formerly the Southern League) was organized to preserve the Southern cultural identity; some members called for secession. That same year, the Republicans, promising a return to limited government, carried the congressional elections.[27]

The Sons of Confederate Veterans, some thirty thousand strong, were most vocal in espousing neo-Confederate values. In the 1990s Ken Burns's eleven-part series *The Civil War* aired, reaching forty million viewers. It raised the ire of some South Carolinians, who did not want their children subjected to a nationalist interpretation of the war. On May 20, 1991, South Carolina Educational Television's *Cross Talk* presented "A Southern Response." The questioners in the audience were mostly members of the Sons of Confederate Veterans. The confrontation caused James Farmer, professor of history at the University of South Carolina, Aiken, to suggest that a more appropriate title for the show should be "The White Southern View."[28]

Some dissident members believed that the Sons of the Confederacy was shelving its prohibition against partisan political activity. They wanted it to disassociate itself from extremists. In 2002 the head of the local chapter in Greensboro, North Carolina, founded "Save the Sons of Confederate Veterans." This group advocated "defending Southern heritage in a non racist way." One of its organizers, from Eutawville, South Carolina, wrote, "If someone wants to attack the government and advocate secession, they can join the League of the South. If they find some sort of warped virtue in racism, then go to the Ku Klux Klan. But this organization," he affirmed, "has rejected racism in the past, and it's time to do it again once and for all." Leaders denied that the Sons of Confederate veterans had violated the prohibitions against political activity.[29]

The national enthusiasm for reenacting American Civil War battles precipitated interest in the war itself. By the late 1990s the United States had more than forty thousand Civil War reenactors. They enjoyed participating in "living history." The Battle of Secessionville, fought on James Island on June 16, 1862, has become especially popular. Each year it has been reenacted in November at Boone Hall Plantation, east of the Cooper River, Mount Pleasant, South Carolina. These reenactments, although not driven by politics, have had political and cultural implications. A four-year-old child at the reenactment of Secessionville in 2000 asked, "Daddy, who do we want to win?" Children also participated in the reenactment of the shelling of Fort Sumter. One nine-year-old boy served as a "Powder-Monkey." By their nature, these nineteenth-century reenactments locked women in traditional roles; few featured women as uniformed soldiers.[30]

The Confederate flag became the central battleground for some in the heritage movement. In 1987 the NAACP led a drive to remove Confederate flags atop state capitols; it threatened economic boycotts. Pro-flag supporters in South Carolina viewed this as the beginning gambit to attack the state's Confederate songs, markers, and monuments. They feared that future generations of schoolchildren might forget their Confederate heritage. The successful legal effort to allow women into the corps at the Citadel, an icon of the Old South, only added fuel to the fire. In the 1990s the Confederate-flag controversy came to a head in South Carolina when a boycott had the potential to hurt seriously the economy of the state. In 1996 Republican Governor David Beasley suggested moving the flag from the capitol dome to a nearby Confederate Soldiers' Monument. A firestorm of criticism ensued. Some clergy proclaimed the flag a "sacred symbol." A social conservative hypothetically wondered how many pro-flag clergy "marched in the South Carolina Pro-Life March and Rally the week before." One irate person complained: "Our Land was illegally invaded; our homes were looted and destroyed. [We were] held captive, by our conqueror for 12 years. [The flag is] a symbol that reminds us of our brave sons who fought for the right of the state to choose for themselves."[31]

Children figured prominently in the controversy. A presentation on South Carolina Educational Television in 1996 featured a debate between Republican Attorney General Charles Condon and Republican Governor David Beasley. Condon best summed up the dilemma: "The root issue of this controversy is not where the Confederate flag flies. The issue is what the flag stands for." He added a rhetorical question, "Are we to regard our state's heritage as essentially good and decent?" Beasley simply asked, "Do we want our children to be debating the Confederate flag in 10 years?" He pleaded: "We must sit down black and white, Republican and Democrat, to ask what is right. And then we must have the courage to do what is right." In 1998, the flag issue, combined with the lottery and other concerns, cost Beasley his reelection bid. During July 1999, the NAACP announced a national boycott to begin January 2000. Democrat Governor Jim Hodges and the legislature reached a compromise that did not please many flag supporters or the NAACP. In July 2000 the flag came down from the dome and was placed alongside the Confederate Soldiers' Monument on the capitol grounds. At that time the legislature made Martin Luther King's birthday a paid state holiday.[32]

Today South Carolina is one of the most military-friendly states in the Union; it is the home of many active and retired military. In 2007 a gala was held aboard the World War II aircraft carrier, the USS Yorktown, at Patriot's Point in the Lowcountry to celebrate the renovation of its museum devoted to the Congressional Medal of Honor. The state's antebellum warrior ethos has resonated with an American military culture that values duty, honor, and country. In 1995 Randolph W. Kirkland Jr. completed an exhaustive compendium of the thousands of South Carolinians who died for the Confederacy. In its scope and design, Broken Fortunes is reminiscent of the Vietnam Memorial Wall in Washington, D.C. In both cases soldiers died in a losing war that was criticized as immoral. Remembering their sacrifice encourages closure.[33]

Likewise, the H. L. Hunley submarine has become an icon for gallantry and death that transcended the war itself. In 1999 when archeologists were searching for members of the Hunley crew who had drowned during trial runs, they discovered the remains of twenty-two Confederate soldiers and sailors under Johnson Hagood Stadium in Charleston. Draped in Confederate flags, the coffins of these remains were placed in eight-horse-drawn military carriages and carried in procession to Charleston's Magnolia Cemetery, where General Micah Jenkins had been buried. Women, acting as widows in period mourning dresses, were in attendance. The commander of the reenactor group, the Palmetto Battalion, solemnly told schoolchildren, "Remember this because you'll never see it again."[34]

A few years later another farewell to the Confederate dead occurred, with luck bringing more closure to the suffering of a destructive war. On Saturday, April 17, 2004, thousands of people participated in the final funeral for the eight-man crew of the *Hunley*. The caskets of the men had lain in state aboard the *USS Yorktown* in Charleston Harbor. Some four thousand reenactors and thousands of others, including children, traveled the 4.5-mile route to Magnolia Cemetery. The crew was placed in a common grave. State Senator Glenn McConnell, chairman of the Hunley Commission, proclaimed: "We are here to give them the burial that fate denied them."[35]

Some black and white male reenactors share a common bond; respect for the courage, sacrifice, and idealism of those fallen in battle. On April 18, 1865, Colonel Artemus Darby Goodwyn's "Home Guard," composed of old men, young boys, and sick soldiers, tried to interdict Yankee troops. Seeing the Fifty-fourth Massachusetts advancing, the colonel ordered fifteen-year-old Burwell H. Boykin to shoot the white Union officer E. L. Stevens, who was leading the black unit. In 1995 the Fifty-fourth Massachusetts Reenactment Unit placed a marker that honored Stevens and Boykin. The unit's Company I also joined with the Twenty-ninth South Carolina and the Tenth South Carolina in reenactments. What bound them together were a shared history and the desire for authenticity. Members of Company I routinely tossed down a few beers with Confederate reenactors after a day of events. In some respects, they were following the tradition of the antebellum South Carolina Militia. Similarly, policemen, including the black former police chief of Charleston, Reuben Greenberg, performed as Confederate reenactors.[36]

South Carolina remains paradoxical about its collective past. A granite and bronze African American History Monument (2001) graces the capitol grounds near the statues of Wade Hampton and Benjamin Tillman. The Charleston area will be the home of a Slave Museum and the Hunley Memorial. While there are markers honoring the "Gullah Heritage" and the "Stono Rebellion" (1739), there is little public awareness of the daily travails of the slaves themselves. The response to Essie Mae Washington Williams, the daughter of Strom Thurmond and Carrie Butler, a sixteen-year-old black family servant, has been especially paradoxical. Her name was added to the names of the other Thurmond children on his monument located on the state capitol grounds in Columbia. The Confederate State Mint, in Florence, featured a likeness of her on a commemorative coin, while South Carolina State University granted the former student an honorary degree. In 2004 Williams contemplated joining the UDC.[37]

In 2007 South Carolina boasted sixty active UDC chapters with more than fifteen hundred members. They were still telling the Children of the Confederacy that the war was not a rebellion and that slavery was not its underlying cause. One of the most prized possessions in the Confederate Museum in Charleston is a punch bowl made from the boiler of the burned *Palmetto State.* Other Lowcountry institutions such as the Charleston Museum reinforce the educational philosophy of the Daughters. In the fall of 2007 the museum sponsored "Home School History Days," which focused on important events and themes of the Lowcountry. The exhibit on the Siege of Charleston was particularly popular. The fall issue of *Provenance,* the museum's newsletter, featured a quiz for young readers on the Civil War, highlighting the exhibit. One question posed: "The 'Swamp Angel' was (A) A nurse who aided the dying and wounded on Morris Island; (B) An alligator who carried off several Union soldiers during the Siege of Charleston; (C) A Union artillery piece which fired on the city; (D) The gun that fired the first shot of the Civil War."[38]

On the eve of the sesquicentennial of the firing on Fort Sumter, the issue of slavery may be the key to the reconciliation of conflicting legacies. On Saturday, January 18, 2003, a mass celebrating the Feast Day of the Confession of St. Peter was held at the Church of the Holy Communion. A. Toomer Porter had founded this church in 1848. The biracial assembly honored the memory of nine slave children advertised for sale at probably the last Charleston auction, held on January 18, 1865. Walter Rhett pleaded that these children and their tribulations are as worthy of remembrance as the crew of the *Hunley.* They are all God's children. However, the debate over the flag remains unresolved. In 2007, the Rev. Joseph A. Darby, the senior pastor of Morris Brown AME Church, called for a compromise on the Confederate flag that "affirms our shared history" and "respects our diverse heritage." He conceded that there were black slaveowners, black Confederates, and Africans who sold other Africans into slavery, but he chided flag proponents for avoiding the central issue. Recalling what "[my] very Southern mother used to say, when I was trying to explain misbehavior on my part," the preacher emphasized, "What you say may be partially right, but it doesn't change the fact you did wrong."[39]

Appendix A: Methodology

The president and the secretary of war of the Confederacy could exempt or detail a limited number of men in the various classes delineated by Congress. National Archives Record Group 109 contains those letters received by the Office of the Confederate Secretary of War from 1861 to 1865 (Microcopy 437, consisting of some 151 microfilm reels). There is also an index of these letters (thirty-four reels identified as Microcopy 409). Note that some letters were not recorded in this series because they were sent to other offices to handle. This just hints at how difficult a logistical problem Record Group 109 poses to the scholar. The letters arrived in various ways, sometimes quite circuitously. While some were sent directly by the persons concerned, others were attached to letters from congressmen with their endorsement. In a few cases a multitude of petitions came from the same individual. An identifying number often opened up a file or packet of petitions, letters, affidavits, endorsements, and official comments. In addition, the method of recording these letters was modified more than once as the war continued and the flow of appeals increased. When I cited CSW, I gave the Microcopy 437 reel number, the initial letter of the writer's surname when given, the identifying number of the letter or packet, and the year. When WD for War Department was noted, I included it, too. Therefore, many citations resembled the following format: CSW, Reel No. 137, N-45–1864, or CSW, Reel No. 137, N-45-WD–1864.

My methodology of analyzing these letters is derived from Donna Rebecca Krug's pathbreaking doctoral dissertation "The Folks Back Home: The Confederate Homefront during the Civil War" (University of California, Irvine, 1990). She sought to determine how the drain of men from the home front and a long-drawn failing war affected the patriarchy. Using a random sample of 2,085 of the 42,839 letters she had read, Krug developed nine categories under the overall classification of "hardship letters." She perceived that hardships involved a shortage of skilled men, problems with slaves, invasions, underage sons in the military, private sufferings of families, the lack of law and order, and family-related requests to leave the Confederacy. She concluded that both the men and the Confederate government were unable to live up to their society's code of honor, which presented them as the natural protectors of the family and the household. However, even in defeat the Southern society still embraced the patriarchal ideal.

From the letters of Record Group 109, I have identified 1,757 dealing with South Carolina. Included were 493 petitions involving exemptions, details, and discharges. Not unusually, petitioners sought release by giving multiple reasons, which included underage, physical disability (unfit for service), and certain classes designated by the Conscription Act (see Appendix B). In those cases of more than one petition from the same person, I just counted the first one. Of the total number of petitions, I noted that 215 were in classes most critical to the functioning of the local community: physicians, blacksmiths, wheelwrights, shoemakers, tanners, millers, and millwrights (see Chapter 7). I have drawn on sixty-three examples from the pool of 493 petitions to discuss family hardships and the physical disabilities experienced by soldiers and civilians. They were the most extreme cases so they vividly reveal the kinds of suffering many households and communities endured between 1862 and 1865.

"Exemption" meant exclusion from conscription. Draftees were sent to Camps of Instruction, which were managed by the Bureau of Conscription. There they were examined for physical disabilities. Some obtained certificates from physicians detailing these disabilities. Skilled artisans were not always aware that they were eligible for exemptions. "Discharge" enabled a soldier to leave the army, usually for reasons of physical unfitness. The wounded and men with serious illness sought furloughs and relief. "Detail" meant army reassignment to somewhere else, based on the needs of the army, the soldier, and the wider community. In cases of family hardship, some were detailed near their homes. Soldiers, such as skilled artisans, sought details on the grounds of community needs. The Office of the Secretary of War had some leeway in determining who fitted all three categories. However, physical disabilities had to be certified by medical boards.

Ordinary people sometimes used the terms "furloughs," "exemptions," "details," and "discharges" interchangeably. The confusion was understandable, since enrolling officers sometimes directly detailed men from the Camps of Instruction; some of them never appeared on company rolls. To complicate matters, the initial Conscription Act was modified several times throughout the war, including just a few days after it was passed. As military needs became desperate, asking for the exemption of a soldier already in the army was tantamount to a denial. Consequently, letter writers adopted a more sophisticated approach. Some petitioners presented the secretary of war with a list of skilled mechanics needed in mills, factories, and tanneries. I have counted such a group of petitions as one. I handled such cases of multiple petitions as one in my statistics. To complicate matters, South Carolina also had its own exemptions and details that the Confederacy did not recognize, such as appointments to the South Carolina Military Academy.

South Carolinians used districts to identify themselves. These districts composed larger areas such as the Lowcountry and Upcountry. Households in the Upcountry suffered the most (see Chapter 7). I have identified the petitions by district, but in some instances, district designations were not very meaningful. Lowcountry refugees traveled to districts all over the state; some listed districts that were not their primary residences. The larger pool of 1,757 letters contained evidence that I have used to measure demoralization over time: complaints against government policies, evidence of desertions, and requests for passports to leave the Confederacy. A significant discovery was the overwhelming sacrifices of communities in the Upcountry districts. On one hand, their suffering sealed their hatred of the Yankees; on the other hand, it exposed the limitations of the Lowcountry.[1]

By late 1861, the reorganization of the Confederate armies was imperative. The enlistment of men who had volunteered for twelve months was about to expire. One hundred forty-eight regiments were affected. On April 16, 1862, Congress declared that all able-bodied males between eighteen and thirty-five years old were eligible for conscription. Those within this age group, already in the army, would have to remain in service for three years or reenlist for the duration of the war. Men underage or overage would have to remain ninety days or until their places could be filled. Youths under eighteen needed the approval of their parents or guardian to volunteer. In February 1864 Congress modified the Conscription Act to include men between the ages of seventeen and fifty liable for military service. Those between seventeen and eighteen and between forty-five and fifty were required to become part of a reserve for state defense and detail duty. (See the Pursley cameo in Chapter 2 to get insight into the hardships this caused families.) At the end of 1864, South Carolina nullified Confederate conscription.

Substitution was allowed under the initial Conscription Act, but the practice elicited a firestorm of criticism, especially after unscrupulous third parties speculated in substitutes, or the "selling" of "white men." Many substitutes were ineligible: aliens, and males under or over the draft age. Congress was forced to make substitutes between the ages of thirty-five and forty subject to the draft. In addition, it required those who had hired them to serve. But this legislation was challenged in state courts. As late as August 1863, South Carolina boys between the ages of sixteen and eighteen were offered "liberal" inducements for their services. Substitution was not abolished until December 1863. Probably no more than a thousand South Carolina males became substitutes.

The multitude of changes to the initial Conscription Act of April 11, 1862, especially regarding exemption, reflected not only the military demands of a debilitating war but also the conflicting interests and maneuverings between the executive and legislative branches of the Confederate government. Members of Congress had to deal with the discontent and needs of their constituencies. The president sought unsuccessfully the power to pursue the war as he saw fit. But Congress jealously guarded its prerogatives with regard to encroachments by the executive. It even revoked the power of the president and the secretary of war to detail men. Engaged in an ongoing kabuki dance, the legislature and the executive tried to balance the need for foodstuffs and manpower by the military on one hand and communities on the other, as well as the demand of slave-owners that the government provide security and the hostility of public opinion toward any concessions to planters with large holdings.

As early as April 21, 1862, and October 11, 1862, the Conscription Act was amended to include exemptions for a long list of men who fell in such "classes" as state officers, ministers, physicians, teachers, postmasters, editors, railroad officials, blacksmiths, shoemakers, tanners, engineers, millwrights, and wagon makers. Men engaged in teaching for two years were exempted. This class also included those teaching twenty or more students. Physicians had to be in prac-tice for five years. On February 17, 1864, the Confederacy raised this number to seven. It excluded doctors under the age of thirty. From April 16, 1862, to Feb-ruary 1865, some 5,839 males (or 39.3 percent) were exempt out of 14,959 South Carolinian conscripts. Many of them suffered from physical disabilities.

Until April 1862, the South Carolina government maintained its right to exempt overseers in the state. Congress subsequently allowed the exemption of overseers on plantations with twenty or more field hands, and an *additional* male for every twenty slaves on two plantations within five miles of one another. This caused a furor among ordinary white South Carolinians, who labeled it the "twenty-nigger law." In May 1863 Congress amended this class to cover "only the plantations of dependents, minors, imbeciles, *femmes soles*, and men in the field." The owner or agent would pay five hundred dollars. This amendment included the exemption of a white male to supervise twenty slaves on two plantations that were within five miles of one another when women, children, and the elderly would otherwise be left abandoned. In addition, the president could exempt persons in districts "deprived of white or slave labor indispensable to the production of grain or provisions necessary for the support of the population remaining at home, and also on account of justice, equity, and necessity." On February 17, 1864, Congress changed the $500 compensation to a bond by which the owner or his agent was required to furnish the govern-ment for each able-bodied slave one hundred pounds of bacon or one hundred pounds of pork and beef at prices set by government agents. Any surplus was to go to the government or to families of the soldiers at prices set by commis-sioners. As late as March 1865, a seventy-two-year-old Abbeville District planter petitioned the secretary of war to get his son returned home as an overseer.[1]

Notes

Introduction: Les Enfants de la Guerre

1. The "New Children's History" emphasizes family, resiliency, and agency. Since the publication of Philippe Ariès's *Centuries of Childhood: A Social History of Family Life* (New York: Vintage Books, 1962), studies of children and childhood have proliferated. The field has become increasingly interdisciplinary. See Paula S. Fass, ed., *Encyclopedia of Children and Childhood in History and Society* (New York: Macmillan Reference USA, 2004), 3 vols.; N. Ray Hiner and Joseph M. Hawes, "History of Childhood United States," is at 2:426–430. Hawes is one of the founders of the Society for the History of Children and Youth. Its program, "Children's Worlds, Children in the World," for its biennial meeting in Milwaukee in August 2005 shows the breadth and scope of the current scholarship. Attending the conference was Steven Mintz. In *Huck's Raft: A History of American Childhood* (Cambridge, Mass.: Harvard University Press, 2004), Mintz divided the history of American childhood into three eras: premodern (colonial to mid-eighteenth century), modern (1750 to 1950), and postmodern (1950 to 2004). In the premodern era, children were seen as adults in training, while in the modern period they were viewed as innocent but capable of being molded.

Scholars like Mintz have demonstrated that age as a category of analysis poses problems. James Marten offered a flexible definition of children as "girls and boys who acted like children" as well as those who reached a majority. He also allowed the subjects to define themselves. See Marten, *The Children's Civil War* (Chapel Hill: University of North Carolina Press, 1998), 244 n. 5. Unlike Marten, I also see underage soldiers as boys and children because that was how the society viewed them. In *Huck's Raft*, viii, Mintz defined childhood as infancy to eighteen. Most of my evidence deals with boys and girls under eighteen. For a stimulating discussion of girlhood in Western Europe, see Mary Jo Maynes, Birgitte Soland, and Christina Benninghaus, eds., *Secret Gardens, Satanic Mills: Placing Girls in European History, 1750–1960* (Bloomington: Indiana University Press, 2005); the authors perceive marriage as a marker ending girlhood.

2. Determining how many soldiers died in the American Civil War is problematic, especially for the Confederacy. In South Carolina, thirteen thousand to eighteen thousand of its white male population over the age of fifteen in 1860 died (i.e., 15–21 percent of 84,157). In York District alone, 18 percent of its entire white male population might have died; this is a figure comparable to the losses Germany suffered during World War II. Marten, *Children's Civil War*, 5; Drew Gilpin Faust, *This Republic of Suffering: Death and the American Civil War* (New York: Knopf, 2008), chapter 8; Randolph W. Kirkland Jr., *Broken Fortunes: South Carolina Soldiers, Sailors and Citizens Who Died in the Service of Their Country and State in the War for Southern Independence, 1861–1865* (Charleston, S.C.: SCHS, 1995), vii, 412; *Population of the United States in 1860, Compiled from the Original Returns of the Eighth Census under the Direction of the Secretary of the Interior, by Joseph C. G. Kennedy, Superintendent of Census* (Washington, D.C.: Government Printing Office, 1864), 448–452; Wolfgang Schivelbusch, *The Culture of Defeat: On National Trauma, Mourning, and Recovery*, trans. Jefferson Chase (New York: Henry Holt, 2003), 37–38; Francis Butler Simkins and Robert Hilliard Woody, *South Carolina During Reconstruction* (Chapel Hill: University of North Carolina Press, 1932), 10.

3. Walter Edgar, *South Carolina: A History* (Columbia: University of South Carolina Press, 1998), 376; *Confederate Baptist*, Columbia, January 20, 1864; Daniel E. Huger Smith, Alice R. Huger Smith, and Arney R. Childs, eds., *Mason Smith Family Letters, 1860–1868* (Columbia: University of South Carolina Press, 1950), 52, 130–138.

4. UDC *Recollections*, vol. 9, "What They're Saying About the Series."

5. *Population of the United States in 1860, Compiled from the Original Returns of the Eighth Census under the Direction of the Secretary of the Interior, by Joseph C. G. Kennedy, Superintendent of Census* (Washington, D.C.: Government Printing Office, 1864), 448–452; United Daughters of the Confederacy, South Carolina Division, *South Carolina Women in the Confederacy* (Columbia, S.C.: State Co., 1903, 1907), 1:156–158; Edmund L. Drago, "Confederate Children and the Commonality of the War Experience: South Carolina as a Test Case," paper, Society for the History of Children and Youth, Marquette University, Milwaukee, August 6, 2005. The title of one of the sessions was "A Children's World." For insight into their world of play, see Howard P. Chudacoff, *Children at Play: An American History* (New York: New York University Press, 2007).

6. Wilbert L. Jenkins, *Climbing Up to Glory: A Short History of African Americans during the Civil War and Reconstruction* (Wilmington, Del.: Scholarly Resources, 2002). Since the 1960s, scholars have produced a plethora of fine works on African Americans in South Carolina. Charleston has been blessed with two monographs: Wilbert L. Jenkins, *Seizing the Day: African Americans in Post–Civil War Charleston* (Bloomington: Indiana University Press, 1998), and Bernard E. Powers Jr., *Black Charlestonians: A Social History, 1822–1865* (Fayetteville: University of Arkansas Press, 1994). There is also W. J. Megginson, *African American Life in South Carolina's Upper Piedmont, 1780–1900* (Columbia: University of South Carolina Press, 2006). See also Leon F. Litwack, *Been in the Storm So Long: The Aftermath of Slavery* (New York: Knopf, 1979); Ira Berlin et al., eds., *Freedom: A Documentary History of Emancipation, 1861–1867* (Cambridge: Cambridge University Press, 1982–90).

7. Eric Foner, *Reconstruction: America's Unfinished Revolution, 1863–1877* (New York: Harper & Row, 1989); Andrew Billingsley, *Yearning to Breathe Free: Robert Smalls of South Carolina and His Families* (Columbia: University of South Carolina Press, 2007), 28, 42–47, 51–52, 61.

8. Billingsley, *Yearning to Breathe Free*, 78, 84, 103, chapters 9–12.

9. The best discussion of the historical, cultural, and economic divisions is Lacy K. Ford Jr., *Origins of Southern Radicalism: The South Carolina Upcountry, 1800–1860* (New York: Oxford University Press, 1988), preface, chapter 2, 371–372. Ford defined the Upcountry as the thirteen districts north and west of the state's fall line. In 1850 they produced 56 percent of the state's cotton while containing only 36 percent of the state's black population. Ford further divided the Upcountry into the Upper Piedmont (Anderson, Greenville, Lancaster, Pickens, Spartanburg, and York districts) and the Lower Piedmont (Abbeville, Chester, Edgefield, Fairfield, Laurens, Newberry, and Union districts). The Lower Piedmont was more involved in the cotton economy; whites composed only 41.3 percent of the population while the Upper Piedmont was 65.5 percent white. The Upcountry was overwhelmingly evangelical; most of the farmers were yeomen.

The historical antipathy for the elite living in the coastal districts of Beaufort, Charleston, Colleton, and Georgetown was shared by other persons living in the Upstate, north of the state capital at Columbia. Upcountry and Upstate became synonymous. Sometimes yeomen in the Lowcountry were simply called country people.

10. Stephanie McCurry, *Masters of Small Worlds: Yeoman Households, Gender Relations, and the Political Culture of the Antebellum South Carolina Low Country* (New York: Oxford University Press, 1997); Stephanie McCurry, "The Politics of Yeoman House-

holds in South Carolina," in Catherine Clinton and Nina Silber, eds., *Divided Households: Gender and the Civil War* (New York: Oxford University Press, 1992), 22–38.

11. David W. Blight, *Race and Reunion: The Civil War in American Memory* (Cambridge, Mass.: Harvard University Press, 2001), 2; Edmund L. Drago, *Hurrah for Hampton! Black Red Shirts in South Carolina During Reconstruction* (Fayetteville: University of Arkansas Press, 1998); W. Fitzhugh Brundage, ed., *Where These Memories Grow: History, Memory, and Southern Identity* (Chapel Hill: University of North Carolina Press, 2000); James C. Cobb, *Away Down South: A History of Southern Identity* (New York: Oxford University Press, 2005). The African American experience was a diverse one, but a certain commonality existed. See Charleston *Post and Courier*, May 22, 2007.

Chapter 1. Children as a Factor in War Strategy

1. Lynda Lasswell Crist, ed., *The Papers of Jefferson Davis* (Baton Rouge: Louisiana State University Press, 1992, 1993), 7:22; A[nthony] Toomer Porter, *Led On! Step by Step Scenes from Clerical, Military, Educational, and Plantation Life in the South, 1828–1898: An Autobiography* (New York: G. P. Putnam's Sons, 1898), 116–117.

2. Anne Sarah Rubin, *A Shattered Nation: The Rise and Fall of the Confederacy, 1861–1868* (Chapel Hill: University of North Carolina Press, 2005), 91–92.

3. Grace B. Elmore Books, vol. 3, rewritten entries, October 18, 1861, SHS; Reid Mitchell, *The Vacant Chair: The Northern Soldier Leaves Home* (New York: Oxford University Press, 1993), 132; "A Boy's Memories of War Time and Other Times by Milledge Lipscomb Bonham," 1–5, Milledge Bonham Collections, Writings, 1913–1920, SCHS; Yorkville *Enquirer*, February 28 and June 5, 1861.

4. Yorkville *Enquirer*, April 4, 1861; Grace B. Elmore Books, April 10, 1861.

5. This summary is based on E. Milby Burton, *The Siege of Charleston, 1861–1865* (Columbia: University of South Carolina Press, 1990), 6–9.

6. Burton, *Siege of Charleston*, 9–11.

7. OR, ser. 1, vol. 1 [1]: 143, 145, 151, 154, 162; Burton, *Siege of Charleston*, 25; Charleston *Daily Courier*, December 18, 1861; February 24, 1862.

8. OR, ser. 1, vol. 1 [1]: 158–159.

9. Emma Holmes, *The Diary of Miss Emma Holmes, 1861–1866*, ed. John F. Marszalek (Baton Rouge: Louisiana State University Press, 1994), 25; Mary Chesnut, *Mary Chesnut's Civil War*, ed. C. Vann Woodward (New Haven: Yale University Press, 1981), 47. Different versions of the event exist; see Holmes, *Diary*, 30, and UDC *Recollections*, 11: 516.

10. A. James Fuller, *Chaplain to the Confederacy: Basil Manly and Baptist Life in the Old South* (Baton Rouge: Louisiana State University Press, 2000), 2–10, 86, 277; *Confederate Baptist*, Columbia, June 3, 1863, September 14, 1864; Yates Snowden, *South Carolina School Books, 1795–1865* (Columbia, S.C., 1910), 14–15; Sarah Law Kennerly, "Confederate Juvenile Imprints: Children's Books and Periodicals Published in the Confederate States of America, 1861–1865" (PhD dissertation, University of Michigan, 1956), 465; James Farmer, *The Metaphysical Confederacy: James Henley Thornwell and the Synthesis of Southern Values* (Macon, Ga.: Mercer University Press, 1986).

11. OR, ser. 4, vol. 3: 1102; Yorkville *Enquirer*, May 30, 1861; September 26, 1861.

12. *Southern Presbyterian Review*, Columbia, 14 (October 1861): 365–398.

13. Charleston *Daily Courier*, May 7, 1861; Holmes, *Diary*, 6–7; UDC *Recollections*, 3: 177–181.

14. Yorkville *Enquirer*, May 2, 1861; October 31, 1862; Charleston *Daily Courier*, April 25, May 1, June 5, and September 30, 1861; May 15 and October 4, 1862; *Confederate Baptist*, Columbia, March 25, 1863; Holmes, *Diary*, 72. The Battle of Antietam occurred on September 17, 1862.

15. Holmes, *Diary*, 58, 71; Charleston *Daily Courier*, June 27, 1861; March 13, 1862. The Battle of First Bull Run occurred on July 21, 1861.

16. Charleston *Daily Courier*, June 25 and August 1, 1862; Chesnut, *Mary Chesnut's Civil War*, 547; Holmes, *Diary*, 263–264; Eugene W. Jones Jr., *Enlisted for the War: The Struggles of the Gallant 24th Regiment, South Carolina Volunteers, Infantry, 1861–1865* (Hightstown, N.J.: Longstreet House, 1997), 36.

17. Charleston *Daily Courier*, February 10 and August 1, 1864.

18. Charleston *Daily Courier*, July 31, 1861; June 24, 1863.

19. Charleston *Daily Courier*, June 26, 1863.

20. *Camden Confederate*, February 28, 1862; Yorkville *Enquirer*, March 30, 1864.

21. OR, ser. 1, vol. 14 [20]: 348, 488–489; *Southern Presbyterian Review*, Columbia, 15 (1862–1863): 479–514.

22. Yorkville *Enquirer*, July 22, 1863; December 7, 1864; Charleston *Daily Courier*, March 17, 1863; June 23, 1866.

23. Drew Gilpin Faust, *Mothers of Invention: Women of the Slaveholding South in the American Civil War* (Chapel Hill: University of North Carolina Press, 1996), 28–29; Charleston *Daily Courier*, March 8, 1862; S. C. Roberts to sister, Charleston, May 10, 1862, Isabella Ann (Roberts) Woodruff Papers, SCWRPL; Holmes, *Diary*, 160.

24. Charleston *Daily Courier*, March 8, 13, 27, 1862; April 10, 18, 21, 1862.

25. Charleston *Daily Courier*, March 26, 1862; April 10, 15, 1862; May 10, 1862; October 11, 29, 1862.

26. Mrs. Sallie [Sarah] F. Chapin, *Fitz-Hugh St. Clair, the South Carolina Rebel Boy: or, It Is No Crime to Be Born a Gentleman* (Charleston, S.C.: John M. Greer, 1872), 19–24; John Hammond Moore, *Southern Homefront, 1861–1865* (Columbia, S.C.: Summerhouse Press, 1998), 95–96; Charleston *Daily Courier*, May 19, 1863.

Chapter 2. Boy Soldiers and Their Families

1. "The Boys of '64" by Marion W. Jones, UDC *Recollections*, 5: 516–517; Susan R. Hull, ed., *Boy Soldiers of the Confederacy* (New York: Neale Publishing, 1905), 13–15; Louisa May Alcott, *Hospital Sketches*, ed. Alice Fahs (New York: Bedford / St. Martin's, 2004), 37; DeAnne Blanton and Lauren M. Cook, *They Fought Like Demons: Women Soldiers in the American Civil War* (Baton Rouge: Louisiana State University Press, 2002), 50–51; Mitchell, *Vacant Chair*, 12; Priscilla Ferguson Clement and Jacqueline S. Reinier, eds., *Boyhood in America: An Encyclopedia* (Santa Barbara, Calif.: ABC-Clio, 2001), 1: xxvii.

My estimate of South Carolina manpower and the number of boy soldiers is based on *Population of the United States in 1860*, 448–451; Janet B. Hewett and Joyce Lawrence, eds., *South Carolina Confederate Soldiers, 1861–1865* (Wilmington, N.C.: Bradfoot, 1998), 1: 358, 372, 375, 643 n. 66, 644 n. 67; Francis Butler Simkins and Robert Hilliard Woody, *South Carolina During Reconstruction* (Chapel Hill: University of North Carolina Press, 1932), 10; Randolph W. Kirkland Jr., *Dark Hours: South Carolina Soldiers, Sailors and Citizens Who Were Held in Federal Prisons During the War for Southern Independence, 1861–1865* (Charleston, S.C.: SCHS, 2002), 523; DeWitt Boyd Stone Jr., *Wandering to Glory: Confederate Veterans Remember Evan's Brigade* (Columbia: University of South Carolina Press, 2002), 11; Jones, *Enlisted for the War*; Mac Wyckoff, *A History of the 2nd South Carolina Infantry, 1861–65* (Fredericksburg, Va.: Sergeant Kirkland's Museum and Historical Society, 1994); Gary Baker, *Cadets in Gray: The Story of the Cadets of the South Carolina Military Academy and Cadet Rangers in the Civil War* (Columbia, S.C.: Palmetto Book Works, 1989), 186–231.

In 1860 there were approximately 77,505 while males in South Carolina between the ages of fifteen and fifty-nine. Estimates of the total number of men who served ranged between 59,000 and 71,000. Jane Hewett and Joyce Lawrence compiled the names of approximately 59,000 troops. Walter Edgar concluded that about 60,000 served. Citing the *Handbook of S.C., 1908*, the two scholars Francis Simkins and Robert Woody placed the number at 71,000. My estimate is around 65,000 because earlier studies were not able to take into full account all units, such as state troops and local and home defense forces, especially toward the very end of the war.

It is even more difficult to determine how many sixteen- and seventeen-year-old soldiers served. Many young men did not give their age at the time of enlistment. Some were undoubtedly trying to conceal it and recruiting officers were mainly interested in filing the ranks. Until February 1864, seventeen-year-olds were not eligible for the draft. Regimental studies, such as Jones's history of the Twenty-fourth Regiment, SCV, Infantry and Wyckoff's one of the Second South Carolina Infantry, indicate that less than 1.6 percent of the members of their respective regiments were under the age of seventeen: 21 / 1,520 (1.4 percent); 26 / 1,583 (1.6 percent). If this percentage is raised to 2.0 percent to include those with no ages given in the two studies, then no more than 1,300 of the 65,000 who served in South Carolina regiments were under seventeen.

Another 1,800 may have served in several all-boy regiments established in the last stages of the war. In late 1865 Governor A. G. Magrath called for the enrollment of sixteen-year-old boys into regiments. For example, a regiment of boy soldiers came from the State Military Academy. Most of the cadets were probably seventeen or older; not all enlisted. The Cadet Rangers and the Battalion of State Cadets totaled 607. Assuming that there were two more all-boy regiments (600 each), then 1,800 teenagers served. The total number of boy soldiers under seventeen did not exceed 5,000.

Sometimes boy soldiers belonged to units that were a mix of old men and youngsters. Most of the local defense forces and militia included old men and boys. Assuming that about 2,000 male children served in such units, the total number of boy soldiers comes to around 5,100. The estimate is an educated guess; the actual number remains unknown.

2. Hull, *Boy Soldiers of the Confederacy*; Charleston *Daily Courier*, October 2, 6, 8, 1862; OR, ser. 4, vol. 1 [125]: 1095, vol. 2 [126]: 1, 160, vol. 3 [127]: 178; Appendix II.

3. Albert Burton Moore, *Conscription and Conflict in the Confederacy* (Columbia: University of South Carolina Press, 1996), 14 n. 5; CSW, Reel No. 19, 8754–1861; Hull, *Boy Soldiers of the Confederacy*, 30–31; Chesnut, *Mary Chesnut's Civil War*, 373. The Battle of Second Bull Run occurred on August 29–30, 1862.

4. *Confederate Baptist*, Columbia, February 3, 1864; Bell Irvin Wiley, *The Life of Johnny Reb: The Common Soldier of the Confederacy* (New York: Bobbs-Merrill, 1943), 331; Porter, *Led On*, 236; Chesnut, *Mary Chesnut's Civil War*, 609, 680; Holmes, *Diary*, 407; Mrs. A. Howell to Dear Friend, June 23, 1864, Mary Y. Harth (Mrs. John) Papers, SCL; David Golightly Harris Farm Journals, 1855–1870, microfilm copy of original, July 2, 1861, SHS. This copy, microfilmed in the 1940s, is complete. In 1979 the journals were given to the Dacus Library at Winthrop University, Rock Hill, South Carolina (DLW). They are listed in the Louise Pettus Archives and Special Collections at DLW as Emily Liles Harris Journals, 1859–1870, 1907–1908, Accession No. 586. As noted, the journals covering the period before May 1859 are not included in the DLW collection. Philip N. Racine has superbly edited the journals in his book, *Piedmont Farmer: The Journals of David Golightly Harris, 1855–1870* (Knoxville: University of Tennessee Press, 1990). His introduction, notes, and annotations make a researcher's task much easier. I have relied heavily on his analysis and works. In the endnotes hereafter I give a short title and the date, e.g. Harris Journals, October 1, 1864. For a description of Emily Harris's mental state during the war, see Philip N. Racine, "Emily Lyles Harris: A Piedmont Farmer During the Civil War," *South Atlantic Quarterly* 79 (Autumn 1980): 386–397.

5. CSW, Reel No. 78, W-749–1862; UDC *Recollections*, 12: 716–718. Moore, *Southern Homefront*, 120 contains a newspaper advertisement, "Substitutes Wanted."

6. Mother [Isabella Wylie Strait] to son [Lafayette Strait], April 1, 1862, Gaston-Strait-Wylie-Baskin Families Papers, SCL; CSW, Reel No. 93, G-146–1863, G-184–1863, Reel No. 127, G-111–1862.

7. Roger Rosenblatt, *Children of War* (Garden City, N.Y.: Anchor Press, 1983), 101; Mitchell, *Vacant Chair*, 12; *Confederate Baptist*, Columbia, December 7, 1864; Frank M. Mixson, *Reminiscences of a Private* (Columbia, S.C.: State Co., 1910), 11, 14–15, 17–18, 130; U.S. Congress, Senate, *South Carolina in 1876: Testimony as to the Denial of the Elective Franchise in South Carolina at the Elections of 1875 and 1876, 44th Congress, 2nd sess., S. Misc. Doc. 48* (Washington, D.C.: Government Printing Office, 1877), 1: 270; Ulysses R. Brooks, *Butler and His Cavalry, 1861–1865* (Columbia, S.C., 1909), 417.

8. CSW, Reel No 8, 3927–1861 with an enclosure, 3926–1861, Reel No. 11, 6347–1861, Reel No. 13, 6833–1861, Reel No. 139, R-138–1864; Petition, Nancy Owens to Governor, February 11, 1865, Letters Received and Sent, 1864–1865, Andrew Gordon Magrath, Governors' Papers, SCDAH.

9. George C. Rable, *Civil Wars: Women and the Crisis of Southern Nationalism* (Champaign: University of Illinois Press, 1991), 75–76; UDC *Recollections*, 6: 218–219.

10. CSW, Reel No. 23, 10074–1862, Reel No. 30, A-WD-455–1862, Reel No. 50, H-225, 1862, Reel No. 64, N-143–1862, Reel No. 106, O-6–1863; CSR, Reel No. 64, Card No. 1502, Reel No. 71, Card No. 1252, Reel No. 198, Card No. 2213, Reel No. 286, Card 533, Reel No. 306, Card 655; Wyckoff, *History of the 2nd South Carolina Infantry*, 247.

11. Charles E. Cauthen, *South Carolina Goes to War, 1860–1865* (Chapel Hill: University of North Carolina Press, 1950), 110; Judith N. McArthur and Orville Vernon Burton, *"A Gentleman and an Officer": A Military and Social History of James B. Griffin's Civil War* (New York: Oxford University Press, 1996), 39; W. Scott Poole, *Never Surrender: Confederate Memory and Conservatism in the South Carolina Upcountry* (Athens: University of Georgia Press, 2004), 25–27; Yorkville *Enquirer*, June 3, 24, 1863, February 17, 1864; Charleston *Daily Courier*, May 6, 1862; S. C. Roberts to sister, May 10, 1862, Woodruff Papers; CSW, Reel No. 83, B-742–1863.

12. Charleston *Daily Courier*, July 2, December 25, 1861; James David Altman, "The Charleston Marine School," *South Carolina Historical Magazine* 88 (April 1987): 76–82; Christine Blanton, "The Life of Mary Amarinthia Snowden," *Preservation Progress* 37 (Fall 1994): 7–11; CSW, Reel No. 125, D-69–1864.

13. OR, ser. 4, vol. 3 [127]: 1120–1122; Jones, *Enlisted for the War*. 339; Charleston *Daily Courier*, March 25, August 21, 1863; *Confederate Veteran*, Nashville, 18 (1910): 214; James Michael Barr and Rebecca Ann Dowling Barr, *Confederate War Correspondence of James Michael Barr and Wife Rebecca Ann Dowling Barr*, compiled by Ruth Barr McDaniel (Taylors, S.C.: Faith Printing Co., 1963), 156; CSR, Reel No. 116, Card 1917.

14. Alexander Samuel Salley Jr., ed., *South Carolina Troops in Confederate Service*, vol. 1 (Columbia, S.C.: R. L. Bryan Co., 1913), vols. 2 and 3 (Columbia, S.C.: State Co., 1914, 1930); David Mallinson, "Armed Only with Their Drums, Union and Confederate Drummer Boys Served Their Causes with Distinction," *America's Civil War* 5 (November 1992): 8, 70–73; W. Chris Phelps, *Charlestonians in War: The Charleston Battalion* (Gretna, La.: Pelican, 2004), 65–66. CSR, Reel No. 160, Card 2021, gives Alex Whisnant, Company B, 2 South Carolina Infantry (2 Palmetto Regiment); Kirkland, *Dark Hours*, 485 lists Alexander Whisenant.

For the black musicians, see Salley, *South Carolina Troops*, 1:318–219; [Gregg's] Bright, John; Dawson, Tobias; Emory, William; Gardner, Seymour; Graves, John; Mazyck, Peter; Mitchell, Arthur; Mitchell, John; Rose, William (slave); Steed, Samuel; Williamson, James; 1: 438, 781; [Hagood's] Green, P.; Larcomb, Oliver; Stuart; Swinton; Williams, J.

15. CSW, Reel No. 90, D-268–1863; UDC *Recollections*, 6: 38, 42, 7: 205–206.

16. D. Augustus Dickert, *History of Kershaw's Brigade, with Complete Roll of Companies, Biographical Sketches, Incidents, Anecdotes, etc.* (Dayton, Ohio: Press of Morningside Bookshop, 1976), 385; UDC *Recollections*, 6: 20, 390–392, 8: 461–462, 9: 570–572.

17. UDC *Recollections*, 8: 59; CSW, Reel No. 77, W-[440]–1862, Reel No. 78, WD-W-734–1862; CSR, Reel No. 269, Card 1805, Reel No. 277, Card 1875; Wyckoff, *History of the 2nd South Carolina Infantry*, 168; McArthur and Burton, *A Gentleman and an Officer*, 54 n. 112.

18. Edgar, *South Carolina*, 358, 360, 375. The figures in table 2.1 were extrapolated from the "Total by Cause" statistics in Kirkland, *Broken Fortunes*, 411. The number 18,639 represents those from all states who died, serving in South Carolina units, but it does not include South Carolinians who joined units in other states. Only 5,601 entries included ages, presumably at the time of their death. This means that 54, or 0.96 percent, died under the age of seventeen. Applying the same percentage to the remaining 13038 entries without ages, suggests another 125 died, bringing the total of young deaths to 179.

19. CSW, Reel No. 131, J-30–1864.

20. Emmy E. Werner, *Reluctant Witnesses: Children's Voices from the Civil War* (Boulder, Colo.: Westview Press, 1998), 117; U.S. Congress, Senate, *South Carolina in 1876*; UDC *Recollections*, 8: 28–29; CSW, Reel No. 25, No. 10544–1862.

21. OR, ser. 1, vol. 6 [6]: 15; *Confederate Veteran*, Nashville, 29 (1921): 442; CSW, Reel No. 36, B-WD-1444–1862; CSR, Reel No. 267, Card 122; Robert S. Seigler, *A Guide to the Confederate Monuments in South Carolina: "Passing the Cup"* (Columbia, S.C.: SCDAH, 1997), 238–239. The Confederate name for Chickahominy was the Battle of Gaines's Mill.

22. Wyckoff, *History of the 2nd South Carolina Infantry*, 210.

23. CSW, Reel No. 17, No. 7922–1861, Reel No. 67, P-751-WD–1862, Reel No. 78, W-WD-734–1862; CSR, Reel No. 158, Card 1980, Reel No. 267, Card 1312; Reel No. 277, Card 75; Kirkland, *Dark Hours*, 360; Kirkland, *Broken Fortunes*, 361.

24. CSW Reel No. 93, G-146–1863, G-184–1863, Reel No. 127, G-111–1864; Kirkland, *Dark Hours*, 179. I have the service record for the father, but it is inaccurate. The service records for W. P. Goodman and W. W. Goodman are inconsistent with the materials in the letters. The letters refer to the son being in prison. See CSR, Reel No. 272, Card 726. It describes a W. P. Goodman, forty years old, in prison. Actually, the father and son were both named William P. Goodman. The son became known as Willie P.

25. Theodore Rosengarten, *Tombee: Portrait of a Cotton Planter with the Journal of Thomas B. Chaplin, 1822–1890* (New York: William Morrow, 1986), 39, 218, 223, 229–230; Kirkland, *Broken Fortunes*, 63 lists the death of Eugene T. Chaplin, "age 19, Beaufort District, PVT, Co. D, 5th South Carolina Volunteer Infantry." He died in prison. Also see UDC *Recollections*, 10: 54–55; CSW, Reel No. 62, M-1185-WD–1862; Kirkland, *Broken Fortunes*, 245; Kirkland, *Dark Hours*, 495; J. L. McCrorey Diary, July 18, 1864, SCL.

26. Mark Mayo Boatner, III, *The Civil War Dictionary*, rev. ed. (New York: David McKay, 1988), 407; W. Scott Poole, *South Carolina's Civil War: A Narrative History* (Macon, Ga.: Mercer University Press, 2005), 140–141; Leonne M. Hudson, "A Confederate Victory at Grahamville: Fighting at Honey Hill," *South Carolina Historical Magazine* 94 (January 1993): 19–33; Baker, *Cadets in Gray*, 29–30, 39, 56, 135, 139, 141–161, 164.

27. UDC *Recollections*, 8: 396–398.

28. Lawrence Whitaker Taylor Papers, SCL.

29. A. G. Magrath, State of South Carolina, Executive Department, to General Hardee, February 7, 1863, A.G. Magrath, State of South Carolina, Executive Department, to Theodore D. Wagener, February 9, 1865, Andrew Gordon Magrath Papers, SHS; reprint in Yorkville *Enquirer*, April 19, 1865; Butler, *Cadets in Gray*, 178; UDC, *South Carolina Women in the Confederacy*, 1:55–56.

30. Mary Frances Jane Pursley Papers, SCWRPL. William R. Erwin Jr., senior reference librarian at Duke University, introduced me to the Pursley Papers. Much of the

biographical material comes from the Card Catalogue Description and Genealogy, "Pursley Family of York," and the letters themselves. There are also J. W. Pursley Letters at SCL. In Population Schedules of the Eighth Census of the United States, 1860, South Carolina [Slave Schedules], Microcopy No. 653, see York District, p. 395, Household 488, which lists a William B. Pursley having a female slave, age 19. He probably was William Pursley's uncle. See also Family Chart, Pursley Papers.

31. S. A. Briant to Jane Pursley (JP), April 20, 1860, S. A. Briant to JP, June 8, 1860, Pursley Letters. Briant mentioned the number of marriages going on before the war, which implied that Jane could have married if she chose. For her weaving skills, see JP to James Warren Pursley (JWP), March 3, 1861. She wove for a neighbor, Mrs. Quinn.

32. JWP to JP, January 8, 19, 1862, JP to JWP, December 16, 1861, June 25, 1862, A. J. Pursley to JWP, May 25, 1862, Pursley Papers.

33. JWP to JP, January 19, June 18, 27, 1862, JP to JWP, June 25, 1862, Pursley Papers.

34. JP to JWP, July 3, 1862, E. J. Pursley to William Pursley, November 28, 1862, JWP to JP, December 20, 1863, Pursley Papers.

35. JP to JWP, April 4, 16, 1862, JP to William Pursley, January 7, 1863 on back side of Elizabeth Pursley to William Pursley, January 4, 1863, JWP to JP, December 11, 1863, Pursley Papers.

36. JP to JWP, April 16, May 16, 23, 1862, William Pursley to Elizabeth Pursley, January 3, 1863, JWP to JP, October 24, 1863, Pursley Papers.

37. JWP to JP May 12, November 1, 1862, March 15, April 5, 1863, February 26, 1864, Pursley Papers.

38. For background on Nathan Evans's brigade, see Stone, *Wandering to Glory;* Jason H. Silverman, Samuel N. Thomas Jr., and Beverly D. Evans, IV, *Shanks: The Life and Wars of General Nathan G. Evans, CSA* (New York: Da Capo Press, 2002); Card Catalogue Description, Pursley Papers; Boatner, *Civil War Dictionary*, 61, 247–249; Crist, *Papers of Jefferson Davis*, 7:428 n. 3; Kirkland, *Broken Fortunes*, xiv. In York District, 183.3 persons per thousand of its white male population died.

39. JWP to JP, August 10, 1862, January 18, 20, February 3, 8, 1864, JWP to William Pursley, January 13, 1864, Card Catalogue, Cards 5 and 8, Pursley Papers; CSR, Reel No. 301, Cards 11–12. Warren bought Jane a thimble.

40. JP to JWP, June 12, 25, July 13, 1862, December 27, 1864 [Jane first dated the letter December 24, but added more on December 27], Pursley Papers.

41. JWP to JP, September 27, 1862, Pursley Papers; CSR, Reel No. 301, Cards 14 and 15.

42. William Pursley to wife, December 26, 1862, William Pursley to E. J. Pursley, January 3, 1863, Elizabeth Pursley to William Pursley, January 4, 1863, JWP to JP, February 25, 1863, Pursley Papers.

43. JWP to JP, February 22, 1863, May 7, 1864, Pursley Papers. In May 1864, eggs were selling for six dollars a dozen.

44. JWP to JP, May 5, June 1863, April 28, 1864, Card Catalogue, Cards 10–15, Pursley Papers.

45. JWP to JP, August 10, September 18, 1864, January 30, March 3, 1865, M. E. James to JWP, July [8?], 1866, Card Catalogue, Cards 15–16, Pursley Papers; CSR, Reel No. 301, Cards 13 and 19.

Chapter 3. Childrearing

1. *Confederate Baptist*, Columbia, July 22, 1863, and January 20, 1864; Yorkville *Enquirer*, July 29, 1863.

2. William C. Davis, *Jefferson Davis: The Man and His Hour* (New York: Harper-Collins, 1991), 62. Davis used this quotation as the title for chapter 4. For the original source, see Haskell M. Monroe Jr. and James T. McIntosh, eds., *The Papers of Jefferson*

Davis (Baton Rouge: Louisiana State University Press, 1971), 1:345. See *Songs of Love and Liberty Compiled by a North Carolina Lady* (Raleigh, N.C.: Branson and Farrar, 1864). Dreams have been a rich source of analysis. See Jean E. Friedman, *The Enclosed Garden: Women and Community in the Evangelical South, 1830–1890* (Chapel Hill: University of North Carolina Press, 1985), xiv, 40, 44–46, 49–51, and James Marten, "Fatherhood in the Confederacy: Southern Soldiers and Their Children," *Journal of Southern History* 63 (May 1997): 269–292. See J[esse] W[alton] Reid, *History of the Fourth Regiment of S.C. Volunteers, from the Commencement of the War Until Lee's Surrender* (Greenville, S.C.: Jesse Walton Reid, 1892), 46–47.

3. McArthur and Burton, *A Gentleman and an Officer*, 155–159; Theodore Honour to wife, May 24, 1862, Theodore A. Honour Papers, SCL.

4. Theodore Honour to wife, September 8, 1863, Honour Papers; Barr and Barr, *Confederate War Correspondence*, 61; Jones, *Enlisted for the War*, 190–191; John Cumming to Carrie [wife], June 6, 1864, John Cumming Papers, SCWRPL; Harris Journals, February 21, 1863.

5. Alonzo A. Vanderford (AAV) to Cynthia (CV), April 25, 1863; July 22, 1863; September 12, 1863; October 7, 1863; November 1, 1863; December 9, 1863; January 2, 1864; Alonzo Adams Vanderford Papers, 1853–1868, SCL.

6. Theodore Honour to Becky, September 5, 18, 23, 1862; August 24, 1863; Honour Papers.

7. Barr and Barr, *Confederate War Correspondence*, 12, 70, 166; Jones, *Enlisted for the War*, 5, 53; Alfred Doby to Mother, March 22, 1862, Alfred Doby to Elisabeth [English] Doby [wife], February 14, March 3, May 1, 18, 1862, Means-English-Doby Families Papers, SCL.

8. Alfred Doby to Elisabeth Doby, February 22, 26, August 24, 1862, Sarah A. Kennedy to Alfred Doby, October 5, 1862, Alfred Doby to wife, December 4, 1862, Biographical Information, Means-English-Doby Families Papers.

9. Theodore Honour to Becky, September 19, 1863, Honour Papers.

10. A. C. Haskell to Ma, June 20, 1863, Alexander Cheves Haskell Papers, SHS. Haskell referred to the infant for an extended period of time as "Baby." See W. J. Box to Margaret Box, January 4, 1863, Box Family Papers, SCL; Harris Journals, July 2, 1861, October 24, 1862.

11. Barr and Barr, *Confederate War Correspondence*, 103; Theodore Honour to Becky, November 7, 1862, Honour Papers. Theodore might have been referring to his older brother who also bore the patriarch's name John Henry Honour. See Boinest Journals, June 8, 1863, in Thaddeus Street Boinest Letters and Journals, SCL; Chesnut, *Mary Chesnut's Civil War*, 280.

12. Sally G. McMillen, *Motherhood in the Old South: Pregnancy, Childbirth, and Infant Rearing* (Baton Rouge: Louisiana State University Press, 1990), 151; Theodore Honour to wife, August 21, 1862, Honour Papers; Donie [Elijah Brown] to Mollie [wife], June 1, 1864, Elijah Webb Brown Papers, 1856–1964, CSC; Barr and Barr, *Confederate War Correspondence*, 166; CV to AAV, January 15, 1864, AAV to CV, February 10, 1864, Vanderford Papers; Frances Box to W. J. Box, May 20, 1862, Box Family Papers.

13. Yorkville *Enquirer*, December 23, 1863; Harris Journals, December 25, 1861, and March 15, 1863; Cindy Dell Clark, "Holidays," in Clement and Reinier, *Boyhood in America*, 1:337–341; Charleston *Daily Courier*, March 23, 1864.

14. Harris Journals, January 30 and April 18, 1862; Dodo [Elijah Brown] to Mollie, April 20, 1862, Elijah Brown Papers.

15. Chesnut, *Mary Chesnut's Civil War*, 245–246, 488–489.

16. Mintz, *Huck's Raft*, 3; Yorkville *Enquirer*, February 28, 1861; March 14, 1861; October 21, 1863; Roblyn Warren, "Discipline," in Clement and Reinier, *Boyhood in America*, 1:201–204.

17. Barr and Barr, *Confederate War Correspondence*, 150.

18. UDC *Recollections*, 8: 293–295; Drago, *Hurrah for Hampton*, 96–97, 122.

19. Diary of Benjamin Ryan Tillman, June 11, 1861, Benjamin Ryan Tillman Papers, 1849–1918, CSC; James F. Smith, "Gambling," in Clement and Reinier, *Boyhood in America*, 1:295–301; Bernard Mergen, "Games," in Clement and Reinier, *Boyhood in America*, 1:301–306; "A Boy's Memories of War Time and Other Times," 35.

20. Diary of Benjamin Ryan Tillman, April 20, 1861; "Journal of Artha Brailsford Wescoat, 1863–1864," ed. Mrs. Sterling Graydon, *South Carolina Historical Magazine* 55 (1954): 71–102; "A Boy's Memories of War Time and Other Times," 5–6; Illustrations, Note Books, Langdon Cheves, III Papers, SCHS. See Note Book One, 14, 18, 21, and Note Book Two, 1–14. The crayon drawings of Yankees retreating have no dates.

21. Theodore Honour to Becky, August 27, 1862, Honour Papers; Reid, *History of the Fourth Regiment*, 50; Harris Journals, June 22, 1863; UDC *Recollections*, 10: 16.

22. Mary [Dawkins] to Sister Kate, January 6, 1862, McLure Family Papers, SCL; Holmes, *Diary*, 426; Camden Archives and Museum, Camden, SC; UDC *Recollections*, 1: 494, 10: 113.

23. Harris Journals, December 18, 1859; June 28, 1860; November 9, 1860; December 16, 1860; February 8, 1862; November 2, 1862; November 14, 1864; "A Boy's Memories of War Time and Other Times," 14, 36. Billy Buttons was the name of David's horse when he courted Emily.

24. James M. McPherson, *Ordeal by Fire: The Civil War and Reconstruction* (New York: McGraw-Hill, 2001), 84, 214; Pauline DeCaradeuc Heyward, *A Confederate Lady Comes of Age: The Journal of Pauline DeCaradeuc Heyward, 1863–1868*, edited by Mary D. Robertson (Columbia: University of South Carolina Press, 1992), 17; Robert K. Ackerman, *Wade Hampton, III* (Columbia: University of South Carolina Press, 2007), chapter 3; John Cumming to Carrie, [May 1864?], Cumming Papers; Alexander C. Haskell to Lewis, November 3, 1863, Alexander Cheves Haskell Papers.

25. Harris Journals, March 21, 1862; Barr and Barr, *Confederate War Correspondence*, 7.

26. Charleston *Daily Courier*, October 16, 1861, September 4, 1862; McArthur and Burton, *A Gentleman and an Officer*, 54 n. 112, 258–259; Jones, *Enlisted for the War*, 69–71.

27. Charleston *Daily Courier*, January 14, 1864; Alexander C. Haskell to Lewis, October 27, 1863, Alexander Cheves Haskell Papers; Yorkville *Enquirer*, October 7, 1863.

28. Charleston *Daily Courier*, April 19, 1861; July 23, 1862; October 3, 1863; AAV to CV, August 9, 1863; March 6, 1864, Vanderford Papers; "Journal of Artha Brailsford Wescoat," 94.

29. *Camden Confederate*, August 2, 1862; Charleston *Daily Courier*, April 30, 1862, and April 2, 1863; Mary Elizabeth Massey, *Ersatz in the Confederacy: Shortages and Substitutes on the Southern Homefront* (Columbia: University of South Carolina Press, 1993), 121; Mark Pendergrast, *For God, Country, and Coca-Cola* (New York: Scribner's, 1993), 27.

30. Yorkville *Enquirer*, September 26, 1862.

31. Yorkville *Enquirer*, June 27, 1861, and July 10, 1862. The correspondent was probably William Washington East, coeditor of the newspaper and a graduate of Erskine College in Abbeville District. He enlisted in the Jasper Light Infantry and was wounded at the Battle of Chickahominy. The twenty-five-year-old soldier, catching a fever, died at his father's home in Laurens District. His widow, whom he had married on a furlough, was from Greenville. See *Confederate Baptist*, Columbia, February 26, 1863; April 22, 1863; November 23, 1864; January 4, 1865.

32. John Cumming to Carrie, March 18, 1863, John Cumming Papers; Holmes, *Diary*, 214.

33. Barr and Barr, *Confederate War Correspondence*, 8–12, 252–253.

34. Edmund L. Drago, *Initiative, Paternalism, and Race Relations: Charleston's Avery Normal Institute* (Athens: University of Georgia Press, 1990), 25. See Holmes, *Diary*, 63–64.

35. For helpful background information, see John F. Marszalek's introduction and "Frequently Mentioned Names" in Holmes, *Diary*.

Chapter 4. "Spilt Milk": Three Family Cameos

1. On Southern honor, see Bertram Wyatt-Brown, *Southern Honor: Ethics and Behavior in the Old South* (New York: Oxford University Press, 1983). All three men were competent managers, unlike planter William McLure, whose heart was not in the details of his large-scale operation. Fortunately, his wife Kate had amazing managerial skills and a flexibility that eluded her husband. See Joan E. Cashin, " 'Since the War Broke Out': The Marriage of Kate and William McLure," in Clinton and Silber, *Divided Houses*, 200–212.

The most subtle and convincing discussion of the impact of the war on the patriarchy is Donna Rebecca Dondes Krug, "The Folks Back Home: The Confederate Homefront during the Civil War" (PhD dissertation, University of California, Irvine, 1990), particularly xi, 14, 175, 229, 235–237, 274, 364–365, 399. The war initially reinforced the value of the patriarchy as men strove to fulfill their roles as protectors of their families. As the war ground on for four years, the resources of local communities were drained, the Confederate government failed to provide the necessary support, and soldiers found themselves unable to fulfill the promise inherent in their Code of Honor. The war, consequently, weakened the patriarchy. However, the ideal prevailed as the men, women, and children of the South tried to put their society back together after the war. Thus, the gender crisis went into remission.

2. Harris, *Piedmont Farmer*, introduction; Racine, "Emily Lyles Harris," 387.

3. Harris, *Piedmont Farmer*, introduction; Harris Journals, November 8, 1864.

4. Harris Journals, November 24, 1862; December 14, 1862; January 28, 1863.

5. Ibid., May 20 and 24, 1864; October 1, 1864; November 18, 1864; December 16 and 30, 1864.

6. Ibid., October 28, 1864; December 14, 1864.

7. Ibid., November 10, 1864. For a more subtle analysis of Emily's mental state, see Racine, "Emily Lyles Harris." In *Piedmont Farmer*, 19, Racine notes that a child probably made the pencil entries. For examples of this, see February 4 and 21, 1865.

8. Harris Journals, June 30, 1863; November 18, 1864; Racine, "Emily Lyles Harris," 393–394, 397; Harris, *Piedmont Farmer*, 17–19.

9. The SCL card catalogue description of the Cumming papers does not note where he came from. The letters themselves mention the main depot at Ridgeville, South Carolina, where Carrie needed to go to pay the taxes. The 1860 census lists the family in St. George, Colleton District. In the Population Schedules of the Eighth Census of the United States, 1860, South Carolina, Microcopy No. 653, see Colleton-Darlington Districts, p. 328. The letters mention three children: Alice, Geneva, and Mitty. I could not find Cumming in the Slave Schedules of the 1860 census. The letters mention the slaves Lewis, Jim, Bob, Joe, Ned, and Rosey.

10. John Cumming to Carrie, March 4 and 18, 1863; April 17 and 19, 1863; May 26, 1863; June 17, 19, and 24, 1863; July 19, 1863, Cumming Papers.

11. John Cumming to Carrie, August 26, 1863; September 7 and 10, 1863, Cumming Papers.

12. John Cumming to Carrie, May 21 and 26, 1864, Cumming Papers.

13. John Cumming to Carrie, May 31, 1864, Cumming Papers.

14. See SCL card catalogue description of Vanderford Papers and Certificate of Commission, dated January 5, 1856, Vanderford Papers.

15. AAV to CV, February 2, 1862; May 28 and 31, 1863; January 13, 1864; CV to AAV, January 15, 1864, Vanderford Papers.

16. AAV to CV, July 5, 1858; July 6, 1863; August 26 and 31, 1863; October 26, 1863; November 1, 1863; December 17, 1863, Vanderford Papers. Vanderford had visited Charleston before the war to attend the ceremony of the laying of the cornerstone of the Calhoun monument. He was familiar with the city and its people.

17. AAV to CV, January 28, 1863; May 3, 28, and 31, 1863; July 12, 15, and 19, 1863; January 31, 1864; February 2, 1864, Vanderford Papers.

18. AAV to CV, August 16, 1863; September 6, 12, and 20, 1863; November 1, 1863; December 20 and 29, 1863; January 5, 1864, Vanderford Papers.

19. AAV to CV, February 2, 1862; November 9, 1862; July 9, 1863; September 20 and 22, 1863, Vanderford Papers.

20. AAV to CV, May 28, 1863; August 31, 1863; September 21 and 22, 1863; October 14, 1863, Vanderford Papers.

21. AAV to CV, February 2 and 10, 1864; April 10, 1864; May 31, 1864; June 4, 1864, Vanderford Papers.

22. AAV to CV, June 20, 1864; CV to AAV, June 20, 1864, Vanderford Papers.

23. N. S. I. Reid to Mrs. Alonzo Vanderford, June 24, 1864; July 21 and 30, 1864; AAV to CV, July 8 and 17, 1864; CV to AAV, July 11 and 22, 1864; S. L. Peltier to Dear Sir, July 24, 1864, handwritten note, August 3, 1864, Vanderford Papers.

Chapter 5. Education and Nation Building

1. Mary Elizabeth Massey, *Bonnet Brigades: American Women and the Civil War* (New York: Knopf, 1966), chapter 6.

2. John Thackston, "Primary and Secondary Education in South Carolina from 1780 to 1860" (PhD dissertation, New York University Graduate Schools, 1908), chapter 5; Jane Turner Censer, *North Carolina Planters and Their Children, 1800–1860* (Baton Rouge: Louisiana State University Press, 1990), 56; Colleen Morse Elliott and Louise Armstrong Moxley, *The Tennessee Civil War Veterans Questionnaires* (Easley, S.C.: Silas Emmett Lucas Jr., 1985), 3:1033–1035, 1160; UDC *Recollections*, 8: 32–33; Thomas H. Pope, *The History of Newberry County, South Carolina* (Columbia: University of South Carolina Press, 1992), 2:173; Laylon Wayne Jordan, "Education for Community: C. G. Memminger and the Origination of Common Schools in Antebellum Charleston," *South Carolina Historical Magazine* 83 (1982): 99–115.

3. OR, ser. 2, vol. 2: 161–162, ser. 4, vol. 1 [125]: 1081, vol. 3 [137]: 179, 1102; Yorkville *Enquirer*, January 6, 1864; Pope, *History of Newberry County*, 2: 173; Jordan, "Education for Community," 108.

4. *Camden Confederate*, December 20, 1861; January 3, 1862; Charleston *Daily Courier*, November 16, 1863.

5. Hull, *Boy Soldiers of the Confederacy*, 170–171; Yorkville *Enquirer*, May 20, 1863; March 2, 1864; *Confederate Baptist*, Columbia, December 9, 1863; February 3, 1864; Boinest Journals, September 7, 1864; Charleston *Daily Courier*, July 4, 1865.

6. Harris Journals, June 14, 1861; October 12, 1861; January 14, 26, and 30, 1862; February 3, 1862.

7. Harris Journals, March 10 and 21, 1862; August 6, 1862; April 25, 1862; December 28 and 30, 1863; January 18, 1864; March 10, 1864; June 23, 1864; November 25, 1864.

8. Harris Journals, November 21, 1864; March 24, 1865; July 24, 1865.

9. Reid, *History of the Fourth Regiment*, 65, 72–73, 120–123, 131, 134.

10. Between October 1861 and May 1864, sixteen South Carolina petitions reached the various Confederate secretaries of war. Most came from the Upcountry. On December 23, 1864, the South Carolina legislature gave the governor the right to grant exemptions and details. Eight teachers sought relief. Six came from the Lowcountry. Of the

eight, six received details, exemptions, or delays. See CSW, Reel No. 132, L-84–1864, Reel 13, No. 6838 and No. 7070.

11. CSW, Reel No. 113, T-51–1863, Reel No. 91, F-103–1863, F-117, 1863; Kirkland, *Broken Fortunes*, 205.

12. Due West Female College, February 1, 1865, Blythwood Female Academy, Fairfield District, February 3, 1865, Petitions for Exemption, 1864–1865, Administrative Records, Adjutant General, SCDAH.

13. CSW, Reel No. 89, D-197–1863, Reel No. 108, R-171–1863, Reel No. 101, M-11, 1863, Petition dated 24 December 1862, Reel No. 120, B-409, 1864, Reel No. 132, L-84–1864.

14. Petitions for Exemption; *South Carolina: The WPA Guide to the Palmetto State* (Columbia: University of South Carolina Press, 1988), 316–317.

15. Yorkville *Enquirer*, February 21, 1861; July 4, 1861; June 3, 1863; Schivelbusch, *Culture of Defeat*, 54–55.

16. J[ames] H[arold] Easterby, *A History of the College of Charleston* (Charleston, S.C.: College of Charleston, 1935), 146–149; Daniel W. Hollis, *University of South Carolina* (Columbia: University of South Carolina Press, 1951), 1:212–224; Yorkville *Enquirer*, April 5, 1865.

17. Holmes, *Diary*, 72; Letter of Reference, signed by John R. Watts and E. G. Simpson, September 5, 1862, W. W. Parker [?] to Miss Pelot, August 29, 1862, Lalla Pelot Papers, SCWRPL; J. L. Kennedy to Mrs. J. E. Hagood, January 12, 1863, James Earle Hagood Papers, SCL; Charleston *Daily Courier*, December 8, 1862.

18. Sara Gossett Crigler (Mrs. Henry Towles), "Education for Girls and Women in South Carolina prior to 1890 with Related Miscellanea," SCL; Edgefield Female Institute, Circular Letter, SCL; William F. Nance to his sisters, January 20, 1859, James Drayton Nance Letters, SCL; Yorkville *Enquirer*, May 3, 1865; Steven M. Stowe, "The Not-So-Cloistered Academy: Elite Women's Education and Family Feeling in the Old South," in Walter J. Fraser, R. Frank Saunders Jr., and Jon L. Wakelyn, *The Web of Southern Social Relations: Women, Family, and Education* (Athens: University of Georgia Press, 1985), 90–106; Judith T. Bainbridge, "'A Nursery of Knowledge': The Greenville Female Academy, 1819–1854," *South Carolina Historical Magazine* 99 (1998): 6–33. The concept of the metaphorical garden comes from Maynes, Soland, and Benninghaus, *Secret Gardens*; see the excellent introduction.

19. Poole, *South Carolina's Civil War*, 152–153; David B. Chesebrough, "'There Goes Your Damned Gospel Shop!' The Churches and Clergy as Victims of Sherman's March Through South Carolina," *South Carolina Historical Magazine* 92 (January 1991): 15–33; Yorkville *Enquirer*, February 1, 1865; May 3, 1865.

20. Holmes, *Diary*, 315–317, 349.

21. Ibid. 332–333, 336–337, 340–341, 378.

22. *Confederate Baptist*, Columbia, August, 31, 1864.

23. Ibid., July 22, 1863; December 7, 1864; Yorkville *Enquirer*, May 11, 1864.

24. C. G. Memminger to Rev. Whitefoord Smith, October 5, 1861, Whitefoord Smith Papers, SCWRPL; Henry Woodbury Moore and James Washington Moore, *"Chained to Virginia While Carolina Bleeds": The Civil War Correspondence of Henry Woodbury Moore and James Washington Moore*, ed. Henry Woodbury Moore (Walterboro, S.C.: Henry Woodbury Moore, 1996), 2, 66–68; James R. Hagood, "Memoirs of the First S.C. Regiment of Volunteer Infantry in the Confederate War for Independence," foreword, 31, James R. Hagood Papers, SCL; Rubin, *Shattered Nation*, 101. In making a case for a viable Confederate nationalism, Rubin argued that "slavery and white supremacy tied the disparate strands of Confederate identity—race, honor, religion—together."

25. CSW, Reel No. 8, #3744, and the introduction to this book, particularly endnote 9. Ford's critique of the Upcountry and secession is compelling.

26. Holmes, *Diary*, 388, 390–392, 400–412, 417–419.

27. Ibid., 186–187; Chesnut, *Mary Chesnut's Civil War*, 394; Charleston *Daily Courier*, December 6, 1862.

28. Theodore Honour to wife, Becky, August 27, 1862, Honour Papers; John Cumming to Carrie, September 8, 1863, Cumming Papers; William Pursley to wife, September 14, 1862, Pursley Papers; Yorkville *Enquirer*, March 18, 1863.

29. William Wylie to his sister, January 2, 1862, Gaston-Strait, Wylie-Baskin Families Papers; *Confederate Baptist*, Columbia, November 5 and 12, 1862; February 26, 1863; May 20, 1863; December 2, 1863.

30. Charleston *Daily Courier*, May 15, 1861; December 7, 1861; *Confederate Baptist*, Columbia, December 14, 1864; Yorkville *Enquirer*, February 1, 1865.

31. Kenneth Moore Startup, *Root of All Evil: The Protestant Clergy and the Economic Mind of the Old South* (Athens: University of Georgia Press, 1997), particularly the epilogue; J. William Jones, *Christ in the Camp, or Religion in the Confederate Army* (Atlanta: Martin and Hoyt Co., 1887), 267; Charleston *Daily Courier*, June 7, 1862; *Confederate Baptist*, Columbia, November 18, 1862; April 8, 1863; July 1, 1863; August 5 and 12, 1863; July 6 and 20, 1864; January 25, 1865; Theodore Honour to Becky, July 26, 1863, Honour Papers; Barr and Barr, *Confederate War Correspondence*, 131.

32. Charleston *Daily Courier*, November 2, 1862; April 20, 1863; February 19, 1864; Yorkville *Enquirer*, March 11, 1863; Chesnut, *Mary Chesnut's Civil War*, 615; Louis P. Towles, ed., *A World Turned Upside Down: The Palmers of South Santee, 1818–1881* (Columbia: University of South Carolina Press, 1996), 364–367; *Confederate Baptist*, Columbia, September 7, 1864; October 5, 1864.

33. Charles E. Leverett, *The Southern Confederacy Arithmetic for Common Schools and Academies with a Practical System of Book-keeping by Single Entry* (Augusta, Ga.: J. T. Patterson and Co., 1864), 122, 151, 193. For the books used in South Carolina, see Snowden, *South Carolina School Books*, 14–15.

34. Yorkville *Enquirer*, February 28, 1861; March 21 and 28, 1861; May 21, 1861; June 27, 1861.

35. M. B. Moore, *The Geographical Reader for the Dixie Children* (Raleigh, N.C.: Branson, Farrar and Co., 1863), 20–21.

36. *Confederate Baptist*, Columbia, October 1, 1862; December 10, 1862; January 14, 1863; July 1, 1863; December 16, 1863.

37. Ibid. January 7, 1863.

38. Ibid., May 6, 1863; June 3 and 10, 1863.

39. Ibid., June 3, 1863; July 22, 1863.

40. Ibid., November 11, 1863; April 13, 1864. For Victorian culture and gender, see Peter Bardaglio, "The Children of Jubilee: African American Childhood in Wartime," in Clinton and Sibler, *Divided Houses*, 228, and Carol Bleser, ed., *In Joy and in Sorrow: Women, Family, and Marriage in the Victorian South, 1830–1900* (New York: Oxford University Press, 1991).

Chapter 6. "Something for the Girls": Marriage Customs and Girlhood

1. Yorkville *Enquirer*, April 13, 1864; March 23, 1865.

2. Chesnut, *Mary Chesnut's Civil War*, 28, 32–33, 47.

3. Orville Vernon Burton, *In My Father's House Are Many Mansions: Family and Community in Edgefield, South Carolina* (Chapel Hill: University of North Carolina Press, 1985), 118–119; Censer, *North Carolina Planters*, 91, table 3. Censer's study of the marriages of planter daughters in North Carolina showed that most married between nineteen and twenty-five years of age. Thirty percent married between twenty-one and twenty-two. Maynes, Soland, and Benninghaus, *Secret Gardens*, offers a valuable and innovative discussion of childhood. This book expands on Mintz's insights. Friedman developed the garden metaphor in *Enclosed Garden*.

4. Holmes, *Diary*, 54, 217, 240; Sallie D. McDowall Books, SHS; UDC *Recollections*, 9: 120.

5. Chesnut, *Mary Chesnut's Civil War*, 565.

6. Diaries, March 9, 1865, Clara Victoria (Dargan) Maclean Papers, SCWRPL; Smith, Smith, and Childs, *Mason Smith Family Letters*, 19.

7. Smith, Smith, and Childs, *Mason Smith Family Letters*, 21; Holmes, *Diary*, 217, 240.

8. Charleston *Daily Courier*, January 1, 1864; Massey, *Bonnet Brigades*, 258–259; Holmes, *Diary*, 362; Baptist Church, Anderson, S.C., Big Creek Minutes, 1801–1936, March 5, 1864, SCL; "Journal of Artha Brailsford Wescoat," 76.

9. *Confederate Baptist*, Columbia, April 8, 1863. For a discussion of fashionable mourning wear for women, see Faust, *Republic of Suffering*, 147–154.

10. Yorkville *Enquirer*, February 21, 1861; July 27, 1864; Faust, *Mothers of Invention*, 226; Chesnut, *Mary Chesnut's Civil War*, 282; Holmes, *Diary*, 248; UDC *South Carolina Women*, 1:174–175, 2:173.

11. *Confederate Baptist*, Columbia, September 23, 1863; Yorkville *Enquirer*, May 11, 1864; Theodore Honour to Becky, April 18, 1864, Letter Book, 305–307, Gerard-Honour Papers, SCHS.

12. Yorkville *Enquirer*, December 23, 1863; Massey, *Ersatz in the Confederacy*, 96; *Confederate Baptist*, Columbia, October 5, 1864.

13. Jenkins, *Climbing Up to Glory*, 62–65; Yorkville *Enquirer*, April 20, 1864; Edward Ball, *Slaves in the Family* (New York: Ballantine, 1999), 271–294; John Hammond Moore, "Getting Uncle Sam's Dollars: South Carolinians and the Southern Claims Commission, 1871–1880," *South Carolina Historical Magazine* 82 (July 1981): 253; John William De Forest, *A Union Officer in the Reconstruction*, ed. James H. Croushore and Davie Morris Potter (New Haven: Yale University Press, 1948), 138. During World War I, Edwin A. Harleston, the grandson of Kate Wilson and William Harleston, became president of the Charleston chapter of the National Association for the Advancement of Colored People (NAACP).

14. "Journal of Artha Brailsford Wescoat," 91; Tute (L. A. Syme) to Richard Jacques, November 18, 1863, Richard E. Jacques Papers, SCWRPL; Sallie Lawton to J. C. Willingham, June 13, 1864, Willingham-Lawton Families Papers, SCL; Alice Boozer (Mrs. Simon P.) Letters, SCL; Yorkville *Enquirer*, September 28, 1864. Trousseau included the wedding dress and other personal attire for the bride.

15. CSW, Reel No. 121, B-595–1864, NA; Kirkland, *Dark Hours*, 177.

16. Ibid.

17. Holmes, *Diary*, 224, 227; Varina Howell Davis, *Jefferson Davis, Ex-President of the Confederate States of America: A Memoir by His Wife* (New York: Belford Co., 1890), 2:326, as cited in Crist, *Papers of Jefferson Davis*, 8:318.

18. [?] to Fannie Aiton, March 6, 1864, [Thomas Aiton?] to sister, April 7, 1863, Thomas Aiton Papers, SCL; Barr and Barr, *Confederate War Correspondence*, 65; J. Nance to Laura, January 22, 1864, Nance Letters; James Conner, *Letters of General James Conner, C.S.A.* (Columbia, S.C.: R. L. Bryan Co., 1950), 123–134; Kirkland, *Broken Fortunes*, 411; Charleston *Daily Courier* as cited in the Yorkville *Enquirer*, June 10, 1863.

19. Krug, "The Folks Back Home," 388: Belle Cory to JP, October 6, 1877, Pursley Papers; Moore, *Southern Homefront*, 193.

20. Chapin, *Fitz-Hugh St. Clair*, 86–87; Brother to Sister (Mrs. A. E. Doby), January 9, 1862, Means-English-Doby Families Papers; UDC *Recollections*, 7: 189–191; South Carolina Confederate Relic Room and Military Museum, Columbia, S.C., Confederate quilt, Item No. 347. The day before his wedding, the groom had to drill for emergency purposes a company of old men and boys, who included the bridesmaids' escorts.

21. Drew Gilpin Faust, "Altars of Sacrifice: Confederate Women and the Narratives of War," in Clinton and Silber, *Divided House*, 192; Catherine T. Brown, August 6, 1869, Admissions, 1828–1876, and Physician's Records, 1860–1874, South Carolina Lunatic Asylum, South Carolina Department of Mental Health, SCDAH; Yorkville *Enquirer*, April 1, 1863.

22. Alice Boozer Letters; Brian Craig Miller, "Reconstructing Manhood: Women and the Experience of Confederate Amputees," paper, Southern Historical Association, Memphis, November 4, 2004; UDC *Recollections*, 10: 89.

23. Conner, *Letters of General James Conner*, 168–169; Holmes, *Diary*, 460, 463; Charleston *Daily Courier*, October 21, 1865; Alice Boozer Letters; Moore, *Southern Homefront*, 236; Belle Cory to JP, October 6, 1877, Pursley Papers.

24. Diaries, January 27, 1862; March 23, 1863; October 11, 1865, Maclean Papers.

25. Dick Simpson and Tally Simpson, *"Far, Far from Home": The Wartime Letters of Dick and Tally Simpson, Third South Carolina Volunteers*, ed. Guy R. Everson and Edward H. Simpson Jr. (New York: Oxford University Press, 1994), 215–218; Friedman, *Enclosed Garden*, 52. Friedman's descriptions of women's dreams as being "consisted of struggles of the center of their being" also applied to men.

26. Simpson and Simpson, *"Far, Far from Home,"* 107–108, 184–186, 264, 271, 283–289.

27. JWP to JP, [June 1863], Pursley Papers.

Chapter 7. "Going Up the Spout":
Converging Defeat on the Battlefield and Home Front

1. Mintz, *Huck's Raft*, 131.

2. The first systematic attempt to gauge the symbiotic relationship between the home front and battlefield was Albert Burton Moore's *Conscription and Conflict*, particularly xiv–xvii, 54, 62, 79–80, 111, 113, 158, 303, 355–356. Writing in the aftermath of World War I and a successful draft in America, Moore laid much of the blame for the South's defeat on its inefficient and porous conscription system; too many men remained out of the battlefield. The historian's emphasis was on policy. Krug's, "The Folks Back Home" dramatically sheds light on the suffering of Confederate households and the devastating impact of the war on morale (see Appendix 1). But the study did not directly link events on the battlefield with what was happening at the home front. In *Southern Homefront*, John Hammond Moore, a World War II veteran, using the words of the participants themselves, did not focus on this symbiotic relationship but rather created a collage of voices that portrayed an iconoclastic view of the war efforts.

This chapter is a modest attempt to show on the regional level how the two fronts were connected in a symbiotic relationship. Efforts to shore up the army in the field had long-term repercussions on the home front. Depleting resources simultaneously hollowed out the Confederate war machine and the home front. By the summer of 1864, South Carolina was ready for collapse. Death provided the most devastating link. The Upcountry bore the brunt of the fatalities. Of the seventeen districts in the state, the ten with the highest soldier mortality rate (the number of soldier deaths per 1,000 white males in the district) came from the Upstate. Six were Upcountry districts: York, 183.8 per 1,000; Spartanburg, 137.7; Newberry, 133.3; Lancaster, 132.9; Abbeville, 124.1; Laurens, 123.1. Compare these with the mortality rate in the Lowcountry: Beaufort, 63.2; Charleston, 71; Georgetown, 73; Colleton, 78.9. For more details, see Kirkland, *Broken Fortunes*, 411–412.

3. Moore, *Southern Homefront*, chapter 3. Moore describes cotton cards as "paddles with metal teeth that were used to comb and clean cotton" (179). Even "destitute soldier families" used them. See Yorkville *Enquirer*, December 17, 1862; November 15, 1864; Harris Journals, January 1, 1862; Charleston *Daily Courier*, April 2, 1862; *Confederate Baptist*,

Columbia, March 11, 1863; Holmes, *Diary*, 378; Massey, *Bonnet Brigades*, 121. Massey cites yearly salaries in Virginia and North Carolina ranging between $400 and $600. Room and board were included.

4. CSW, Reel No. 39, C-WD-746–1862, C-WD-821–1862, Reel No. 62, M-WD-1359–1862.

5. CSW, Reel No. 52, H-WD-837–1862, Reel No. 82, B-315–1863, Reel No. 100, L-336–1863.

6. CSW, Reel No. 103, M-380–1863, M-532–1863, Reel No. 105, M-906–1863.

7. CSW, Reel No. 32, B-WD-430–1862, Reel No. 57, L-WD-361–1862, Reel No. 117, W-575–1863, Reel No. 145, W-293–1864.

8. Ford, *Origins of Southern Radicalism*, 45–56, table 2–1; CSW, Reel No. 38, C-WD-540–1862.

9. CSW, Reel No. 52, H-WD-1028–1862, Reel No. 49, G-WD-698–1862, Reel No. 47, F-WD-526–1862, Reel No. 105, N-56–1863, Reel No. 93, G-385–1863, Reel No. 92, F-265–1863.

10. CSW, Reel No. 67, P-WD-775–1862, Reel No. 101, M-75–1863, Reel No. 115, W-116–1863, Reel No. 135, M-279–1864.

11. Rable, *Fredericksburg*, 91–92; CSW, Reel No. 84, B-900–1863, Reel No. 131, J-61–1864.

12. CSW, Reel No. 127, G-38–1864, Reel No. 107, P-394–1863, Reel No. 137, N-45–1864, Reel No. 143, T-67–1864, Reel No. 126, F-66–1864.

13. CSW, Reel No. 51, H-WD-367–1862, Reel No. 51, H-WD-493–1862, Reel No. 77, W-WD-346–1862, Reel No. 30, A-WD-299–1862, Reel No. 77, H-WD-501–1862, Reel No. 63, M-1578–1862, Reel No. 109, R-257–1863; Moore, *Conscription and Conflict*, 73, 88, 144–145, 151.

14. Charles E. Cauthen, ed., *Journals of the South Carolina Executive Councils of 1861 and 1862* (Columbia, S.C.: SCDAH, 1956), 262–267. Issued on September 22, 1862, the Emancipation Proclamation declared that slaves in states still in rebellion on January 1, 1863, would be free. This gave the Confederacy at least three months to seek peace negotiations or risk the slaves' getting out of hand.

15. Wayne K. Durrill, *War of Another Kind: A Southern Community in the Great Rebellion* (New York: Oxford University Press, 1990), 69; Jenkins, *Climbing Up to Glory*, 32, 58–59; CSW, Reel No. 75, T-534–1862, T-WD- 551–1862.

16. CSW, Reel No. 75, T-537–1862, Reel No. 145, W-387–1864.

17. CSW, Reel No. 110, S-27–1863, Reel No. 102, M-105–1863, Reel No. 151, W-WD-43–1865.

18. CSW, Reel No. 93, G-247–1863.

19. See the introduction to this book, particularly endnote 9.

20. CSW, Reel No. 114, T-302–1863.

21. CSW, Reel No. 46, F-WD-220–1862, Reel No. 64, O-WD-121–1862. Reel No. 111, S-314–1863, Reel No. 107, P-209–1863.

22. CSW, Reel No. 62, M-WD-1042–1862, Reel No. 71, S-600–1862.

23. CSW, Reel No. 69, R-497–1862, Reel No. 141, S-273–1864.

24. OR, ser. 4, vol. 2 [126]: 408–409.

25. CSW, Reel No. 37, B-WD-1563–1862, Reel No. 107, P-378–1862.

26. CSW, Reel No. 64, O-100–1862, Reel No. 81, B-143–1863, Reel No. 35-B-WD-1077–1862.

27. CSW, Reel No. 22, 9808–1862, Reel No. 33, B-WD-660–1862.

28. CSW, Reel No. 33, B-WD-660–1862, Reel No. 91, F-61–1863; OR, ser. 4, vol. 3 [127]: 182, 1104–1106.

29. CSW, Reel No. 79, Z-12–1862, Reel No. 44, D-WD-554–1862, Reel No. 89, D-124–1863, Reel No. 141, S-202–1864.

30. Yorkville *Enquirer*, October 29, 1862; JWP to JP, December 11, 1863, Pursley Papers.

31. CSW, Reel No. 29, A-WD-148–1862, Reel No. 51, H-WD-384–1862; Moore, *Conscription and Conflict*, 121, 307.

32. CSW, Reel No. 129, H-213–1864, Reel No. 131, J-100–1864, Reel No. 140, R-214–1864.

33. CSW, Reel No. 84, B-789–1863, Reel No. 83, B-722–1863; Massey, *Ersatz in the Confederacy*, 24–26.

34. CSW, Reel No. 127, G-7–1864, Reel No. 144, W-74–1864, Reel No. 137, P-68–1864, Reel No. 122, C-116–1864.

35. CSW, Reel No. 52, H-WD-838–1862, Reel No. 124, C-444–1864, Reel No. 127, G-123–1864; Reports of the Soldiers Board of Relief, Newberry County [District], January 2, 1862, August 5, 1863, State and County Records, Soldiers Board of Relief, State Auditor Papers, Records of the Comptroller Board, SCDAH.

36. James Moore Goode, "The Rise of Manufacturing in South Carolina during the Civil War," 6, 12–13, SCL; Charleston *Daily Courier*, April 29, 1863; Harris Journals, April 11, 1863, October 1, 1864.

37. Chesnut, *Mary Chesnut's Civil War*, 317, 547; CSW, Reel No. 84, B-900–1863, Reel No. 135, M-205–1864.

38. CSW, Reel No. 118, A-208–1864, Reel No. 146, A-7–1865.

39. CSW, Reel No. 89, D-248–1863, Reel No. 141, S-266–1864, Reel No. 120, B-460–1864, Reel No. 138, P-135–1864, P-272–1864; OR, ser. 4, vol. 2 [126]: 769–775.

The extent of Confederate desertions remains elusive. In *The Confederate War* (Cambridge, Mass.: Harvard University Press, 1997), Gary W. Gallagher notes that most Confederate soldiers remained amazingly loyal until the Union army crushed them. On the other hand, in *More Damning Than Slaughter: Desertions in the Confederate Army* (Lincoln: University of Nebraska Press, 2005), Mark A. Weitz argues that disunity and division thoroughly permeated the Confederate society. Except in the mountain districts bordering North Carolina, the presence of a black majority in the rest of South Carolina probably discouraged mass desertions from its ranks. One conservative estimate for this state is roughly 3,600. See Ella Lonn, *Desertion During the Civil War* (Gloucester, Mass.: Peter Smith, 1966), 65, 231.

Early in the war, six hundred mountaineers, living in the northwest region of the state (designated as the "Dark Corner"), threatened to march on the Lowcountry to keep South Carolina in the Union. They eventually surrendered their arms, and many were forced to enlist in the Confederate army. In late 1861 and early 1862, Eliza Fludd of Charleston took refuge in the village of Gowansville, located in the upper part of Greenville District, which was part of the Dark Corner. Her children warned her not to live in the mountains with the uneducated and uncouth country people. However, they welcomed her, even supplying her with meat and vegetables. See De Forest, *A Union Officer in the Reconstruction*, 162; Eliza Fludd to Sister, Charleston, December 11, 1865, Eliza Fludd Papers, SCWRPL.

For a sophisticated analysis interweaving race and class on the local level, see Durrill, *War of Another Kind*. Washington County, North Carolina, was a hotbed of Unionist resistance.

40. CSW, Reel No. 81, B-220–1863, Reel No. 126, E-8–1864, Reel No. 137, O-83–1864; Kirkland, *Broken Fortunes*, 101.

41. CSW, Reel No. 96, H-464–1863, Reel No. 132, L-21–1864, L-69, 1864, Reel No. 136, M-413–1864; Moore, *Conscription and Conflict*, 31 n. 16, 61.

42. CSW, Reel No. 124, C-582–1864.

Chapter 8. Baptism by Fire

1. For more about the ironclad *Palmetto State*, see chapter 5. Greek fire was "an incendiary material . . . placed inside a special shell that was designated to explode over a target and start a fire." The Yankees used two types. See Stephen R. Wise, *Gate of Hell: Campaign for Charleston Harbor, 1863* (Columbia: University of South Carolina Press, 1994), 148.

2. "A Boy's Memories of War Time and Other Times," 35; CSW, Reel No. 138, P-273–1864.

3. Charleston *Mercury*, January 3, 1865; Grace Brown Elmore, *A Heritage of War: The Civil War Diary of Grace Brown Elmore, 1861–1868*, ed. Marli F. Weiner (Athens: University of Georgia Press, 1997), 88–96, 200–201 n. 5; UDC, *South Carolina Women in the Confederacy*, 1:243–247; Moore, *Southern Homefront*, 241–246; John Hammond Moore, *Columbia and Richland Country: A South Carolina Community, 1740–1990* (Columbia: University of South Carolina Press, 1993), 199.

4. *Confederate Baptist*, Columbia, January 18, 1865.

5. Marion Brunson Lucas, *Sherman and the Burning of Columbia* (College Station: Texas A&M University Press, 1976), 54, 70–71, 106, 128; Mrs. Emily Caroline Ellis Diary, February 16, 1865, pp. 24–25, SCL; George Ward Nichols, *The Story of the Great March: From the Diary of a Staff Officer* (New York: Harper and Brothers, 1865), 364; George F. Cram, *Soldiering with Sherman: The Civil War Letters of George F. Cram*, ed. Jennifer Cain Bohrnstedt (DeKalb: Northern Illinois University Press, 2000), 161–162. Charles Royster offered the most vivid and compelling account of the burning of Columbia in *The Destructive War: William Tecumseh Sherman, Stonewall Jackson, and the Americans* (New York: Knopf, 1991), chapter 1.

6. Joseph LeConte, *'Ware Sherman: A Journal of Three Months' Personal Experience in the Last Days of the Confederacy* (Berkeley: University of California Press, 1937), 140–142; Chapin, *Fitz-Hugh St. Clair*, chapter 12.

7. Chapin, *Fitz-Hugh St. Clair*, 87, 104–109.

8. August Conrad, *The Destruction of Columbia, S.C.*, translated from German by Wm. H. Pleasants (Roanoke, Va.: Stone Printing and Manufacturing Co., 1902), 18–22; Lucas, *Sherman and the Burning of Columbia*, 128; OR, ser. 1, vol. 53 [11]: 53.

9. Rable, *Civil Wars*, 172; Royster, *Destructive War*, 342.

10. J. S. Middleton, "Reminiscences, ca. 1880s," SCHS; Chesnut, *Mary Chesnut's Civil War*, 802.

11. Mrs. H. H. Simons Recollection, "The Burning of Columbia," SCL.

12. Notebook, February 1864, Sallie D. McDowall Books; Eliza Fludd to Mrs. Jolliffe, Charleston, September 25, 1865, Eliza Fludd to Sister, Charleston, December 11, 1865, Fludd Papers.

13. Smith, Smith, and Childs, *Mason Smith Family Letters*, 209–212; UDC *Recollections*, 7: 91–95; UDC, *South Carolina Women in the Confederacy*, 2: 163–164.

14. UDC, *South Carolina Women in the Confederacy*, 2: 145, 154–156, 163; UDC Recollections, 6: 86–87, 10: 17; Confederate Museum, Charleston, S.C., Item No. 501.

15. UDC *Recollections*, 9: 489–490, 10: 78–80; Sarah H. Bryce, *The Personal Experiences of Mrs. Campbell Bryce during the Burning of Columbia, South Carolina, by W. T. Sherman's Army, February 17, 1865* (Philadelphia: J. P. Lippincott Co., 1899), 33.

16. Winnsboro *Fairfield News and Herald*, ca. 1937; Grace B. Elmore Books.

17. John Cheesborough to wife, August 7, 1861, John Cheesborough Papers, SHS; Cauthen, *South Carolina Goes to War*, 137–139; Chesnut, *Mary Chesnut's Civil War*, 266; Walter J. Fraser, Jr., *Charleston! Charleston! The History of a Southern City* (Columbia: University of South Carolina Press, 1989), 253–255; Charleston *Daily Courier*, January 8,

9, 1862; *Camden Confederate*, December 20, 1861; Charleston Police Records, December 1861–March 1863, entry March 8, 1862, CLS.

18. Other planned depot centers were Greenville, Spartanburg, Anderson, Pickens, Pendleton, Hamburg, Chester, and York. See City of Charleston Commission Minute Books, 1862–1863, 6–7, 15, 32, 50–51, 59, Commission for the Removal of Negroes and Other Noncombatants from the City of Charleston, SCDAH; S. C. Roberts to sister, May 10, 1862, Woodruff Papers.

19. John Cheesborough to wife, August 2, 1862, John Cheesborough Papers; Conner, *Letters of General James Conner*, 76, 79, 94–95.

20. Burton, *Siege of Charleston*, 144, 163–177; Charleston *Daily Courier*, August 18, 1863.

21. OR, ser. 1, vol. 28, pt. 2 [47]: 57–61.

22. Wise, *Gate of Hell*, 148; Heyward, *Confederate Lady Comes of Age*, 22–23; OR, ser. 1, vol. 28, pt. 1 [46]: 682–684; Susan L. King, ed., *History and Records of the Charleston Orphan House, 1860–1899* (Columbia, S.C.: SCMAR, 1994), 1–5. See also George P. Rawick, ed., *The American Slave: A Composite Autobiography*, reprint, ser. 1, vol. 2, *South Carolina Narratives*, pts. 1 and 2; vol. 3, *South Carolina Narratives*, pts. 3 and 4 (Westport, Conn.: Greenwood, 1972), vol. 3, pt. 3: 214–216.

23. Burton, *Siege of Charleston*, 186, 200, 251–263; Charleston *Daily Courier*, March 11, 1864.

24. Burton, *Siege of Charleston*, 256; Porter, *Led On*, 146; OR, ser. 1, vol. 35, pt. 1 [65]: 43, pt. 2 [66]: 43, 131–312, 145, vol. 53 [111]: 105–106.

25. Charleston *Mercury*, June 9, 13, 1864; Charles Reagan Wilson, *Baptized in Blood: The Religion of the Lost Cause, 1865–1920* (Athens: University of Georgia Press, 1980), 51. The monument was a cenotaph.

26. Burton, *Siege of Charleston*, xvi; Theodore Honour to Becky, August 28, 1863, Honour Papers; Heyward, *Confederate Lady Comes of Age*, 26–27; UDC, *South Carolina Women in the Confederacy*, 1: 163; *New York Times*, February 22, 1865; Holmes, *Diary*, 396.

27. *New York Times*, March 18, 1865; Charleston *Daily Courier*, February 20, 1865; Burton, *Siege of Charleston*, 321; UDC, *South Carolina Women in the Confederacy*, 1:165–167; Board of Health Death Records, Charleston, vol. 21, October 20, 1861 to June 30, 1866, entries, February 12–25, 1865, CCL; Simkins and Woody, *South Carolina During Reconstruction*, 6; David Duncan Wallace, *South Carolina: A Short History, 1520–1948* (Columbia: University of South Carolina Press, 1984), 554. Initially Northern accounts blamed a Rebel soldier for entering the depot and igniting the gunpowder. This inaccurate report is an example of the kind of propaganda that comes out of the fog of war.

28. Reprint in Yorkville *Enquirer*, March 29, 1865. See also Yorkville *Enquirer*, April 12, 1865; Fraser, *Charleston*, 310 (Courtenay); Simkins and Woody, *South Carolina During Reconstruction*, 30; Charleston *Daily Courier*, May 2, 1865; King, *Charleston Orphan House, 1860–1899*, 1–5. Courtenay became one of Charleston's most successful mayors.

Chapter 9. Widows and Orphans

1. Yorkville *Enquirer*, May 11, 1864. On May 25, 1864 the newspaper reprinted an item on Jenkins from the Charleston *Daily Courier*. See Seigler, *Guide to Confederate Monuments*, 111, 120, 133, 159; Faust, *Republic of Suffering*, 154, 238, 242–243; Ladies Memorial Association, *Confederate Memorial Day at Charleston, S.C.: Reinterment of the Carolina Dead from Gettysburg* (Charleston, S.C.: William G. Maczyck, 1871), 1, 7.

2. *Confederate Baptist*, Columbia, May 6, 1863.

3. Charleston *Daily Courier*, July 12, 1862; April 29, 1863; May 8, 1863; Yorkville *Enquirer*, May 27, 1863; Towles, *A World Turned Upside Down*, 1023; Harris Journals, May 13, 1864.

4. *Confederate Baptist*, Columbia, June 3, 1863, September 14, 1864; Snowden, *South Carolina School Books*, 14–15; De Forest, *A Union Officer in the Reconstruction*, xxix–xxx; *Proceedings of the First and Second Annual Meetings of the Survivors' Association of the State of South Carolina and Oration of General John S. Preston, Delivered before the Association, November 10th, 1870* (Charleston, S.C.: Walker, Evans and Cogswell, 1870), 3–10.

5. Elise Doby to her mother (Mrs. Alfred Doby), December 6, 1867, Means-English-Doby Families Papers; CSW, Reel No. 77, W-367–1862.

6. Dickert, *History of Kershaw's Brigade*, 103; Chapin, *Fitz-Hugh St. Clair*, 100–101; circular, dated October 4, 1865, in Yorkville *Enquirer*, October 19, 1865. After the war, the Freedmen's Bureau allowed the apprenticing of black children under state laws as long as there was no distinction based on race. There has been no comprehensive study of white apprenticeship in South Carolina after the war.

7. Ruth Bordin, "Chapin, Sarah Flournoy," in John A. Garraty and Mark C. Carnes, eds., *American National Biography* (New York: Oxford University Press, 1999), 4:696–697; Anne King Gregorie, "Chapin, Sarah Flournoy," in Edward T. James, ed., *Notable American Women, 1607–1950: A Biographical Dictionary* (Cambridge, Mass.: Harvard University Press, 1971), 1:231–232.

8. Camden Orphan Society Records, SCL; Ladies' Benevolent Society for Orphan and Destitute Children, Columbia, Treasurer's Book, 1839–1936, and other collections filed under this nomenclature, SCL; King, *Charleston Orphan House, 1860–1899*, 1–5; Hebrew Orphan Society, Charleston, Records, SCL; Charleston *Daily Courier*, February 3, 1862; W. Martin Hope and Jason H. Silverman, *Relief and Recovery in Post–Civil War South Carolina: A Death by Inches* (Lewiston, N.Y.: Edwin Mellon Press, 1997), 112.

9. Susan L. King, "Children of the City: The First One Hundred Years of the Charleston Orphan House," MS, ca. November 2005, copy in author's possession, 14–15; Barbara L. Bellows, *Benevolence Among Slaveholders: Assisting the Poor in Charleston, 1670–1840* (Baton Rouge: Louisiana State University Press, 1993), chapter 5.

10. King, *Charleston Orphan House, 1860–1899*, 95. King's book offers an alphabetical list of the names of the orphans and brief summaries of their cases. I base my statistics on these data. The examples are from the same source. See King's excellent introduction.

11. Ibid., 127, 140.

12. Ibid., 10–11, 16.

13. Ibid., 10–11, 32–33.

14. Hope and Silverman, *Relief and Recovery*, 115–116, 119; Porter, *Led On*, chapter 26; Drago, *Initiative, Paternalism, and Race Relations*, 75. In 1891 Jenkins approached the city council for help in housing his orphans. Two years later the orphanage opened on Franklin Street.

15. Blanton, "The Life of Mary Amarinthia Snowden," 37: 7–11; Confederate College, Charleston, table of statistics, and postcard of Confederate College, SCL.

16. Charleston *Daily Courier*, April 16, 1866; Charleston Police Records, December 1861–March 1863, entry January 10, 1862, CLS; Bellows, *Benevolence Among Slaveholders*, chapter 3. This summary is based on Hope and Silverman, *Relief and Recovery*, 259–263.

17. South Carolina General Assembly, *An Act to Provide a Pension Fund for Confederate Veterans and Their Widows and to provide the Distribution thereof: An Act to provide for Pensions for Certain Faithful Negroes who were Engaged in the Service for the State in the War between the States* (Columbia: South Carolina General Assembly, 1923).

Chapter 10. Reconstruction and Redemption: The Civil War, Part II

1. See quotation in review of Tanner's *An Apology for African Methodism* in *Southern Presbyterian Review*, Columbia, S.C., 19 (April 1868): 305–312; Porter, *Led On*, 188.

2. Joel Williamson, *After Slavery: The Negro in South Carolina During Reconstruction, 1861–1877* (Hanover, N.H.: University Press of New England, 1990); Thomas Holt,

Black Over White: Negro Political Leadership in South Carolina During Reconstruction
(Champaign: University of Illinois Press, 1979), 1.

3. Porter, *Led On,* 230.

4. "Sunday School Literature—An Important Question," *Religious Herald,* April
12, 1863, as quoted in Sally G. McMillen, *To Raise Up the South: Sunday Schools in Black
and White Churches, 1865–1915* (Baton Rouge: Louisiana State University Press, 2001), 1;
Proceedings of the First and Second Annual Meetings of the Survivors' Association, 3–5;
Hampton as quoted in Richard Gray, *Writing the South: Ideas of an American Region*
(New York: Cambridge University Press, 1986), 76.

5. Edgar, *South Carolina,* 376, chapter 17, "The Civil War: Part II, 1865–1877."

6. John B. Patrick Diary, June 5, 1863, SCL; Smith, Smith, and Childs, *Mason Smith
Family Letters,* 52–53, 130–138, 280–281; W. Eric Emerson, *Sons of Privilege: The Charleston Light Dragoons in the Civil War* (Columbia: University of South Carolina Press,
2005), xv–xvi, 103–104.

7. Kirkland, *Broken Fortunes,* 411, Patrick J. McCawley, *Artificial Limbs for Confed-
erate Soldiers* (Columbia, S.C.: SCDAH, 1992), 9–40; Edgar, *South Carolina,* 644 n. 68;
Conner, *Letters of General James Conner,* 205–206; Eric T. Dean Jr., *Shook Over Hell:
Post-Traumatic Stress, Vietnam, and the Civil War* (Cambridge, Mass.: Harvard Univer-
sity Press, 1997), chapter 6. See also John T. Jackson, October 2, 1861, Admissions; James
Green, July 4, 1866, Physician's Records; Joseph D. Ferguson, no date; [Olin?] Festner,
February 18, 1868, Physician's Records, SCDMH.

8. Mary E. Eason, January 21, 1862, Admissions and Physician's Records; Harriet
Bibb, July 3, 1863, Admissions and Physician's Records; Ann Eliza Meyer, February 2,
1865, Admissions and Physician's Records; Martha Harben, March 28, 1864, Admissions
and Physician's Records; Martha J. Bird, February 20, 1866, Admissions and Physician's
Records, SCDMH.

9. Heyward, *Confederate Lady Comes of Age,* 76; Ellen Cooper Johnson Memoirs,
11, SCL.

10. Manson S. Jolly Papers, 1861–1865, CSC; UDC *Recollections,* 1: 452–453; Heyward,
Confederate Lady Comes of Age, 113; JWP to JP, December 24, 1862, Elizabeth Pursley to
husband, January 4, 1863, Pursley Papers. Confederate family folklore includes stories of
revenge with an undercurrent of anger, bitterness, and resentment for the war. Manson
Jolly's story brought not only vicarious pleasure but also release for these strong emotions. In March 1867 the body of George Heyward was found on a public road with a
shot through the head. Blacks were blamed for the assassination of the former Confederate officer. The economic hardships caused by the patriarch's death forced the family to
relocate to Savannah. Years later in Alabama an old veteran who had served under Captain Heyward confessed on his deathbed to the murder as revenge for a reprimand. In
modern times, this was fragging. Stories of invading Yankees ripping necessities from
whites and then doling these items to blacks justified one Confederate officer and his
men to take things they needed from blacks.

11. Hope and Silverman, *Relief and Recovery,* xi–xii, 12, 23, 34, chapter 1; Charleston
Daily News, May 8, 16, 1867; Poole, *Never Surrender,* 75; Simkins and Woody, *South Car-
olina During Reconstruction,* 163, Williamson, *After Slavery,* 381–392; Mark Wahlgren
Summers, *The Gilded Age, or, the Hazard of New Functions* (Upper Saddle River, N.J.:
Prentice Hall, 1997), 77; Lewis P. Jones, *South Carolina: A Synoptic History for Laymen,*
rev. ed. (Orangeburg, S.C.: Sandlapper, 1971), 199; Drago, *Initiative, Paternalism, and
Race Relations,* 79; Kyle S. Sinisi, *Sacred Debts: State Civil War Claims and American
Federalism, 1861–1880* (New York: Fordham University Press, 2003), 39–40.

12. Massey, *Bonnet Brigades,* 325; "An Account of the Experiences of the Family of
the Rev. and Mrs. Paul Trapier during and after the War between the States" by T. D.

(Mrs. Paul) Trapier, Paul Trapier Papers, SCAL; Simkins and Woody, *South Carolina During Reconstruction*, 18; Porter, *Led On*, 188, Rosengarten, *Tombee*, 25–36, 295; Blanton, "The Life of Mary Amarinthia Snowden," 7–11; Mary Elizabeth Massey, *Refugee Life in the Confederacy* (Baton Rouge: Louisiana State University Press, 1964), 275.

13. Chapin, *Fitz-Hugh St. Clair*, chapters 16–22.

14. C. Vann Woodward, *Origins of the New South, 1877–1913* (Baton Rouge: Louisiana State University Press, 1971), 19; Simkins and Woody, *South Carolina During Reconstruction*, 18; Pope, *History of Newberry County*, 2:30–31; "Journal of Artha Brailsford Wescoat," 71.

15. Towles, *A World Turned Upside Down*, 2, 622–624, 761, 992–993; Harriet Palmer, March 9, 1869, SCDMH; Elizabeth Buescher, "'I Must Have Something': Childhood, the Civil War and the Campbell R. Bryce Family," SCL.

16. Heyward, *Confederate Lady Comes of Age*, xviii, 5–6, 17, 82; Kirkland, *Broken Fortunes*, 90.

17. Heyward, *Confederate Lady Comes of Age*, chapter 11, prologue, epilogue; Kirkland, *Dark Hours*, 214. Pauline's father gave her $500 for her wedding outfit. Her wedding gown came from Baltimore. She had additional dresses made for her in Augusta. One was cut too short for her hoop.

18. Fludd Papers; Porter, *Led On*, 112–113; Anne Middleton Holmes, *The New York Ladies' Southern Relief Association, 1866–1867* (New York: Mary Mildred Sullivan Chapter, United Daughters of the Confederacy, 1926), 29; Charleston *Daily Courier*, September 19, 1865, May 14, 1887; *South Carolina Genealogies: Articles from The South Carolina Historical (and Genealogical) Magazine* (Spartanburg, S.C.: Reprint Co., 1983), 4:308; Ethel Trenholm Seabrook Nepveux, *George A. Trenholm, Financial Genius of the Confederacy: His Associates and His Ships That Ran the Blockade* (Anderson, S.C.: privately printed, 1999), 7: Ethel Trenholm Seabrook Nepveux, *George Alfred Trenholm: The Company That Went to War, 1861–1865* (Charleston, S.C.: Comprint, 1973), 4; Charleston County Death Records, 1821–1926, entries C. Trenholm, September 18, 1865 and Eliza Fludd, May 13, 1887, CCL. Circular Congregational Church Records, SCHS. My forthcoming monograph on Eliza Fludd gives more details and insight into her life.

19. As cited in Drago, *Hurrah for Hampton*, 17. Also see Simkins and Woody, *South Carolina During Reconstruction*, 19.

20. Richard Zuczek, *State of Rebellion: Reconstruction in South Carolina* (Columbia: University of South Carolina Press, 1996), 74; Allen W. Trelease, *White Terror: The Ku Klux Klan Conspiracy and Southern Reconstruction* (Baton Rouge: Louisiana State University Press, paperback, 1999), 363, 367; Lou Falkner Williams, *The Great South Carolina Ku Klux Klan Trials, 1871–1872* (Athens: University of Georgia Press, 1996), 2, 21 (map), 28, 32–39, 47, 74, 76–77, 105–106, 120. Williams offers a chilling account of the Klan's atrocities, especially on women and children.

21. Rawick, *American Slave*, vol. 2, pt. 1, 336, pt. 2, 46–47, vol. 3, pt. 3, 248–250, pt. 4, 215–217.

22. KKK Reports 5:1,866–1,868.

23. Simkins and Woody, *South Carolina During Reconstruction*, 459–460; Williams, *Great South Carolina Ku Klux Klan Trials*, 35, 62; KKK Reports 5:1,744–1,745. Jerry L. West, *The Reconstruction Ku Klux Klan in York County, South Carolina, 1865–1877* (Jefferson, N.C.: McFarland and Co., 2002) is the best account of the Klan in York.

24. KKK Reports 5:1,861–1,862.

25. KKK Reports 5:1,951–1,955. For Edward T. Avery, see Williams, *Great South Carolina Ku Klux Klan Trials*, 78, 95–100.

26. Williams, *Great South Carolina Ku Klux Klan Trials*, 1, 40–59, 63–66, 103–111; Trelease, *White Terror*, 403–408, West, *Reconstruction Ku Klux Klan*, ch. 7.

27. KKK Reports 5: 1,972–1,990; Williams, *Great South Carolina Ku Klux Klan Trials*, 93; West, *Reconstruction Ku Klux Klan*, appendixes 1 (Klan Constitution) and 6 (profile of those from York County sent to the federal penitentiary in Albany, New York). Those sentenced to the penitentiary seemed older.

28. KKK Reports 5:1983. For the argument that Klansmen were responding against challenges to their manhood, see Rubin, *Shattered Nation*, 171.

29. KKK Reports 5:1,985, 1,989–1,990.

30. Bond as cited in Williams, *Great South Carolina Ku Klux Klan Trials*, 116–117. See also West, *Reconstruction Ku Klux Klan*, 137, appendix 9.

31. Williams, *Great South Carolina Ku Klux Klan Trials*, 106–111, 121–125; West, *Reconstruction Ku Klux Klan*, 116–117.

32. Drago, *Hurrah for Hampton*, 1–28, 37; Simkins and Woody, *Reconstruction in South Carolina*, 474–513.

33. John S. Reynolds, *Reconstruction in South Carolina, 1865–1877* (New York: Negro Universities Press, 1969), 357–358; Drago, *Hurrah for Hampton*, 10; UDC *Recollections*, 1: 506–607; John B. Edmunds Jr., *Francis W. Pickens and the Politics of Destruction* (Chapel Hill: University of North Carolina Press, 1986), 140–141; W. W. Ball, *A Boy's Recollections of the Red Shirt Campaign of 1876 in South Carolina, Paper Read Before the Kosmos Club of Columbia, S.C., by W. W. Ball, January 21, 1911*, pamphlet (Columbia, S.C.: Kosmos Club, 1911), 8, 11; *Newberry Herald*, September 20, 1876.

34. See Drago, *Hurrah for Hampton*.

Chapter 11. The Last Phoenix: Conflicting Legacies, 1890–2007

1. Karen L. Cox, *Dixie's Daughters: The United Daughters of the Confederacy and the Preservation of Confederate Culture* (Gainesville: University Press of Florida, 2003), 1, 121, 134–135.

2. This section is based on Ronald D. Burnside, "Racism in the Administrations of Governor Cole Blease," in George C. Rogers Jr., ed., *Proceedings of the South Carolina Historical Association, 1964* (Columbia: South Carolina Historical Association, 1964), 43–57; David L. Carlton, *Mill and Town in South Carolina, 1880–1920* (Baton Rouge: Louisiana State University Press, 1982); Drago, *Initiative, Paternalism, and Race Relations*; Stephen Kantrowitz, *Ben Tillman and the Reconstruction of White Supremacy* (Chapel Hill: University of North Carolina Press, 2000); I. A. Newby, *Plain Folk in the New South: Social Change and Cultural Persistence, 1880–1915* (Baton Rouge: Louisiana State University Press, 1989); Poole, *Never Surrender*, 173; Francis Butler Simkins, *Pitchfork Ben Tillman: South Carolinian* (Baton Rouge: Louisiana State University Press, 1967); Joel Williamson, *The Crucible of Race: Black-White Relations in the American South Since Emancipation* (New York: Oxford University Press, 1984), 108–110, 428–429, chapter 4; Orville Vernon Burton, "The Black Squint of the Law: Racism in South Carolina," in David R. Chesnutt and Clyde N. Wilson, eds., *The Meaning of South Carolina History: Essays in Honor of George C. Rogers, Jr.* (Columbia: University of South Carolina Press, 1991), 161–185. See Mrs. Sallie [Sarah] F. Chapin, *Fitz-Hugh St. Clair*, reprint, 1873, autographed copy with MS presentation to Benjamin R. Tillman, SCL.

3. Burton, "Black Squint," 173.

4. Benjamin E. Mays, *Born to Rebel: An Autobiography* (Athens: University of Georgia Press, 1987), 1, 26, 243; Mamie Garvin Fields, with Karen Fields, *Lemon Swamp and Other Places: A Carolina Memoir* (New York: Free Press, 1983), 47–50; Burnside, "Racism in the Administrations of Governor Cole Blease." For a secondary account of the Phoenix Riot, see Kantrowitz, *Ben Tillman*, 257–258. According to John Hammond Moore, ed., *South Carolina Newspapers* (Columbia: University of South Carolina Press, 1988), 130, Greenwood County was formed in 1897 from sections of Abbeville and Edgefield counties. The life span of Racial Radicals Benjamin Tillman (1847–1918), Coleman Blease

(1868–1942), and their spiritual heir Strom Thurmond (1902–2003) covers a century and a half.

5. Cox, *Dixie's Daughters*, 14, 35–36, 39–41, 121, 134–140; David Goldfield, *Still Fighting the Civil War: The American South and Southern History* (Baton Rouge: Louisiana State University Press, 2002), 112; Mrs. Henry Davis Allen, ed., *Catechism on the History of the Confederate States of America, 1861–1865* (Richmond, Va.: UDC, 1954, reprint, 1990); *Confederate Veteran*, Nashville, vol. 23 (1915), masthead; 31 (1923): 193–194. See Cornelia Branch Stone, *U.D.C. for Children Arranged for the Veuve Jefferson Davis Chapter* (Galveston, Tex.: n.p., 1904). The author received valuable assistance from the Daughters Margaret Murdock and Brenda Latham at the UDC Archives in Richmond.

6. Lancaster *Ledger*, February 20, 1861–March 13, 1861; Charleston *Daily Courier*, July 16, 1861.

7. *Confederate Veteran*, Nashville, 28 (1920): 74; 35 (1927): 32; Cox, *Dixie's Daughters*, 138–139. The UDC Archives in Richmond has photocopies of some of the state catechisms. The 1954 version by Allen was reprinted in 1955–1957, 1972, 1974, 1984, 1987, and 1990. Another version, entitled *Catechism of the Confederate States of America, 1861–1865*, was published in 1999.

8. Allen, *Catechism* (1990); Cox, *Dixie's Daughters*, 14–15; *Confederate Veteran*, Nashville, 8 (1900): 90. For a sophisticated account of Winnie Davis, see Joan E. Cashin, *First Lady of the Confederacy: Varina Davis's Civil War* (Cambridge, Mass.: Harvard University Press, 2006).

9. "The State Reunion of South Carolina Volunteers, S.C., May 18–19, 1921," in Benjamin S. Williams Papers, SCWRPL; Address, ca. 1912 , by Mildred Lewis Rutherford, in Anna Louisa Salmond Papers, SCWRPL; Virginia L. Daily, ed., *A Sampler of Women's Studies Resources*, SCWRPL; Sarah H. Case, "The Historical Ideology of Mildred Lewis Rutherford: A Confederate Historian's New South Creed," *Journal of Southern History* 68 (August 2002): 599–628; Joan Marie Johnson, "Sisters of the South: Louisa and Mary Poppenheim and South Carolina Clubwomen," in *Proceedings of the South Carolina Historical Association, 1997* (Columbia: South Carolina Historical Association, 1998), 77–95; Cox, *Dixie's Daughters*, 39–41; *Confederate Veteran*, Nashville, 15 (1907): 154–155; 25 (1917): 282; 29 (1921): 397–398; 36 (1928): 354–355. See also Mildred Lewis Rutherford, *Address Delivered by Miss Mildred Lewis Rutherford, Historian-General, United Daughters of the Confederacy* (Washington, D.C., 1912).

10. *Confederate Veteran*, Nashville, 15 (1907) has a picture of the choir; debates in 15 (1907): 154–155, 344 and 17 (1909): 7, 11, 138, 268–269. For illustration of young women in Texas with toy rifles, see Cox, *Dixie's Daughters*, 92.

11. UDC, South Carolina Division, Black Oak Chapter Minute Books, 1900–1915, SCWRPL.

12. Ibid.

13. Seigler, *Guide to Confederate Monuments*, 20, 24–25, 94–96, 298. Seigler documents the role of women in the monument and marker movements.

14. Cox, *Dixie's Daughters*, 107–108.

15. Thomas Dixon Jr., *The Clansman: An Historical Romance of the Ku Klux Klan* (New York: Doubleday, Page and Co., 1905), 3–18, 29–35, 180–188. 190–191, 196–197, 205, 216–217, 284–285, 302–326; Williamson, *Crucible of Race*, 140, 153, 172–175; Drago, *Initiative, Paternalism, and Race Relations*, 128; John Hammond Moore, "South Carolina's Reaction to the Photoplay, The Birth of a Nation," in George C. Rogers Jr., ed. *Proceedings of the South Carolina Historical Association, 1963* (Columbia: South Carolina Historical Association, 1964), 30–40.

16. Ibid.

17. Moore, "South Carolina's Reaction to the Photoplay, The Birth of a Nation."

18. Drago, *Initiative, Paternalism, and Race Relations*, 101, 128, 172–176.

19. Ibid., 197 (citation of Charleston *News and Courier*, March 21, 1937), 238–241; Richard Kluger, *Simple Justice: The History of Brown v. Broad of Education and Black America's Struggle for Equality* (London: André Deutsch, 1977), 334.

20. Kluger, *Simple Justice*; Ball, *Slaves in the Family*, 380–381; Charleston *News and Courier*, October 9, 1955, as quoted in Drago, *Initiative, Paternalism, and Race Relations*, 273.

21. This section is based on William J. Cooper Jr. and Thomas E. Terrill, *The American South: A History* (New York: McGraw-Hill, 1991); David Halberstam, *The Children of the Movement* (New York: Random House, 1998), 51, 217, 255, 431–432, 438–441, 483–484, 491, 641; Drago, *Initiative, Paternalism, and Race Relations*, chapter 6; Mays, *Born to Rebel*, chapter 21; Jack Bass and Jack Nelson, *The Orangeburg Massacre*, 2nd ed. (Macon, Ga.: Mercer University Press, 2002); I. A. Newby, *Black Carolinians: A History of Blacks in South Carolina from 1895 to 1968* (Columbia: University of South Carolina Press, 1973). See also Peter F. Lau, *Democracy Rising: South Carolina and the Fight for Black Equality Since 1865* (Lexington: University of Kentucky Press, 2006); Mintz, *Huck's Raft*, chapter 5.

22. Mays, *Born to Rebel*, chapter 21 (part of the chapter title); Newby, *Black Carolinians*, chapter 8; Drago, *Initiative, Paternalism, and Race Relations*, 272–280.

23. Bass and Nelson, *Orangeburg Massacre*, vi–xi, 16, 68–71; Philip G. Grose, *South Carolina at the Brink: Robert McNair and the Politics of Civil Rights* (Columbia: University of South Carolina Press, 2006), chapter 10; Drago, *Initiative, Paternalism, and Race Relations*, 282–286; Fraser, *Charleston*, 428–429; Newby, *Black Carolinians*, 360.

24. Jack Bass and Marilyn W. Thompson, *Ol' Strom: An Unauthorized Biography of Strom Thurmond* (Atlanta: Longstreet Press, 1998), chapter 3.

25. Ibid., chapters 8 and 10; Charleston *News and Courier*, August 20, 1956, in Howard H. Quint, *Profile in Black and White: A Frank Portrait of South Carolina* (Washington, D.C.: Public Affairs Office, 1958), 40, chapter 4 entitled "The White Folks Fight Back."

26. Bass and Thompson, *Ol' Strom*, introduction, 256–261, 281–282, 298, 308–309.

27. Seigler, *Guide to Confederate Monuments*, 23–28; Kirkland, *Broken Fortunes*, 411; Cartoon, Charleston *Post and Courier*, November 13, 1999; Tony Horwitz, *Confederates in the Attic: Dispatches from the Unfinished Civil War* (New York: Pantheon Books 1998), 105, 112; Goldfield, *Still Fighting the Civil War*; K. Michael Prince, *Rally 'Round the Flag, Boys! South Carolina and the Confederate Flag* (Columbia: University of South Carolina Press, 2004), 54, 57–62, 66, 85–86, 239.

28. Robert Brent Toplin, ed., *Ken Burns's The Civil War* (New York: Oxford University Press, 1996), introduction; "The Southern Response" on "Cross Talk," South Carolina Educational Television, May 20, 1991, video. For the numbers, see Charleston *Post and Courier*, March 23, 2003.

29. "Racial Agenda Splits Civil War Group," Charleston *Post and Courier*, November 24, 2002.

30. Horwitz, *Confederates in the Attic*, 10, 126; Charleston *Post and Courier*, April 13, 1997; November 12, 2000; Blanton and Cook, *They Fought Like Demons*. The 2006 reenactment featured an all-women Home Guard.

31. Horwitz, *Confederates in the Attic*, 105–106; Catherine S. Mangegold, *In Glory's Shadow: The Citadel, Shannon Faulkner, and a Changing America* (New York: Vintage Books, 2001); Goldfield, *Still Fighting the Civil War*, 312–314; Prince, *Rally 'Round the Flag*, 133, 175–194; Charleston *Post and Courier*, December 12, 1996; February 2, 1997; July 29, 1999; February 26, 2000. On March 12, 2000, the Charleston *Post and Courier* highlighted "Dixie Divided."

32. Charleston *Post and Courier*, November 27, 1996; Goldfield, *Still Fighting the Civil War*, 313; Prince, *Rally 'Round the Flag*, 198, 246, chapters 5–6, postlude.

33. Charleston *Post and Courier*, May 23, 1007; David Hackett Fischer, *Albion's Seed: Four British Folkways in America* (New York: Oxford University Press, 1989), as discussed in Bertram Wyatt-Brown, "The Ethic of Honor in National Crises: The Civil War, Vietnam, Iraq, and the Southern Factor," *Journal of the Historical Society* 4 (December 2005): 431–460.

34. Charleston *Post and Courier*, November 11, 1999; November 13, 1999; March 19, 2000; April 12, 2004.

35. Charleston *Post and Courier*, April 18, 2004; Mt. Pleasant *Moultrie News*, April 14, 2000.

36. Seigler, *Guide to Confederate Monuments*, 84–88; Charleston *Post and Courier*, April 18, 2004; communication from Marvin W. Dulaney, executive director, Avery Research Center, College of Charleston, Charleston, S.C., to the author, September 2006.

37. Charleston *Post and Courier*, May 8, 2004; May 13, 2004; item entitled "Adding a Simple 'Essie Mae,' Thurmond's Biracial Daughter Recognized on Monument," July 2, 2004. Also see *New York Times*, July 2, 2004; Prince, *Rally 'Round the Flag*, 251.

38. South Carolina Division, UDC, website, October 11, 2007.

39. Porter, *Led On*, 188–189; Walter Rhett, "The Confession of St. Peter and the Children of the Auction Block," flyer, ca. January 17, 2003; Charleston *Post and Courier*, May 22, 2007.

Appendixes A and B: Conscription

1. Appendix A and Appendix B are based on Cauthen, *South Carolina Goes to War*, 166–172; Charleston *Daily Courier*, June 25, 1862; Edgar, *South Carolina*, 372; Harris, *Piedmont Farmer*, 542–543 n. 49; Krug, "The Folks Back Home," xi–xii, 426–462; Moore, *Conscription and Conflict*, 6, 13–14, 53, 56, 67–68, 73–74, 83–84, 107–109, 117, 302–304, 308–310, 341; OR, ser. 4, vol. 1 [125]: 1081, 1095–1097, vol. 2 [126]: 161–168, 408–409, 553–554, vol. 3 [127]: 178–183, 1100–1102; Moore, *Southern Homefront*, 114–120; Index to Letters Received by the Confederate Secretary of War, 1861–1865, Record Group 109, Microcopy No. 409, NA; CSW, Reel No. 147, C-85-1865.

Bibliography

Manuscripts and Collections

Camden Archives and Museum, Camden, S.C.
  Handkerchief Baby Dolls
Charleston City Archives, Charleston, S.C. (CCA)
  Charleston Orphan House Papers
Charleston County Library, Main Branch, Charleston, S.C. (CCL)
  Board of Health Death Records, Charleston. Vol. 21, October 20, 1861, to June
    30, 1866
  Charleston County Death Records, 1821–1926
Charleston County Probate Court, Charleston, S.C.
  Record of Wills
Charleston Library Society Charleston, S.C. (CLS)
  Charleston Police Records, December 1861–March 1863
Confederate Museum, Charleston, S.C.
  Punch bowl made from boiler of burned *Palmetto State*. Item No. 501
National Archives, Washington, D.C. (NA)
  Compiled Service Records of Confederate Soldiers Who Served in Organiza-
    tions from the State of South Carolina, Microcopy No. 267 (CSR)
  Consolidated Index to Compiled Service Records of Confederate Soldiers,
    Microcopy No. 253
  Index to Letters Received by the Confederate Secretary of War, 1861–1865,
    Record Group 109, Microcopy No. 409
  Letters Received by the Confederate Secretary of War, 1861–1865, Record
    Group 109, Microcopy No. 437, 151 reels (CSW)
  Population Schedules of the Eighth Census of the United State, 1860, South
    Carolina, Microcopy No. 653
  Southern Claims Commission
South Carolina Confederate Relic Room and Military Museum, Columbia, S.C.
  Confederate quilt, Item No. 347
South Carolina Department of Archives and History, Columbia, S.C. (SCDAH)
  Adjutant General, Administrative Records
    List of Draft Substitutes, 1862

Petitions for Exemption, 1864–1865
Commission for the Removal of Negroes and Other Noncombatants from
    the City of Charleston
City of Charleston Commission Minute Book, 1862–1863
Records of the Comptroller General, State Auditor Papers
    Soldiers' Board of Relief, State and County Records, Newberry County
        [District], Reports of Soldiers Board of Relief
General Assembly Petitions
Governors' Papers
Milledge Luke Bonham, Letters Received and Sent, 1862–1864
Lawrence Chamberlain, Letters Received
Andrew Gordon Magrath, Letters Received and Sent, 1864–1865
Applications for Furlough, 1865
Benjamin Franklin Perry, Letters Received and Sent, 1865
Francis Wilkinson Pickens, Letters Received and Sent, 1860–1862
John H. Moore, "South Carolina and the Southern Claims Commission, 1871–
    1880" (ca. 1975, 1 vol.)
South Carolina Department of Mental Health. South Carolina Lunatic Asylum
    (SCDMH)
Admissions, 1828–1876
Physicians' Records, 1860–1874
South Carolina State Population Census Schedules, 1869
South Carolina Historical Society, Charleston, S.C. (SCHS)
Milledge Bonham Collections, Writings, 1913–1920, "A Boy's Memories of
    War Time and Other Times by Milledge Lipscomb Bonham"
Langdon Cheves III Papers
Circular Congregational Church Records
Gerard-Honour Papers
J. S. Middleton, "Reminiscences, ca. 1880s"
South Caroliniana Library, University of South Carolina, Columbia, S.C. (SCL)
Thomas Aiton Papers
Leonardo Andrea [Genealogical] Collection (see Mary Frances Jane Pursley
    Papers, SCWRPL)
Baptist Church, Anderson, S.C., Big Creek Minutes, 1801–1936
Thaddeus Street Boinest Letters and Journals (see Lutheran Church, New-
    berry County Records for biographical information on Boinest)
Alice Boozer (Mrs. Simon P.) Letters
Box Family Papers
Mary Davis Brown Diary
Bryce Family Papers

Elizabeth Buescher, "'I Must Save Something': Childhood, the Civil War and the Campbell R. Bryce Family"

Camden Orphan Society Records

Mrs. Sallie [Sarah] F. Chapin, *Fitz-Hugh St. Clair*, reprint, 1873; autographed copy with MS presentation to Benjamin R. Tillman, Jr. (see Chapin under Books for additional information)

Esther B. Cheesborough Notebook

W. F. Clayton, "Recital of our Services during the War for Southern Independence"

Confederate College, Charleston, Table of statistics, Postcard of Confederate College

Sara Gossett Crigler (Mrs. Henry Towles), "Education for Girls and Women in South Carolina prior to 1890 with Related Miscellanea"

Edgefield Female Institute, Circular Letter

Mrs. Emily Caroline Ellis Diary

Gaston-Strait-Wylie-Baskin Families Papers

James Moore Goode, "The Rise of Manufacturing in South Carolina during the War."

Greenville Ladies' Association Records, 1861–1865

James Earle Hagood Papers

James R. Hagood Papers

Mary Y. Harth (Mrs. John) Papers

Hebrew Orphan Society, Charleston, Records

Theodore Honour Papers

Ellen Cooper Johnson Memoirs

Ladies' Benevolent Society for Orphan and Destitute Children, Columbia, Treasurer's Book, 1839–1936; other collections under this nomenclature

Emma Florence LeConte (1848–1901) Journal, 1864–1865

Joseph LeConte Journal of Three Months Personal Experience during the Last Days of the Confederacy

Lutheran Church, Newberry County, Bethlehem, Pomaria, and Lutheran Church of the Redeemer (formerly Luther Chapel), Newberry, Records (see Thaddeus Street Boinest Letters and Journals)

J. L. McCrorey Diary

McLure Family Papers

Andrew Gordon Magrath (1813–1893) Papers

Means-English-Doby Families Papers

James Drayton Nance Letters

John B. Patrick Diary

J. W. Pursley Letters (see Mary Frances Jane Pursley Papers, SCWRPL)

Mrs. H. H. Simons recollection, "The Burning of Columbia," and letter
Mary Amarinthia Snowden Papers
Yates Snowden Collection, "Burning of Columbia," miscellaneous manu-
    scripts and printed materials
Society for Orphan and Destitute Children, Columbia Records (see Ladies'
    Benevolent Society for Orphans and Destitute Children, Columbia)
Lawrence Whitaker Taylor Papers
United Daughters of the Confederacy, Secessionville Chapter, James Island
    Records
Alonzo Adams Vanderford Papers, 1853–1868
Willingham-Lawton Families Papers
Southern Historical Collection, Wilson Library, University of North Carolina,
    Chapel Hill, N.C. (SHS)
John Cheesborough Papers
Grace B. Elmore Books
David Golightly Harris Farm Journals, 1855–1870, microfilm copy of original
Alexander Cheves Haskell Papers
Sallie D. McDowall Books
Andrew Gordon Magrath Papers
Special Collections, Clemson University Libraries, Clemson, S.C. (CSC)
Elijah Webb Brown Papers, 1856–1964
Manson S. Jolly Papers, 1861–1865
Music Books, MS No. 18
Benjamin Ryan Tillman Papers, 1849–1918; Diary of Benjamin Ryan Tillman
Louise Pettus Archives and Special Collections, Dacus Library, Winthrop Uni-
    versity, Rock Hill, S.C. (DLW)
Emily Liles Harris Journals, 1859–1870, 1907–1908, Accession No. 586
Special Collections, Marlene and Nathan Addlestone Library, College of
    Charleston, Charleston, S.C. (SCAL)
"An Account of the Experiences of the Family of the Rev. and Mrs. Paul
    Trapier during and after the War between the States" by T. D. (Mrs.
    Paul) Trapier, Paul Trapier Papers
Special Collections, William R. Perkins Library, Duke University, Durham,
    N.C. (SCWRPL)
John Cumming Papers
Virginia L. Daily, ed., *A Sampler of Women's Studies Resources*
Eliza Fludd Papers
Richard E. Jacques Papers
Clara Victoria (Dargan) Maclean Papers

Lalla Pelot Papers

Louisa Bouknight Poppenheim and Mary Barnett Poppenheim Papers

Mary Frances Jane Pursley Papers

Ann Louisa Salmond Papers (see Daily's *Sampler*, SCWRPL, and *Address* by
Mildred Lewis Rutherford under Books)

Whitefoord Smith Papers

United Daughters of the Confederacy. South Carolina Division, Black Oak
Chapter Minute Books, 1900–1915

United Daughters of the Confederacy, South Carolina Division, Edgefield
Chapter Papers

Benjamin S. Williams Papers

Isabella Ann (Roberts) Woodruff Papers

Government Documents

*Population of the United States in 1860, Compiled from the Original Returns of
the Eighth Census under the Direction of the Secretary of the Interior, by
Joseph C. G. Kennedy, Superintendent of Census*. Washington, D.C.: Government Printing Office, 1864.

South Carolina General Assembly. *An Act to Provide a Pension Fund for Confederate Veterans and Their Widows and to provide the Distribution thereof: An
Act to provide for Pensions for Certain Faithful Negroes who were Engaged
in the Service for the State in the War between the States*. Columbia: South
Carolina General Assembly, 1923.

Statutes at Large of South Carolina. Vol. 13, *Containing the Acts from December,
1861, to December, 1866, Arranged Chronologically, Published under Authority of the Legislature*. Reprint. Columbia, S.C.: Republican Printing Co.,
1875.

U.S. Congress. *Testimony Taken by the Joint Select Committee to Inquire into the
Condition of Affairs in the Late Insurrectionary States*, vols. 3–5. Washington, D.C.: Government Printing Office, 1872.

U.S. Congress. *Senate, South Carolina in 1876: Testimony as to the Denial of the
Elective Franchise in South Carolina at the Elections of 1875 and 1876, 44th
Congress, 2nd sess., S. Misc. Doc. 48*, 1:270. Washington, D.C.: Government
Printing Office, 1877.

*The War of the Rebellion: A Compilation of the Official Records of the Union and
Confederate Armies*. 128 vols. Washington, D.C.: Government Printing
Office, 1880–1901; additions and corrections inserted in each volume, 1902.

Newspapers and Periodicals

Augusta, Ga.
  Southern Christian Advocate (see Charleston)
  Southern Presbyterian (see Columbia)
Camden, S.C.
  Camden Confederate
Charleston, S.C.
  Charleston Medical Journal and Review, 1848–1860 (formerly *Southern Journal of Medicine and Pharmacy*, 1846–1847, Charleston)
  Daily Courier
  Mercury
  News and Courier
  Post and Courier
  Preservation Progress for the Preservation Society of Charleston
  Provenance, The Charleston Museum Newsletter (Fall 2007)
  Southern Christian Advocate, 1861–1865 (see Augusta)
Columbia, S.C.
  Confederate Baptist
  Daily South Carolinian
  Daily Southern Guardian
  Daily Union-Herald
  Phoenix
  Southern Presbyterian (see Augusta)
  Southern Presbyterian Review
  Tri-Weekly Carolinian
Edgefield, S.C.
  Advertiser
Greenville, S.C.
  Mountaineer
Lancaster, S.C.
  Ledger
Louisville, Ky.
  Southern Bivouac
Mt. Pleasant, S.C.
  Moultrie News
Nashville, Tenn.
  Confederate Veteran
Newberry, S.C.
  Herald

New York, N.Y.
  Times
  Tribune
Raleigh, N.C.
  Deaf Mute Casket
Richmond, Va.
  Children's Friend
Spartanburg, S.C.
  Carolina Spartan
Sumter, S.C.
  Tri-Weekly Watchman
Winnsboro, S.C.
  Daily News
York, S.C.
  Yorkville Enquirer

Books and Pamphlets

Ackerman, Robert K. *Wade Hampton III*. Columbia: University of Carolina Press, 2007.

Alcott, Louisa May. *Hospital Sketches*. Ed. Alice Fahs. New York: Bedford / St. Martin's, 2004.

Allen, Mrs. Henry Davis, ed. *Catechism on the History of the Confederate States of America, 1861–1865*. Richmond, Va.: United Daughters of the Confederacy, 1954, reprint, 1990; reissue, 1999, as *Catechism of the Confederate States of America, 1861–1865*.

Ariès, Philippe. *Centuries of Childhood: A Social History of Family Life*. New York: Vintage Books, 1962.

Ash, Stephen V. *When the Yankees Came: Conflict and Chaos in the Occupied South, 1861–1865*. Chapel Hill: University of North Carolina Press, 1995.

Avery, Catherine B., ed. *The New Century Handbook of Greek Mythology and Legend*. New York: Meredith, 1972.

Ayers, Edward L. *In the Presence of Mine Enemies: The Civil War in the Heart of America, 1859–1863*. New York: Norton, 2003.

Baird, Washington. *The Confederate Spelling Book*. Macon, Ga.: Burke, Boykin and Co., 1864.

Baker, Gary. *Cadets in Gray: The Story of the Cadets of the South Carolina Military Academy and Cadet Rangers in the Civil War*. Columbia, S.C.: Palmetto Book Works, 1989.

Ball, Edward. *Slaves in the Family.* New York: Ballantine, 1999.

Ball, W. W. *A Boy's Recollections of the Red Shirt Campaign of 1876 in South Carolina. Paper Read before the Kosmos Club of Columbia, S.C., by W. W. Ball, January 21, 1911.* Pamphlet. Columbia, S.C.: Kosmos Club, 1911.

Bardaglio, Peter. *Reconstructing the Household: Families, Sex, and the Law in the Nineteenth Century South.* Chapel Hill: University of North Carolina Press, 1995.

Barney, William L. *The Making of a Confederate: Walter Lenoir's Civil War.* New York: Oxford University Press, 2008.

Barr, James Michael, and Rebecca Ann Dowling Barr. *Confederate War Correspondence of James Michael Barr and Wife Rebecca Ann Dowling Barr.* Ed. Ruth Barr McDaniel. Taylors, S.C.: Faith Printing, 1963.

Bass, Jack, and Marilyn W. Thompson. *Ol' Strom: An Unauthorized Biography of Strom Thurmond.* Atlanta: Longstreet Press, 1998.

Bass, Jack, and Jack Nelson. *The Orangeburg Massacre.* 2nd ed. Macon, Ga.: Mercer University Press, 2002.

Bellows, Barbara L. *Benevolence among Slaveholders: Assisting the Poor in Charleston, 1670–1840.* Baton Rouge: Louisiana State University Press, 1993.

Berlin, Ira, et al., eds. *Freedom: A Documentary History of Emancipation, 1861–1867.* Cambridge: Cambridge University Press, 1982–1990.

Billingsley, Andrew. *Yearning to Breathe Free: Robert Smalls of South Carolina and His Families.* Columbia: University of South Carolina Press, 2007.

Blanton, DeAnne, and Lauren M. Cook. *They Fought Like Demons: Women Soldiers in the American Civil War.* Baton Rouge: Louisiana State University Press, 2002.

Bleser, Carol, ed. *In Joy and in Sorrow: Women, Family, and Marriage in the Victorian South, 1830–1900.* New York: Oxford University Press, 1991.

Blight, David W. *Race and Reunion: The Civil War in American Memory.* Cambridge, Mass.: Harvard University Press, 2001.

Boatner, Mark Mayo, III. *The Civil War Dictionary.* Rev. ed. New York: David McKay, 1988.

Boylan, Anne M. *Sunday School: The Formation of an American Institution, 1790–1880.* New Haven: Yale University Press, 1988.

Brooks, Ulysses R. *Butler and His Cavalry, 1861–1865.* Columbia, S.C.: n.p., 1909.

Brown, Thomas J., ed. *Reconstruction: New Perspectives on the Postbellum United States.* New York: Oxford University Press, 2006.

Brundage, W. Fitzhugh. *The Southern Past: A Clash of Race and Memory.* Cambridge, Mass.: Harvard University Press, 2005.

Brundage, W. Fitzhugh, ed. *Where These Memories Grow: History, Memory, and Southern Identity.* Chapel Hill: University of North Carolina Press, 2000.

Bryce, Sarah H. *The Personal Experiences of Mrs. Campbell Bryce During the Burning of Columbia, South Carolina, by General W. T. Sherman's Army, February 17, 1865.* Philadelphia: J. P. Lippincott Co., 1899.

Burton, E. Milby. *The Siege of Charleston, 1861–1865.* Columbia: University of South Carolina Press, 1990.

Burton, Orville Vernon. *In My Father's House Are Many Mansions: Family and Community in Edgefield, South Carolina.* Chapel Hill: University of North Carolina Press, 1985.

Bynum, Victoria E. *Unruly Women: The Politics of Social and Sexual Control in the Old South.* Chapel Hill: University of North Carolina Press, 1992.

Caldwell, J[ames] F[itz] J[ames]. *The History of a Brigade of South Carolinians, Known First as "Gregg's" and Subsequently as "McGowan's Brigade."* Ed. Lee A. Wallace Jr. Dayton, Ohio: Morningside Press, 1984.

Calvert, Karin. *Children in the House: The Material Culture of Early Childhood, 1600–1900.* Boston: Northeastern University Press, 1992.

Carlton, David L. *Mill and Town in South Carolina, 1880–1920.* Baton Rouge: Louisiana State University Press, 1982.

Cashin, Joan E. *A Family Venture: Men and Women on the Southern Frontier.* New York: Oxford University Press, 1991.

———. *First Lady of the Confederacy: Varina Davis's Civil War.* Cambridge, Mass.: Harvard University Press, 2006.

Cauthen, Charles E., ed. *Journals of the South Carolina Executive Councils of 1861 and 1862.* Columbia, S.C.: SCDAH, 1956.

———. *South Carolina Goes to War, 1860–1865.* Chapel Hill: University of North Carolina Press, 1950.

Censer, Jane Turner. *North Carolina Planters and Their Children, 1800–1860.* Baton Rouge: Louisiana State University Press, 1990.

Chapin, Mrs. Sallie [Sarah] F. *Fitz-Hugh St. Clair, the South Carolina Rebel Boy: or, It Is No Crime to Be Born a Gentleman.* Charleston, S.C.: John M. Greer, 1872.

Chesnut, Mary. *Mary Chesnut's Civil War.* Ed. C. Vann Woodward. New Haven: Yale University Press, 1981.

Chesnutt, David R., and Clyde N. Wilson, eds. *The Meaning of South Carolina History: Essays in Honor of George C. Rogers, Jr.* Columbia: University of South Carolina Press, 1991.

Children of the Confederacy of the United Daughters of the Confederacy. *Minutes of the Annual Meeting of the Annual Convention.* Richmond, Va.: United Daughters of the Confederacy. 1955–2008.

Chudacoff, Howard P. *Children at Play: An American History.* New York: New York University Press, 2007.

Cimbala, Paul A. *Under the Guardianship of the Nation: The Freedmen's Bureau and the Reconstruction of Georgia, 1865–1870.* Athens: University of Georgia Press, 1997.

Cisco, Walter Brian. *Wade Hampton: Confederate Warrior, Conservative Statesman.* Washington, D.C.: Brassey's, 2004.

Clement, Priscilla Ferguson, and Jacqueline S. Reinier, eds. *Boyhood in America: An Encyclopedia.* 2 vols. Santa Barbara, Calif.: ABC-Clio, 2001.

Clemson, Floride. *A Rebel Came Home: The Diary and Letters of Floride Clemson, 1863–1866.* Ed. Charles M. McGee Jr. and Ernest M. Lander. Rev. ed. Columbia: University of South Carolina Press, 1989.

Clinton, Catherine, and Nina Silber, eds. *Divided Houses: Gender and the Civil War.* New York: Oxford University Press, 1992.

Cobb, James C. *Away Down South: A History of Southern Identity.* New York: Oxford University Press, 2005.

The Confederate Sunday School Hymn Book, Compiled by a Superintendent at Greenville, S.C. Greenville, S.C.: G. E. Elford's Press, 1863.

Conner, James. *Letters of General James Conner, C.S.A.* Ed. Mary Conner Moffett. Columbia, S.C.: R.L. Bryan Co., 1950.

Connolly, James A. *Three Years in the Army of the Cumberland: The Letters and Diary of Major James A. Connolly.* Ed. Paul M. Angle. Bloomington: Indiana University Press, 1959.

Conrad, August. *The Destruction of Columbia, S.C.* Trans. W. H. Pleasants. Roanoke, Va.: Stone Printing and Manufacturing Co., 1902.

Cooper, William J., Jr., and Thomas E. Terrill. *The American South: A History.* New York: McGraw-Hill, 1991.

Cox, Karen L. *Dixie's Daughters: The United Daughters of the Confederacy and the Preservation of Confederate Culture.* Gainesville: University Press of Florida, 2003.

Cram, George F. *Soldiering with Sherman: The Civil War Letters of George F. Cram.* Ed. Jennifer Cain Bohrnstedt. DeKalb: Northern Illinois University Press, 2000.

Crawford, Richard. *The Civil War Songbook: Complete Original Sheet Music for 37 Songs.* New York: Dover Publications, 1977.

Crist, Lynda Lasswell, ed. *The Papers of Jefferson Davis*, vols. 7 and 8. Baton Rouge: Louisiana State University Press, 1992–93.

Daniel, Robert N. *Furman University: A History.* Greenville, S.C.: Furman University, 1951.

Davis, William C. *Jefferson Davis: The Man and His Hour.* New York: HarperCollins, 1991.

Dawson, Francis Warrington. *Our Women in the War*. Charleston, S.C.: Walker, Evans and Cogswell, 1887.

Dean, Eric T., Jr. *Shook Over Hell: Post-Traumatic Stress, Vietnam, and the Civil War*. Cambridge, Mass.: Harvard University Press, 1997.

De Forest, John William. *A Union Officer in the Reconstruction*. Ed. James H. Croushore and David Morris Potter. New Haven: Yale University Press, 1948.

Dickert, D. Augustus. *History of Kershaw's Brigade, with Complete Roll of Companies, Biographical Sketches, Incidents, Anecdotes, etc.* Dayton, Ohio: Press of Morningside Bookshop, 1976.

Dixon, Thomas, Jr. *The Clansman: An Historical Romance of the Ku Klux Klan*. New York: Doubleday, Page, 1905.

Drago, Edmund L. *Hurrah for Hampton! Black Red Shirts in South Carolina During Reconstruction*. Fayetteville: University of Arkansas Press, 1998.

———. *Initiative, Paternalism, and Race Relations: Charleston's Avery Normal Institute*. Athens: University of Georgia Press, 1990. Reissued as *Charleston's Avery Center: From Education and Civil Rights to Preserving the African American Experience*, 2006.

Durrill, Wayne K. *War of Another Kind: Southern Community in the Great Rebellion*. New York: Oxford University Press, 1990.

Easterby, J[ames] H[arold]. *A History of the College of Charleston*. Charleston, S.C.: College of Charleston, 1935.

Edmunds, John B., Jr. *Francis W. Pickens and the Politics of Destruction*. Chapel Hill: University of North Carolina Press, 1986.

Edgar, Walter. *South Carolina: A History*. Columbia: University of South Carolina Press, 1998.

Edwards, Laura. *Gendered Strife and Confusion: The Political Culture of Reconstruction*. Champaign: University of Illinois Press, 1997.

Elliott, Colleen Morse, and Louise Armstrong Moxley. *The Tennessee Civil War Veterans Questionnaires*. Easley, S.C.: Silas Emmett Lucas Jr., 1985.

Elmore, Grace Brown. *A Heritage of War: The Civil War Diary of Grace Brown Elmore, 1861–1868*. Ed. Marli F. Weiner. Athens: University of Georgia Press, 1997.

Emerson, W. Eric. *Sons of Privilege: The Charleston Light Dragoons in the Civil War*. Columbia: University of South Carolina Press, 2005.

Farmer, James. *The Metaphysical Confederacy: James Henley Thornwell and the Synthesis of Southern Values*. Macon, Ga.: Mercer University Press, 1986.

Fass, Paula S., ed. *Encyclopedia of Children and Childhood in History and Society*. 3 vols. New York: Macmillan Reference USA, 2004.

Faust, Drew Gilpin. *Mothers of Invention: Women of the Slaveholding South in the American Civil War*. Chapel Hill: University of North Carolina Press, 1996.

———. "'A Riddle of Death': Mortality and Meaning in the American Civil War." 34th Annual Robert Fortenbaugh Memorial Lecture, Gettysburg College, 1995.

———. *This Republic of Suffering: Death and the American Civil War*. New York: Knopf, 2008.

Fellman, Michael. *Inside War: The Guerilla Conflict in Missouri During the American Civil War*. New York: Oxford University Press, 1989.

Fields, Mamie Garvin, with Karen Fields. *Lemon Swamp and Other Places: A Carolina Memoir*. New York: Free Press, 1983.

Fischer, David Hackett. *Albion's Seed: Four British Folkways in America*. New York: Oxford University Press, 1989.

Fleming, Robert. *The Revised Elementary Spelling Book: The Elementary Spelling Book, Revised and Adapted to the Youth of the Southern Confederacy, Interspersed with Bible Readings on Domestic Slavery*. Atlanta: J. J. Toon, 1863.

Foner, Eric. *Reconstruction: America's Unfinished Revolution, 1863–1877*. New York: Harper & Row, 1989.

Ford, Lacy K., Jr. *Origins of Southern Radicalism: The South Carolina Upcountry, 1800–1860*. New York: Oxford University Press, 1988.

Foster, Gaines M. *Ghosts of the Confederacy: The Lost Cause and the Emergence of the New South, 1865–1913*. New York: Oxford University Press, 1987.

Fowler, A[bijah]. J. *The Southern School Arithmetic: or Youth's Assistant*. Revised by M. Gibson. Richmond, Va.: West and Johnston, 1864.

Fox, William F. *Regimental Losses in the American Civil War, 1861–1865: A Treatise on the Extent and Nature of the Mortuary Losses in the Union Regiments, with Full and Exhaustive Statistics Compiled from the Official Records on File in the United States Bureaus and at Washington*. 4th ed. Albany, N.Y.: Albany Publishing Co., 1898.

Fraser, Walter J., Jr. *Charleston! Charleston! The History of a Southern City*. Columbia: University of South Carolina Press, 1989.

Fraser, Walter J., R. Frank Saunders Jr., and Jon L. Wakelyn. *The Web of Southern Social Relations: Women, Family, and Education*. Athens: University of Georgia Press, 1985.

Friedman, Jean E. *The Enclosed Garden: Women and Community in the Evangelical South, 1830–1890*. Chapel Hill: University of North Carolina Press, 1985.

Fuller, A. James. *Chaplain to the Confederacy: Basil Manly and Baptist Life in the Old South*. Baton Rouge: Louisiana State University Press, 2000.

Gallagher, Gary W. *The Confederate War*. Cambridge, Mass.: Harvard University Press, 1997.

———. "'The Progress of Our Arms': Whither Civil War Military History?" 44th Annual Robert Fortenbaugh Memorial Lecture, Gettysburg College, 2005.

Gallman, J. Matthew. *The North Fights the Civil War: The Home Front*. Chicago: Ivan R. Dee, 1994.

Gaston, John Thomas. *Confederate War Diary of John Thomas Gaston*. Ed. Alifaire (Allie) Gaston Walden. Columbia, S.C.: Vogue Press, 1960.

Goldfield, David. *Still Fighting the Civil War: The American South and Southern History*. Baton Rouge: Louisiana State University Press, 2002.

Gray, Richard. *Writing the South: Ideas of an American Region*. New York: Cambridge University Press, 1986.

Grose, Philip G. *South Carolina at the Brink: Robert McNair and the Politics of Civil Rights*. Columbia: University of South Carolina Press, 2006.

Halberstam, David. *The Children*. New York: Random House, 1998.

Hanawalt, Barbara A. *Growing Up in Medieval London: The Experience of Childhood in History*. New York: Oxford University Press, 1995.

Harris, David Golightly. *Piedmont Farmer: The Journals of David Golightly Harris, 1855–1870*. Ed. Philip N. Racine. Knoxville: University of Tennessee Press, 1990.

Hawes, Joseph M., and Ray N. Hiner, eds. *American Childhood: A Research Guide and Historical Handbook*. Westport, Conn.: Greenwood, 1985.

Heller, J. Roderick, III, and Carolynn Ayres Heller, eds. *The Confederacy Is on Her Way Up the Spout: Letters to South Carolina, 1861–1864*. Athens: University of Georgia Press, 1992.

Hewett, Janet B., and Joyce Lawrence, eds. *South Carolina Confederate Soldiers, 1861–1865*. 2 vols. Wilmington, N.C.: Broadfoot, 1998.

Heyward, Pauline DeCaradeuc. *A Confederate Lady Comes of Age: The Journal of Pauline DeCaradeuc Heyward, 1863–1888*. Ed. Mary D. Robertson. Columbia: University of South Carolina Press, 1992.

Hollis, Daniel W. *University of South Carolina*, vol. 1. Columbia: University of South Carolina Press, 1951.

Holmes, Anne Middleton. *The New York Ladies' Southern Relief Association, 1866–1867*. New York: Mary Mildred Sullivan Chapter, United Daughters of the Confederacy, 1926.

Holmes, Emma. *The Diary of Miss Emma Holmes, 1861–1866*. Ed. John F. Marszalek. Baton Rouge: Louisiana State University Press, 1994.

Holt, Thomas. *Black Over White: Negro Political Leadership in South Carolina During Reconstruction*. Champaign: University of Illinois Press, 1979.

Hope, W. Martin, and Jason H. Silverman. *Relief and Recovery in Post–Civil War South Carolina: A Death by Inches.* Lewiston, N.Y.: Edwin Mellon Press, 1997.

Horwitz, Tony. *Confederates in the Attic: Dispatches from the Unfinished Civil War.* New York: Pantheon Books, 1998.

Hull, Susan R., ed. *Boy Soldiers of the Confederacy.* New York: Neale Publishing Co., 1905.

Janney, Carolina E. *Burying the Dead but Not the Past: Ladies' Memorial Associations and the Lost Cause.* Chapel Hill: University of North Carolina, 2008.

Jenkins, Wilbert L. *Climbing Up to Glory: A Short History of African Americans During the Civil War and Reconstruction.* Wilmington, Del.: Scholarly Resources, 2002.

———. *Seizing the Day: African Americans in Post–Civil War Charleston.* Bloomington: Indiana University Press, 1998.

Jones, Eugene W., Jr. *Enlisted for the War: The Struggles of the Gallant 24th Regiment, South Carolina Volunteers, Infantry, 1861–1865.* Hightstown, N.J.: Longstreet House, 1997.

Jones, J. William. *Christ in the Camp, or Religion in the Confederate Army.* Atlanta: Martin and Hoyt, 1887.

Jones, Lewis P. *South Carolina: A Synoptic History for Laymen.* Rev. ed. Orangeburg, S.C.: Sandlapper, 1971.

Kantrowitz, Stephen. *Ben Tillman and the Reconstruction of White Supremacy.* Chapel Hill: University of North Carolina Press, 2000.

Keith-Lucas, Alan. *A Legacy of Caring: The Charleston Orphan House, 1790–1990.* Charleston, S.C.: Charleston Orphan House / Wyrick and Co., 1991.

Kett, Joseph F. *Rites of Passage: Adolescence in America, 1790 to the Present.* New York: Basic Books, 1977.

King, Susan L., ed. *The History and Records of the Charleston Orphan House, 1790–1860.* Easley, S.C.: Southern Historical Press, 1984.

———. *History and Records of the Charleston Orphan House, 1860–1899.* Columbia, S.C.: SCMAR, 1994.

King, Wilma. *African American Childhoods: Historical Perspectives from Slavery to Civil Rights.* New York: Palgrave Macmillan, 2005.

———. *Stolen Childhood: Slave Youth in Nineteenth-Century America.* Bloomington: Indiana University Press, 1995.

Kirkland, Randolph W., Jr. *Broken Fortunes: South Carolina Soldiers, Sailors and Citizens Who Died in the Service of Their Country and State in the War for Southern Independence, 1861–1865.* Charleston: SCHS, 1995.

———. *Dark Hours: South Carolina Soldiers, Sailors and Citizens Who Were Held in Federal Prisons During the War for Southern Independence, 1861–1865.* Charleston: SCHS, 2002.

Kluger, Richard. *Simple Justice: The History of Brown v. Board of Education and Black America's Struggle for Equality.* London: André Deutsch, 1977.

Ladies Memorial Association. *Confederate Memorial Day at Charleston, S.C.: Reinterment of the Carolina Dead from Gettysburg.* Charleston, S.C.: William G. Maczyck, 1871.

Lander, S. *Our Own School Arithmetic.* Greensboro, N.C.: Sterling, Campbell and Albright, 1863; Richmond, Va.: W. Harvey White, 1863.

Lau, Peter F. *Democracy Rising: South Carolina and the Fight for Black Equality since 1865.* Lexington: University of Kentucky Press, 2006.

LeConte, Emma. *When the World Ended: The Diary of Emma LeConte.* Ed. Earl Schenck Miers. New York: Oxford University Press, 1957.

LeConte, Joseph. *Autobiography of Joseph LeConte.* Ed. William Dallam Armes. New York, 1903.

———. *'Ware Sherman: A Journal of Three Months' Personal Experience in the Last Days of the Confederacy.* Berkeley: University of California Press, 1937.

Leverett, Charles E. *The Southern Confederacy Arithmetic for Common Schools and Academies with a Practical System of Book-keeping by Single Entry.* Augusta, Ga.: J. T. Patterson and Co., 1864.

Litwack, Leon F. *Been in the Storm So Long: The Aftermath of Slavery.* New York: Knopf, 1979.

Longacre, Edward G. *Gentleman and Soldier: A Biography of Wade Hampton, III.* Nashville, Tenn.: Rutledge Hill Press, 2003.

Lonn, Ella. *Desertion During the Civil War.* Gloucester, MA: Peter Smith, 1966.

Lucas, Marion Brunson. *Sherman and the Burning of Columbia.* College Station: Texas A&M University Press, 1976.

Mangegold, Catherine S. *In Glory's Shadow: The Citadel, Shannon Faulkner, and a Changing America.* New York: Vintage Books, 2001.

Marten, James. *Children for the Union: The War Spirit on the Northern Homefront.* Chicago: Ivan R. Dee, 2004.

———. *The Children's Civil War.* Chapel Hill: University of North Carolina Press, 1998.

———, ed. *Lessons of War: The Civil War in Children's Magazines.* Wilmington, Del.: Scholarly Resources Imprint, 1999.

Massey, Mary Elizabeth. *Bonnet Brigades: American Women and the Civil War.* New York: Knopf, 1966.

————. *Ersatz in the Confederacy: Shortages and Substitutes on the Southern Homefront*. Columbia: University of South Carolina Press, 1993.

————. *Refugee Life in the Confederacy*. Baton Rouge: Louisiana State University Press, 1964.

Maynes, Mary Jo, Birgitte Soland, and Christina Benninghaus, eds. *Secret Gardens, Satanic Mills: Placing Girls in European History, 1750–1960*. Bloomington: Indiana University Press, 2005.

Mays, Benjamin E. *Born to Rebel: An Autobiography*. Athens: University of Georgia Press, 1987.

McArthur, Judith N., and Orville Vernon Burton. *"A Gentleman and an Officer": A Military and Social History of James B. Griffin's Civil War*. New York: Oxford University Press, 1996.

McCawley, Patrick J. *Artificial Limbs for Confederate Soldiers*. Columbia, S.C.: SCDAH, 1992.

McCurry, Stephanie. *Masters of Small Worlds: Yeoman Households, Gender Relations, and the Political Culture of the Antebellum South Carolina Low Country*. New York: Oxford University Press, 1997.

McMillen, Sally G. *Motherhood in the Old South: Pregnancy, Childbirth, and Infant Rearing*. Baton Rouge: Louisiana State University Press, 1990.

————. *To Raise Up the South: Sunday Schools in Black and White Churches, 1865–1915*. Baton Rouge: Louisiana State University Press, 2001.

McPherson, James M. *Cross Roads of Freedom: Antietam*. New York: Oxford University Press, 2002.

————. *For Cause & Comrades: Why Men Fought in the Civil War*. New York: Oxford University Press, 1997.

————. *Ordeal by Fire: The Civil War and Reconstruction*. New York: McGraw-Hill, 2001.

Megginson, W. J. *African American Life in South Carolina's Upper Piedmont, 1780–1900*. Columbia: University of South Carolina Press, 2006.

Mintz, Steven. *Huck's Raft: A History of American Childhood*. Cambridge, Mass.: Harvard University Press, 2004.

Mitchell, Reid. *Civil War Soldiers*. New York: Viking Penguin, 1988.

————. *The Vacant Chair: The Northern Soldier Leaves Home*. New York: Oxford University Press, 1993.

Mixson, Frank M. *Reminiscences of a Private*. Columbia, S.C.: State Co., 1910.

Monroe, Haskell M., Jr., and James T. McIntosh, eds. *The Papers of Jefferson Davis*, vol. 1, *1808–1840*. Baton Rouge: Louisiana State University Press, 1971.

Moore, Albert Burton. *Conscription and Conflict in the Confederacy*. Columbia: University of South Carolina Press, 1996.

Moore, Henry Woodbury, and James Washington Moore. *"Chained to Virginia While Carolina Bleeds": The Civil War Correspondence of Henry Woodbury Moore and James Washington Moore.* Walterboro, S.C.: Henry Woodbury Moore, 1996.

Moore, John Hammond. *Columbia and Richland Country: A South Carolina Community, 1740–1990.* Columbia: University of South Carolina Press, 1993.

———. *Southern Homefront, 1861–1865.* Columbia, S.C.: Summerhouse Press, 1998.

Moore, John Hammond, ed. *South Carolina Newspapers.* Columbia: University of South Carolina Press, 1988.

Moore, M. B. *Dixie Primer, for the Little Folks.* 3rd ed. Raleigh, N.C.: Branson, Farrar and Co., 1863.

———. *Dixie Speller, to Follow the First Dixie Reader.* Raleigh, N.C.: Branson and Farrar, 1864.

———. *The Geographical Reader, for the Dixie Children.* Raleigh, N.C.: Branson, Farrar and Co., 1863.

Mulligan, A[lfred] B. *"My Dear Mother & Sisters": Civil War Letters of Capt. A. B. Mulligan, Co. B, 5th South Carolina Cavalry—Butler's Division—Hampton's Corps, 1861–1865.* Ed. Olin Fulmer Hutchinson Jr. Spartanburg, S.C.: Reprint Co., 1992.

Nelson, Scott Reynolds, and Carol Sheriff. *A People at War: Civilians and Soldiers in America's Civil War, 1854–1877.* New York: Oxford University Press, 2008.

Nepveux, Ethel Trenholm Seabrook. *George A. Trenholm, Financial Genius of the Confederacy: His Associates and His Ships That Ran the Blockade.* Anderson, S.C.: Privately printed, 1999.

———. *George Alfred Trenholm: The Company That Went to War, 1861–1865.* Charleston, S.C.: Comprint, 1973.

Newby, I. A. *Black Carolinians: A History of Blacks in South Carolina from 1895 to 1968.* Columbia: University of South Carolina Press, 1973.

———. *Plain Folk in the New South: Social Change and Cultural Persistence, 1880–1915.* Baton Rouge: Louisiana State University Press, 1989.

Nichols, George Ward. *The Story of the Great March: From the Diary of a Staff Officer.* New York: Harper and Brothers, 1865.

Pease, Jane H., and William H. Pease. *A Family of Women: The Carolina Petigrus in Peace and in War.* Chapel Hill: University of North Carolina Press, 1999.

———. *James Louis Petigru: Southern Conservative, Southern Dissenter.* Athens: University of Georgia Press, 1995.

————. *The Web of Progress: Private Values and Public Styles in Boston and Charleston, 1828–1843.* Athens: University of Georgia Press, 1991.

Pendergrast, Mark. *For God, Country, and Coca-Cola.* New York: Charles Scribner's Sons, 1993.

Phelps, W. Chris. *Charlestonians in War: The Charleston Battalion.* Gretna, La.: Pelican, 2004.

Phillips, Jason. *Diehard Rebels: The Confederate Culture of Invincibility.* Athens: University of Georgia Press, 2007.

Poole, W. Scott. *Never Surrender: Confederate Memory and Conservatism in the South Carolina Upcountry.* Athens: University of Georgia Press, 2004.

————. *South Carolina's Civil War: A Narrative History.* Macon, Ga.: Mercer University Press, 2005.

Pope, Thomas H. *The History of Newberry County, South Carolina,* vol. 2, *1860–1990.* Columbia: University of South Carolina Press, 1992.

Porter, A[nthony] Toomer. *Led On! Step by Step Scenes from Clerical, Military, Educational, and Plantation Life in the South, 1828–1898: An Autobiography.* New York: G. P. Putnam's Sons, 1898.

Powers, Bernard E., Jr. *Black Charlestonians: A Social History, 1822–1865.* Fayetteville: University of Arkansas Press, 1994.

Prince, K. Michael. *Rally 'Round the Flag, Boys! South Carolina and the Confederate Flag.* Columbia: University of South Carolina Press, 2004.

Proceedings of the First and Second Annual Meetings of the Survivors' Association of the State of South Carolina and Oration of General John S. Preston, Delivered before the Association, November 10th, 1870. Charleston, S.C.: Walker, Evans, and Cogswell, 1870.

Quint, Howard H. *Profile in Black and White: A Frank Portrait of South Carolina.* Washington, D.C.: Public Affairs Press, 1958.

Rable, George C. *Civil Wars: Women and the Crisis of Southern Nationalism.* Urbana: University of Illinois Press, 1991.

————. *Fredericksburg! Fredericksburg!* Chapel Hill: University of North Carolina Press, 2002.

Rawick, George P., ed. *The American Slave: A Composite Autobiography.* 11 volumes. Westport, Conn.: Greenwood, 1972–77.

Reid, J[esse] W[alton]. *History of the Fourth Regiment of S.C. Volunteers, from the Commencement of the War until Lee's Surrender.* Greenville, S.C.: Shannon and Co., 1892.

Reinier, Jacqueline S. *From Virtue to Character: American Childhood, 1750–1850.* New York: Twayne, 1996.

Reynolds, John S. *Reconstruction in South Carolina, 1865–1877.* New York: Negro Universities Press, 1969.

Rhea, Gordon C. *Carrying the Flag: The Story of Private Charles Whilden, the Confederacy's Most Unlikely Hero.* New York: Basic Books, 2003.

Rosen, Robert N. *The Jewish Confederates.* Columbia: University of South Carolina Press, 2000.

Rosenblatt, Roger. *Children of War.* Garden City, N.Y.: Anchor Press, 1983.

Rosengarten, Theodore. *Tombee: Portrait of a Cotton Planter with the Journal of Thomas B. Chaplin, 1822–1890.* New York: William Morrow, 1986.

Royster, Charles. *The Destructive War: William Tecumseh Sherman, Stonewall Jackson, and the Americans.* New York: Knopf, 1991.

Rubin, Anne Sarah. *A Shattered Nation: The Rise and Fall of the Confederacy, 1861–1868.* Chapel Hill: University of North Carolina Press, 2005.

Rubin, Hyman, III. *South Carolina Scalawags.* Columbia: University of South Carolina Press, 2006.

Rutherford, Mildred Lewis. *Address Delivered by Miss Mildred Lewis Rutherford, Historian-General, United Daughters of the Confederacy.* Pamphlet. Washington, D.C., 1912.

Salley, Alexander Samuel, Jr., ed. *South Carolina Troops in Confederate Service.* 3 vols. Columbia, S.C.: State Co., 1913–30.

Schivelbusch, Wolfgang. *The Culture of Defeat: On National Trauma, Mourning, and Recovery.* Trans. Jefferson Chase. New York: Henry Holt, 2003.

Schwalm, Leslie A. *"A Hard Fight for We": Women's Transition from Slavery to Freedom in South Carolina.* Champaign: University of Illinois Press, 1997.

Seigler, Robert S. *A Guide to the Confederate Monuments in South Carolina: "Passing the Cup."* Columbia, S.C.: SCDAH, 1997.

Silverman, Jason H., Samuel N. Thomas Jr., and Beverly D. Evans, IV. *Shanks: The Life and Wars of General Nathan G. Evans, CSA.* New York: Da Capo Press, 2002.

Simkins, Francis Butler. *Pitchfork Ben Tillman: South Carolinian.* Baton Rouge: Louisiana State University Press, 1967.

Simkins, Francis Butler, and Robert Hilliard Woody. *South Carolina During Reconstruction.* Chapel Hill: University of North Carolina Press, 1932.

Simkins, Francis Butler, and James Welch Patton. *The Women of the Confederacy.* Richmond, Va.: Garrett and Massie, 1936.

Simon, Bryant. *A Fabric of Defeat: The Politics of South Carolina Millhands, 1910–1948.* Chapel Hill: University of North Carolina Press, 1998.

Simpson, Dick, and Tally Simpson. *"Far, Far from Home": The Wartime Letters of Dick and Tally Simpson, Third South Carolina Volunteers.* Ed. Guy R. Everson and Edward H. Simpson Jr. New York: Oxford University Press, 1994.

Sinha, Manisha. *The Counterrevolution of Slavery: Politics and Ideology in Ante-bellum South Carolina.* Chapel Hill: University of North Carolina Press, 2000.

Sinisi, Kyle S. *Sacred Debts: State Civil War Claims and American Federalism, 1861–1880.* New York: Fordham University Press, 2003.

Smith, Daniel E. Huger, Alice R. Huger Smith, and Arney R. Childs, eds. *Mason Smith Family Letters, 1860–1868.* Columbia: University of South Carolina Press, 1950.

[Smith, R. M.] *The Confederate First Reader: Containing Selections in Prose and Poetry, as Reading Exercises for the Young Children in the Schools and Fami-lies of the Confederate States.* Richmond, Va.: G. L. Bidgood, 1864.

———. *The Confederate Spelling Book, with Reading Lessons for the Young, Adapted to the Use of Schools or for Private Instruction.* 5th ed. Richmond, Va.: George L. Bidgood, 1865.

Snay, Mitchell. *Gospel of Disunion: Religion and Separatism in the Antebellum South.* Chapel Hill: University of North Carolina Press, 1997.

Snowden, Yates. *Marching with Sherman: A Review by Yates Snowden of the Let-ters and Campaign Diaries of Henry Hitchcock.* Columbia, S.C.: n.p., 1929.

———. *South Carolina School Books, 1795–1865.* Columbia, S.C.: n.p., 1910.

Songs of Love and Liberty Compiled by a North Carolina Lady. Raleigh, N.C.: Branson and Farrar, 1864.

South Carolina: The WPA Guide to the Palmetto State. Columbia: University of South Carolina Press, 1988.

South Carolina Genealogies: Articles from The South Carolina Historical (and Genealogical) Magazine. Spartanburg, S.C.: Reprint Co., 1983.

Startup, Kenneth Moore. *Root of All Evil: The Protestant Clergy and the Eco-nomic Mind of the Old South.* Athens: University of Georgia Press, 1997.

Sterling, Richard. *Our Own Fourth Reader: For the Use of Schools and Families.* Greensboro, N.C.: Sterling and Albright, 1865; New York: Owens and Agar, 1865.

Stokes, William. *Saddle Soldiers: The Civil War Correspondence of General Wil-liam Stokes of the 4th South Carolina Cavalry.* Ed. Lloyd Halliburton. Orangeburg, S.C.: Sandlapper, 1993.

Stone, Cornelia Branch. *U.D.C. for Children Arranged for the Veuve Jefferson Davis Chapter.* Galveston, Tex.: n.p., 1904.

Stone, DeWitt Boyd, Jr. *Wandering to Glory: Confederate Veterans Remember Evans' Brigade.* Columbia: University of South Carolina Press, 2002.

Summers, Mark Wahlgren. *The Gilded Age, or, the Hazard of New Functions.* Upper Saddle River, N.J.: Prentice-Hall, 1997.

Toplin, Robert Brent, ed. *Ken Burns's The Civil War*. New York: Oxford University Press, 1996.

Towles, Louis P., ed. *A World Turned Upside Down: The Palmers of South Santee, 1818–1881*. Columbia: University of South Carolina Press, 1996.

Trelease, Allen W. *White Terror: The Ku Klux Klan Conspiracy and Southern Reconstruction*. Baton Rouge: Louisiana State University Press, 1999.

United Daughters of the Confederacy, South Carolina Division. *Recollections and Reminiscences, 1861–1865 through World War I*. 12 vols. N.p., 1990–2002. (UDC *Recollections*)

———. *South Carolina Women in the Confederacy*. 2 vols. Columbia, S.C.: State Co., 1903, 1907.

Upson, Theodore F. *With Sherman to the Sea: The Civil War Letters, Diaries, and Reminiscences of Theodore F. Upson*. Ed. Oscar Osburn Winter. Bloomington: Indiana University Press, 1958.

Walker, Clarence E. *Deromanticizing Black History: Critical Essays and Reappraisals*. Knoxville: University of Tennessee Press, 1991.

Wallace, David Duncan. *South Carolina: A Short History, 1520–1948*. Columbia: University of South Carolina Press, 1984.

Weiner, Marli F. *Mistresses and Slaves: Plantation Women in South Carolina, 1830–80*. Urbana: University of Illinois Press, 1998.

Weitz, Mark A. *More Damning Than Slaughter: Desertion in the Confederate Army*. Lincoln: University of Nebraska Press, 2005.

Werner, Emmy E. *Reluctant Witnesses: Children's Voices from the Civil War*. Boulder, Colo.: Westview Press, 1998.

West, Elliott, and Paula Petrik, eds. *Small Worlds: Children and Adolescents in America, 1850–1950*. Lawrence: University Press of Kansas, 1992.

West, Jerry L. *The Reconstruction Ku Klux Klan in York County, South Carolina, 1865–1877*. Jefferson, N.C.: McFarland and Co., 2002.

Whites, LeeAnn. *The Civil War as a Crisis in Gender: Augusta, Georgia, 1860–1890*. Athens: University of Georgia Press, 1995.

Wiley, Bell Irvin. *The Life of Johnny Reb: The Common Soldier of the Confederacy*. New York: Bobbs-Merrill, 1943.

Williams, Lou Falkner. *The Great South Carolina Ku Klux Klan Trials, 1871–1872*. Athens: University of Georgia Press, 1996.

Williamson, Joel. *After Slavery: The Negro in South Carolina during Reconstruction, 1861–1877*. Hanover, N.H.: University Press of New England, 1990.

———. *The Crucible of Race: Black-White Relations in the American South Since Emancipation*. New York: Oxford University Press, 1984.

Wilson, Charles Reagan. *Baptized in Blood: The Religion of the Lost Cause, 1865–1920*. Athens: University of Georgia Press, 1980.

Wise, Stephen R. *Gate of Hell: Campaign for Charleston Harbor, 1863*. Columbia: University of South Carolina Press, 1994.

Woodward, C. Vann. *Origins of the New South, 1877–1913*. Baton Rouge: Louisiana State University Press, 1971.

Wyatt-Brown, Bertram. *Southern Honor: Ethics and Behavior in the Old South*. New York: Oxford University Press, 1983.

Wyckoff, Mac. *A History of the 2nd South Carolina Infantry, 1861–65*. Fredericksburg, Va.: Sergeant Kirkland's Museum and Historical Society, 1994.

Zuczek, Richard. *State of Rebellion: Reconstruction in South Carolina*. Columbia: University of South Carolina Press, 1996.

Articles and Contributions to Edited Volumes

Altman, James David. "The Charleston Marine School." *South Carolina Historical Magazine* 88 (April 1987): 76–82.

Bainbridge, Judith T. "'A Nursery of Knowledge': The Greenville Female Academy, 1819–1854." *South Carolina Historical Magazine* 99 (1998): 6–33.

Bardaglio, Peter. "The Children of Jubilee: African American Childhood in Wartime." In Clinton and Silber, *Divided Houses*, 213–229. (See Books for all contributions to edited volumes.)

Blanton, Christine. "The Life of Mary Amarinthia Snowden." *Preservation Progress* 37 (Fall 1994): 7–11.

Bordin, Ruth. "Chapin, Sarah Flournoy." In John A. Garraty and Mark C. Carnes, eds., *American National Biography* (New York: Oxford University Press, 1999), 4: 696–697.

Brookes, Barbara. "Menarche." In Fass, *Children and Childhood*, 2: 594–595.

Burnside, Ronald, D. "Racism in the Administrations of Governor Cole Blease." In George C. Rogers Jr., ed., *Proceedings of the South Carolina Historical Association, 1964*, 43–57. Columbia: South Carolina Historical Association, 1964.

Burton, Orville Vernon. "The Black Squint of the Law: Racism in South Carolina." In Chesnutt and Wilson, *Meaning of South Carolina History*, 161–185.

———. "The Effects of the Civil War and Reconstruction on the Coming of Age of Southern Males, Edgefield County, South Carolina." In Fraser, Saunders, and Wakelyn, *Web of Southern Social Relations*, 204–224.

Case, Sarah H. "The Historical Ideology of Mildred Lewis Rutherford: A Confederate Historian's New South Creed." *Journal of Southern History* 68 (August 2002): 599–628.

Cashin, Joan E. "'Since the War Broke Out': The Marriage of Kate and William McLure." In Clinton and Silber, *Divided Houses*, 200–212.

———. "An 'Unbroken Stallion' Comes Home from the Civil War." *Manuscripts* 44 (Fall 1992): 307–314.

Chesebrough, David B. "'There Goes Your Damned Gospel Shop!' The Churches and Clergy as Victims of Sherman's March through South Carolina." *South Carolina Historical Magazine* 92 (January 1991): 15–33.

Clark, Cindy Dell. "Holidays." In Clement and Reinier, *Boyhood in America*, 1:337–341.

Faust, Drew Gilpin. "Altars of Sacrifice: Confederate Women and the Narratives of War." In Clinton and Silber, *Divided Houses*, 171–199.

———. "The Civil War Soldiers and the Art of Dying." *Journal of Southern History* 57 (2004): 3–38.

———. "'Trying to Do a Man's Business': Slavery, Violence and Gender in the American Civil War." *Gender and History* 4 (Summer 1992): 197–214.

Gillis, John R. "Rites of Passage." In Fass, *Children and Childhood*, 2:714–716.

Gregorie, Anne King. "Chapin, Sarah Flournoy." In Edward T. James, ed., *Notable American Women, 1607–1950: A Biographical Dictionary*, 1:231–232. Cambridge, Mass.: Harvard University Press, 1971.

Hiner, N. Ray, and Joseph M. Hawes. "History of Childhood United States." In Fass, *Children and Childhood*, 2:426–430.

Hudson, Leonne M. "A Confederate Victory at Grahamville: Fighting at Honey Hill." *South Carolina Historical Magazine* 94 (January 1993): 19–33.

Johnson, Joan Marie. "Sisters of the South: Louisa and Mary Poppenheim and South Carolina Clubwomen." In *Proceedings of the South Carolina Historical Association, 1997*, 77–95. Columbia: South Carolina Historical Association, 1998.

Jordan, Laylon Wayne. "Education for Community: C.G. Memminger and the Origination of Common Schools in Antebellum Charleston." *South Carolina Historical Magazine* 83 (1982): 99–115.

"Journal of Artha Brailsford Wescoat, 1863–1864." Ed. Mrs. Sterling Graydon. *South Carolina Historical Magazine* 55 (1954): 71–102.

Mallinson, David. "Armed Only with Their Drums, Union and Confederate Drummer Boys Served Their Causes with Distinction." *America's Civil War* 5 (November 1992): 8, 70–73.

Marten, James. "Fatherhood in the Confederacy: Southern Soldiers and Their Children." *Journal of Southern History* 63 (May 1997): 269–292.

McCurry, Stephanie. "The Politics of Yeoman Households in South Carolina." In Clinton and Silber, *Divided Houses*, 22–38.

Mergen, Bernard. "The Discovery of Children's Play." *American Quarterly* 27, no. 4 (October 1975): 399–421.

———. "Games." In Clement and Reinier, *Boyhood in America*, 1:301–306.

Moore, John Hammond. "Getting Uncle Sam's Dollars: South Carolinians and the Southern Claim Commission, 1871–1880." *South Carolina Historical Magazine* 82 (July 1981): 248–262.

———. "South Carolina's Reaction to the Photoplay, The Birth of a Nation." In George C. Rogers Jr., ed., *Proceedings of the South Carolina Historical Association, 1963* 30–40. Columbia: South Carolina Historical Association, 1964.

Racine, Philip N. "Emily Lyles Harris: A Piedmont Farmer During the Civil War." *South Atlantic Quarterly* 79 (Autumn 1980): 386–397.

Schmidt, Kirsten. "Dolls." In Fass, *Children and Childhood*, 1:279–282.

Schrum, Kelly. "Teenagers." In Fass, *Children and Childhood*, 3:808–809.

Smith, James F. "Gambling." In Clement and Reinier, *Boyhood in America*, 1:295–301.

Stowe, Steven M., "The Not-So Cloistered Academy: Elite Women's Education and Family Feeling in the Old South." In Fraser, Saunders, and Wakelyn, *Web of Southern Social Relations*, 90–106.

Warren, Roblyn. "Discipline." In Clement and Rainier, *Boyhood in America*, 1:201–204.

Wyatt-Brown, Bertram. "The Ethic of Honor in National Crises: The Civil War, Vietnam, Iraq, and the Southern Factor." *Journal of the Historical Society* 4 (December 2005): 431–460.

Papers, Theses, Dissertations, Videos, and Miscellaneous Works

Drago, Edmund L. "Confederate Children and the Commonality of the War Experience: South Carolina as a Test Case." Paper, Society for the History of Children and Youth, Marquette University, Milwaukee, August 6, 2005.

Feimster, Crystal. "'How Are the Daughters of Eve Punished?' Rape During the Civil War." Paper, Southern Historical Association Meeting, Atlanta, November 5, 2005.

Frank, Lisa Tendrich. "I Am a Southern Woman." Paper, Southern Historical Association Meeting, Baltimore, November 8, 2002.

Honour, Katherine Lyons. "Theodore A. Honour: His Life and Letters of the Civil War Period." MA thesis, East Tennessee University, 1979. Manuscript Department, SCL.

Kennerly, Sarah Law. "Confederate Juvenile Imprints: Children's Books and Periodicals Published in the Confederate States of America, 1861–1865." PhD dissertation, University of Michigan, 1956.

King, Susan L. "Children of the City: The First One Hundred Years of the Charleston Orphan House." MS, ca. November 2005. Copy in author's possession.

Krug, Donna Rebecca Dondes. "The Folks Back Home: The Confederate Homefront during the Civil War." PhD dissertation, University of California, Irvine, 1990.

McNamara, Vanessa. "The Evolution of Women's Benevolence Work in Nineteenth Century, Charleston, SC: A Case Study." MA thesis, College of Charleston and The Citadel, 2007.

Miller, Brian Craig. "Reconstructing Manhood: Women and the Experience of Confederate Amputees." Paper, Southern Historical Association Meeting, Memphis, November 4, 2004.

Rhett, Walter. "The Confession of St. Peter and the Children of the Auction Block." Flyer, ca. January 17, 2003.

"The Southern Response" on "Cross Talk," South Carolina Educational Television, May 20, 1991. Video.

Thackston, John. "Primary and Secondary Education in South Carolina from 1780 to 1860." PhD dissertation, New York University Graduate Schools, 1908.

Index

RECONSTRUCTING AMERICA SERIES
Paul A. Cimbala, series editor

1. Hans L. Trefousse, *Impeachment of a President: Andrew Johnson, the Blacks, and Reconstruction.*

2. Richard Paul Fuke, *Imperfect Equality: African Americans and the Confines of White Ideology in Post-Emancipation Maryland.*

3. Ruth Currie-McDaniel, *Carpetbagger of Conscience: A Biography of John Emory Bryant.*

4. Paul A. Cimbala and Randall M. Miller, eds., *The Freedmen's Bureau and Reconstruction: Reconsiderations.*

5. Herman Belz, *A New Birth of Freedom: The Republican Party and Freedmen's Rights, 1861 to 1866.*

6. Robert Michael Goldman, *"A Free Ballot and a Fair Count": The Department of Justice and the Enforcement of Voting Rights in the South, 1877–1893.*

7. Ruth Douglas Currie, ed., *Emma Spaulding Bryant: Civil War Bride, Carpetbagger's Wife, Ardent Feminist—Letters, 1860–1900.*

8. Robert Francis Engs, *Freedom's First Generation: Black Hampton, Virginia, 1861–1890.*

9. Robert F. Kaczorowski, *The Politics of Judicial Interpretation: The Federal Courts, Department of Justice, and Civil Rights, 1866–1876.*

10. John Syrett, *The Civil War Confiscation Acts: Failing to Reconstruct the South.*

11. Michael Les Benedict, *Preserving the Constitution: Essays on Politics and the Constitution in the Reconstruction Era.*

12. Andrew L. Slap, *The Doom of Reconstruction: The Liberal Republicans in the Civil War Era.*

RECONSTRUCTING AMERICA SERIES
Paul A. Cimbala, series editor